How Large
Language Models
Can Help
Your Search Project

Alessandro Benedetti

How Large Language Models Can Help Your Search Project

Alessandro Benedetti
Sease Ltd.
London, UK

ISBN 978-3-032-01562-4   ISBN 978-3-032-01563-1   (eBook)
https://doi.org/10.1007/978-3-032-01563-1

© The Editor(s) (if applicable) and The Author(s), under exclusive license to Springer Nature Switzerland AG 2025

This work is subject to copyright. All rights are solely and exclusively licensed by the Publisher, whether the whole or part of the material is concerned, specifically the rights of translation, reprinting, reuse of illustrations, recitation, broadcasting, reproduction on microfilms or in any other physical way, and transmission or information storage and retrieval, electronic adaptation, computer software, or by similar or dissimilar methodology now known or hereafter developed.
The use of general descriptive names, registered names, trademarks, service marks, etc. in this publication does not imply, even in the absence of a specific statement, that such names are exempt from the relevant protective laws and regulations and therefore free for general use.
The publisher, the authors and the editors are safe to assume that the advice and information in this book are believed to be true and accurate at the date of publication. Neither the publisher nor the authors or the editors give a warranty, expressed or implied, with respect to the material contained herein or for any errors or omissions that may have been made. The publisher remains neutral with regard to jurisdictional claims in published maps and institutional affiliations.

This Springer imprint is published by the registered company Springer Nature Switzerland AG
The registered company address is: Gewerbestrasse 11, 6330 Cham, Switzerland

If disposing of this product, please recycle the paper.

Preface

The inception of this book dates back to a dark November night in London, 2023, during the Search Solutions conference hosted by the British Computer Society's Information Retrieval Specialist Group.

I was hosting a tutorial, "How Large Language Models Can Improve Your Search Project", and was approached to make a book out of it.

Fast forward to 2025, roughly 19 months and 200 pages later and here we are, the book is a reality.

I've been writing theses, essays, blogs and papers, but never a book... until now! What a ride!

I really enjoyed the writing experience and genuinely hope you enjoy the reading as much as I enjoyed the writing.

I've always been a big fan of education since university, where I was tutoring younger students, and I put it into practice via training sessions (private and public) across many venues (both academic and industrial).

I wrote multiple blog posts and a paper, sharing ideas, best practices and research topics, but being able to condense knowledge in a useful book format has been a completely different story.

The primary scope of this book is to communicate the current state of the art of large language model applications in the domain of information retrieval and search with a pragmatic perspective on industrial adoption via open source software.

You'll find some references to commercial large language models, but the big emphasis is on open source technologies.

Open source is very dear to me: I genuinely believe it to be the right place to implement innovation and foster human progress, and collaboration, transparently.

I am personally part of the open source community, acting as a committer of the Apache Lucene and Solr projects (the people who have rights to change the code and documentation of the project) and as the chair of the Apache Solr Project Management Committee (PMC).

I genuinely hope this book will encourage new people to take this path.

Open source always looks for new energy and perspectives: not talking only about code and documentation here, anything, including ideas and discussions, is valuable.

The intended audience of this book is anyone curious to learn how large language models can be applied to improve a search project.

Ideally, you are:

- a beginner or intermediate in the field of information retrieval and artificial intelligence.
- an expert in artificial intelligence who is now approaching the search world.
- an expert in search who is now approaching large language models.
- a search practitioner curious to learn about the latest trends, research and industrial applications around search and large language models.

The book is organised as follows:

- **Part I** gives an introduction to artificial intelligence and large language models, including an overview of open source and commercial options.
- **Part II** describes techniques and strategies to integrate large language models in your search project, including how to choose the right model for your use case and how to avoid the classic mistakes that can happen in the process.
- **Part III** gives an overview of open source technologies to interact with large language models and gives a detailed survey of how the most popular open source search engines support them.

I would like to wrap up the preface with some acknowledgements: Thanks to my colleagues at Sease, Andrea Gazzarini, Elia Porciani, Anna Ruggero, Ilaria Petreti, Lisa Biella, and Daniele Antuzi; this book wouldn't have been possible without the hours of discussions we had on countless open source projects and client work: you are an inspiration.

Thanks to John T. Kane for the webinar we did together in June 2023, one of the first explorations I did on the topic, which definitely inspired me to explore it more, give the tutorial, and eventually write the book.

Thanks to all my clients and people in the field, you indirectly made this book possible.

I hope you enjoy the ride and learn something useful!

London, UK Alessandro Benedetti
June 2025

Declarations

Competing Interests The author has no competing interests to declare that are relevant to the content of this manuscript.

Contents

Part I Large Language Models

1 Introduction to Large Language Models 3
   1.1   Artificial Intelligence, Machine Learning and Deep Learning 3
   1.2   Generative Artificial Intelligence 8
   1.3   What Is a Large Language Model? 11
   1.4   Fine-tuned for... 12
        1.4.1   Following Instructions 13
        1.4.2   Text Vectorisation 14
        1.4.3   Summarisation 15
        1.4.4   Translation 16
   1.5   Limitations and How to Mitigate Them 17
   References 20

2 The Open Source Landscape 23
   2.1   What Does "Open" Mean for a Large Language Model? 23
        2.1.1   License 24
        2.1.2   Datasets: Pre-training and Fine-tuning 25
        2.1.3   Code: Pre-training, Fine-Tuning and Inference 26
        2.1.4   Architecture 26
        2.1.5   Weights: Base Model and Fine-Tuned Model 26
        2.1.6   Paper 27
        2.1.7   Documentation 27
        2.1.8   APIs 27
   2.2   Open Source General Purpose Large Language Models 28
   2.3   Partially Open Large Language Models 30
   2.4   Domain-Specific Language Models 33
        2.4.1   Bioscience and Chemistry 34
        2.4.2   Biomedicine and Healthcare 35
        2.4.3   Coding Assistance 36
   2.5   Repositories 37
   References 38

3	**The Commercial Landscape**		41
	3.1 Business Paradigms		41
	3.2 OpenAI: ChatGPT		43
		3.2.1 o Models	44
		3.2.2 GPT Models	45
		3.2.3 Text to Vector	45
		3.2.4 APIs	45
	3.3 Google: Gemini		46
		3.3.1 Text to Vector	47
		3.3.2 APIs	47
	3.4 Cohere: Command		48
		3.4.1 Text to Vector	49
		3.4.2 APIs	49
	3.5 Anthropic: Claude		50
		3.5.1 APIs	50
	References		51

Part II Large Language Models and Search

4	**Applying Large Language Models to Search**		55
	4.1 Vector Search		55
		4.1.1 Sparse and Dense First-Stage Retrieval	57
		4.1.2 Quantisation and Binary Vectors	59
		4.1.3 First-Stage Learned Sparse Retrieval	63
		4.1.4 Late Interaction Models	64
		4.1.5 Reranking	66
		4.1.6 Vector Search in Production	67
	4.2 Retrieval Augmented Generation		70
		4.2.1 Naive	71
		4.2.2 Advanced	72
		4.2.3 Modular	84
		4.2.4 Evaluation	84
		4.2.5 Current Limitations	86
	4.3 Query/Document Expansion		87
	4.4 Semantic Neural Highlighting		90
	4.5 Spellchecking and Autocompletion		92
		4.5.1 Spellchecking	93
		4.5.2 Autocompletion	94
	4.6 Multi-modal Search		95
	4.7 Multi-lingual Search		99
	4.8 From Natural Language to Structured Queries		100
		4.8.1 Query Parsing Approach	103
		4.8.2 Filtering Suggestions Approach	105
		4.8.3 Document Enrichment Approach	106
		4.8.4 Conclusions and Evaluation	106

	4.9	Reranking	110
		4.9.1 Top-k and Context	113
	4.10	Search Quality Evaluation	115
		4.10.1 Queries	116
		4.10.2 Ratings and Rationale	118
	References		120

5 What Large Language Model Is the Best for You? ... 125
- 5.1 Start from the Task You Need to Solve ... 125
- 5.2 Validate the License ... 127
- 5.3 Analyse the Training Data ... 130
- 5.4 How to Compare Large Language Models ... 132

6 Rabbit Holes ... 135
- 6.1 Not Measuring Search Quality Metrics ... 135
- 6.2 Choosing the Wrong Tech Stack ... 139
- 6.3 Choosing the Wrong Large Language Model ... 144
- References ... 145

Part III How to Use Open Source Software to Interact with Large Language Models

7 Open Source Frameworks and Projects ... 149
- 7.1 LangChain ... 149
  - 7.1.1 Should You Use LangChain? ... 151
- 7.2 Haystack ... 152
  - 7.2.1 Should You Use Haystack? ... 153
- 7.3 LangChain4j ... 154
  - 7.3.1 Should You Use It? ... 155
- 7.4 Comparisons ... 156

8 Popular Open Source Search Engines ... 159
- 8.1 Apache Lucene ... 159
- 8.2 Apache Solr ... 166
  - 8.2.1 Text Vectorisation ... 166
  - 8.2.2 Vector Search ... 168
  - 8.2.3 Future Work ... 169
- 8.3 OpenSearch ... 170
  - 8.3.1 Text/Multi-modal Vectorisation ... 171
  - 8.3.2 Vector Search ... 172
  - 8.3.3 Nested Vectors Search ... 175
  - 8.3.4 Learned Sparse Retrieval ... 178
  - 8.3.5 Cross-encoders for Reranking ... 179
  - 8.3.6 Semantic Highlighting ... 181
  - 8.3.7 Retrieval Augmented Generation with Conversation History ... 181

	8.4	Elasticsearch	184
		8.4.1 Vector Search	184
		8.4.2 Nested Vectors Search	186
	8.5	Vespa	188
		8.5.1 Text/Multi-modal Vectorisation	189
		8.5.2 Vector Search	191
		8.5.3 Multi-vectors Search	193
		8.5.4 Learned Sparse Retrieval	194
		8.5.5 Cross-encoders and Late Interaction Models for Reranking	195
		8.5.6 Local or Remote LLMs	196
		8.5.7 Retrieval Augmented Generation	198
		8.5.8 Document Enrichment	199
	8.6	Qdrant	201
	8.7	Milvus	202
	8.8	Weaviate	203
	References		204

Glossary 205

Acronyms

I genuinely hate acronyms, so this list is as small as possible and contains only acronyms that are extremely well-known.

AI   Artificial Intelligence
LLM Large Language Model
GPT Generative Pre-trained Transformer
RAG Retrieval Augmented Generation
HNSW Hierarchical Navigable Small World Graph

Part I

Large Language Models

- What are large language models, and how were humans able to build them?
- How does open source apply to this new technology?
- What are the most prominent open and commercial options available?

The first part of the book aims to answer these questions to introduce the reader to the world of Artificial Intelligence and language modelling.

The first three chapters don't dedicate too much space to concepts repeated many times already across different sources, but it's fundamental to lay the right foundations and references to guarantee a pleasant fruition of the book to anyone, independently of different backgrounds and levels of exposure to the subject.

Building upon the artificial intelligence introduction, the focus will shift to an aspect that is often neglected: what it means to be open source in the domain of large language modelling.

Being an active open source advocate and contributor, this part is extremely dear to the author. In the last couple of years, we've seen tens of examples of mislabelled LLMs (sometimes genuine mistakes, sometimes marketing), and there is a need to bring clarity.

To wrap up this first part, we'll also go through the most popular open and commercial large language models out there: if initially it was pretty much just OpenAI and ChatGPT, nowadays there is a plethora of options, extremely difficult to differentiate and compare when it comes to performance, costs and quality.

Part I is organised as follows:

- Chapter 1 presents the introduction on artificial intelligence, machine learning and language modelling.
  If the reader is a subject expert already, the first chapter can be skipped (or considered a nice refresher of the basics); if not, the reader will get a solid introduction that covers all the information needed to enjoy the following chapters at the right level of detail.
- Chapter 2 details how the open source model can be applied to LLMs, the controversies and examples of open LLMs.

- Chapter 3 wraps up the first part, describing the commercial offering and its business model.

By the end of this part, the reader is expected to learn:

The *LLM foundations*—the basic internal working of large language models and how they are designed, trained and fine-tuned to display human-like natural language capabilities.

The *Open source*—the importance of different layers of transparency in this emerging ecosystem.

The *Commercial options*—who were the pioneers in the commercial landscape, their products and the key differences among each other.

Introduction to Large Language Models

Abstract

This chapter introduces the reader to the domain of artificial intelligence, machine learning and deep learning to give a high-level understanding of how LLMs are designed, trained and fine-tuned. It explores the variety of tasks these models can solve: from generating text following user instructions to estimating sentences' semantic similarity (how similar in terms of meaning two sentences are); from text summarisation to content translation and much more. The chapter closes with current known limitations and how the research community and the industry are working to mitigate them.

1.1 Artificial Intelligence, Machine Learning and Deep Learning

Learn the foundational principles at the base of large language models, starting from the definition of artificial intelligence, what is machine learning, how it solves problems and how the implementation of deep neural networks has revolutionised the field, opening the doors to Deep Learning.

Artificial intelligence is a branch of computer science that aims to reproduce human-like intellectual capabilities through computers.

The *artificial* side of the denomination is clear to the public: from Latin *artificium* it literally means *done by hand* and in a broader sense is used nowadays to indicate something done by humans and not by nature.

What we mean by "intelligence" is more complicated.

We could simplify *intelligence* as the ability of a system to perform a task effectively and efficiently, hence minimising resource consumption (including time).

Following this simple definition, general intelligence would be the ability of a system to perform **any** task effectively and efficiently.

In nature, intelligence is achieved by living beings through various skills:

Causality understanding—The ability to associate causes with effects.

Abstract thinking—The ability to recall and manipulate information mentally, it has various degrees of complexity, from a basic representation of the world (what's here and now) to spatial and time abstraction (what's there and yesterday/tomorrow) and imagination (fiction, myths, nations, companies, etc.).

Language—The ability to express information and communicate internal thinking vocally, visually or textually; it has various degrees of complexity, from using a basic, limited set of units to the ability to concatenate such units of language indefinitely.

Cooperation—The ability to collaborate with other systems to achieve the task.

Learning—The ability to improve the task execution based on experience.

Memory—The ability to persist and retrieve information when necessary.

The origins of artificial intelligence go back to Alan Turing and his paper "Computing Machinery and Intelligence" [22] from 1950, where the British polymath discussed possible approaches to building and testing intelligent machines.

As a discipline, it is widely regarded to find its roots in the Dartmouth Summer Research Project on Artificial Intelligence (DSRPAI) conference, hosted by John McCarthy and Marvin Minsky in 1956.

Since then, AI has passed periods of excitement and development (AI Summers) and periods with a substantial decline in enthusiasm and funding (AI Winters).

High expectations are built during AI Summers, and subsequent failure to achieve them causes disillusionment and has a big impact on research and development efforts and funding around the world.

Early approaches to artificial intelligence focused on building machine translation and speech understanding software using perceptrons (an early version of neural networks) [19] and lexical graph exploration [14].

Perceptrons are a form of software (that later became physical machines) that simulates how visual perception works (according to the knowledge of those days).

Their main focus was to represent linear functions with adjustable weights to be used in classification problems to recognise patterns in data (audio and visual).

Despite encouraging results (e.g. the HARPY automatic speech recognition system [14] could recognise around 1,000 words with good accuracy), these primordial AI systems were not good enough for daily use (not to mention military use, where the vast majority of funding was coming from).

The visible dissatisfaction from the sponsors and numerous controversies raised in books and reports of the time [8, 15] brought an increasing scepticism in AI, a reduction of funding, and general interest faded at the beginning of the 1970s.

1.1 Artificial Intelligence, Machine Learning and Deep Learning

We have to wait until the late 1970s and early 1980s to see an AI resurgence with the development of expert systems [9].

The new focus was on knowledge; specifically, these new systems were designed to solve narrow tasks, leveraging knowledge bases and rules.

In the 1980s, they became widely used in the industry, with many of the main corporations around the globe using them in daily business activities.

However, they had problems, and, once again, the ideal of reaching general artificial intelligence through them faded quickly: it was difficult to write and maintain the rules to reflect the knowledge of experts (most of the time it was Boolean logic and conditional if/else statements manually written).

The clamour and expectations around expert systems were growing much faster than the results they were delivering.

Furthermore, the dedicated AI hardware market suffered from the competition of newly available general-purpose machines from Apple and IBM, and the collapse was inevitable: reduction of funding and an AI Winter again in the 1990s.

The early 2000s marked the end of the second AI Winter with more pragmatic development of machine learning, more powerful computational hardware and easy access to large datasets and the Web.

Machine learning is a sub-discipline of artificial intelligence that studies the design, development and application of statistical algorithms that learn from (past) data to predict unseen data without explicit new instructions.

It started theoretically as early as the initial AI studies: the denomination has its roots in 1959, and many of its statistical and mathematical foundations derive from those years.

The reason machine learning became popular again in the 2000s is the shift in its own paradigms: moving from tackling the vague and complex artificial general intelligence (AGI) problem to focusing on practical tasks, working on the strong foundation of statistics, fuzzy logic and probability theory.

The current artificial intelligence resurrection surpassed by a large margin any other AI summer, and multiple factors played a role:

- *Ease of access to theoretical information*—Research papers, surveys and books are easily accessible on the Web, most of the time for free, to any individual (not only academic researchers).
- *Ease of access of computational hardware*—Bare metal is way cheaper, making it more accessible to both research laboratories and individuals.
  Even better, spinning up virtual machines powered by powerful graphical processing units is now almost instantaneous, decently cheap and available on the Web on demand (so you can use it for the limited amount of time you need it).
- *Open source software*—There is a huge variety of machine learning software freely readable, modifiable and extensible.
  International communities of individuals unite their efforts freely and openly: the only entry point is a consumer computer.

- *Managed services*—Many machine learning components are available as services on the Web, so there's no need to rewrite them from scratch, and they can be easily integrated into more complex solutions.
- *Open repositories*—Trained models are available on the Web on public repositories, and they can be used and improved by any individual.

How does machine learning work? We can identify three main approaches:

Supervised learning—A predictive algorithm is trained on a dataset where each data sample is labelled by a supervisor.
The scope of the algorithm is to learn how to predict the label of unseen data.
An example is a system that predicts the price of a house.
The training dataset will be a list of samples, where each sample could represent an existing house with the size, location and known price labelled by a supervisor.
The system will generalise and predict the price of unknown houses, given their size and location.

Unsupervised learning—No labelled training dataset is given to the algorithm, which needs to find the structure of its input on its own.
Examples of unsupervised algorithms are clustering (where data points are divided into groups based on their similarity) and language models (that learn the probability of a word given the surrounding or preceding context).

Reinforcement learning—The algorithm interacts with an environment (could be the real world or other simulations) to perform a task.
A reward/feedback is given depending on how successful it was, the feedback modifies the algorithm itself, and new iterations can happen.
Examples of reinforcement learning are algorithms that are capable of playing games such as chess, pong or go.

One of the most successful and flexible mathematical models used by Machine Learning algorithms is the Artificial Neural Network.
A model vaguely inspired by biological animal brains, composed of processing units (neurons) and edges connecting them (synapses) (Fig. 1.1).
Each neuron receives an input (real number) from connected neurons, processes it through some non-linear function and returns an output (that can be used by other neurons).
How neurons are connected and the weight associated with each edge is learned during the training phase.
Neurons are organised in layers that separate the input from the output.
Numbers move from the first layer (the input layer) to the last layer (the output layer), possibly passing through multiple layers (hidden layers).

1.1 Artificial Intelligence, Machine Learning and Deep Learning

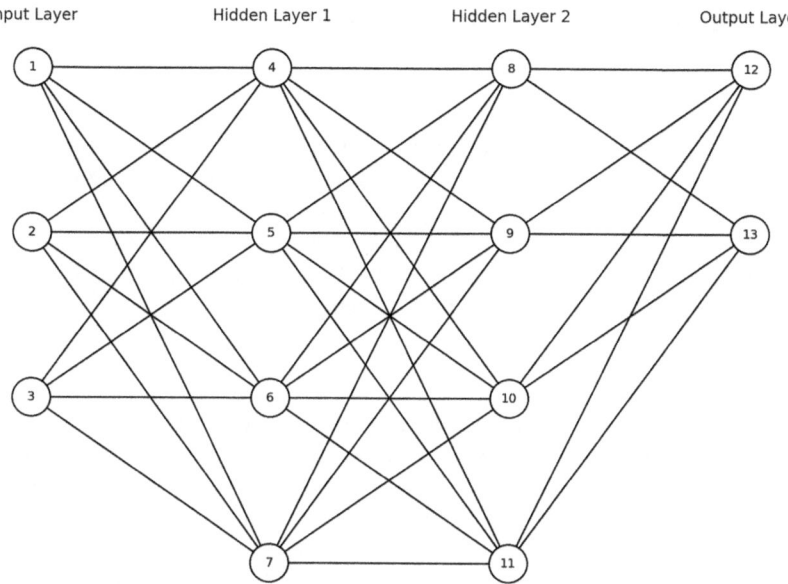

Fig. 1.1 Deep neural network example

A network with a minimum of two hidden layers is called a deep neural network. Deep learning studies the architecture, design, development and application of deep neural networks.

The success of production-grade applications in various domains such as image and speech recognition, natural language processing, robotics and autonomous driving has brought a significant and lasting impact on both the industry and society.

> **Key Takeaways**

- Artificial intelligence is a branch of computer science that studies and develops computer systems able to exhibit intelligent behaviours and problem-solving skills.
- Machine learning is a branch of AI that studies and develops algorithms and software solutions that learn from (past) data how to predict (future) unseen data and perform tasks with no need for explicit instructions.
- Deep learning is a branch of machine learning that leverages deep neural networks (models inspired by biological neuroscience) to perform AI tasks.

1.2 Generative Artificial Intelligence

> Can an artificial system generate a poem or draw a digital painting with minimal explicit instructions? The boom of AI in the 2020s has demonstrated that what was once a dream for many years is now a reality.
>
> Learning from training data, AI software acquires the patterns of natural language, art, audio and video and is able to produce original content inspired by "experience" and make an impact on many aspects of our lives.

Generative AI (not to be confused with artificial general intelligence) is a branch of AI that makes use of generative models to produce text, video, audio and images.

A generative model is trained on large amounts of data to grasp its patterns, structures and building blocks. It also learns how to generate new data by following user instructions and requirements (often expressed in natural language statements).

The history of generative algorithms goes hand in hand with the inception of artificial intelligence, finding its roots in the development of hidden Markov models [5]: statistical models able to produce sequences of words.

However, it wasn't until the advancements in deep learning that generative models saw relevant progress in quality, scalability and adoption.

The first breakthroughs arrived in 2014 with generative adversarial networks [4], among the first models successfully able to generate images in opposition to just labelling and classifying them.

In a generative adversarial architecture, two models are in competition: a generative one that produces data candidates and a discriminative one that evaluates if such data candidates are genuine training data or artificially synthesised.

It's a zero-sum game: the generative network's training target is to increase the error rate of the discriminative network, basically becoming increasingly good at generating data that looks credible and difficult to discern from the original data distribution.

In 2017, we observed another milestone with transformer models [24] leading to the first generative pre-trained transformer (GPT), known as GPT-1, in 2018 [17].

The reason transformers were so foundational for the improvement of generative AI is that they capture relationships between terms far away in the text and can process in parallel long contexts with a huge boost both in performance, scalability and efficiency.

Key in the process is the self-attention mechanism: instead of processing data in sequence, one element at a time, it allows the training to focus on various sections of the sequence all at once and determine which parts are most important.

This new architecture allowed large neural networks to be trained using unsupervised learning or semi-supervised learning, rather than the expensive supervised approach typical of previous discriminant models.

1.2 Generative Artificial Intelligence

Unsupervised learning removed the necessity for humans to manually label data, allowing for larger networks to be trained at a fraction of the human cost.

We'll see later that this statement applies to the pre-training phase, which builds the foundational model from a huge amount (Web-scale) of unlabelled data (Web pages, images datasets, audio/video datasets); human feedback still has a vital role in how large language models are refined (fine-tuned).

Transformers can be divided into two major sub-families:

Bidirectional—Also known as Masked Language Models, during the unsupervised pre-training on a large amount of text, some terms in the sentences are hidden (masked) and the model learns how to fill the gaps leveraging both the words preceding and following the missing ones (hence bidirectional). An example of these models is BERT [2].

Generative pre-trained—They are based on the autoregressive foundation, which means that they are trained to predict the next word based on all the preceding words.

Both family of transformers base their architecture on the encoder/decoder neural network mechanism:

Encoding phase—The encoder neural network processes the entire text in input and represents it as a single vector, condensing its semantics. This is the final hidden state of the encoder.

Decoding phase—The decoder neural network uses the vector as its input hidden state and generates the output text one token at a time.

As language models evolved, different sub-families of transformers ended up using these two main mechanisms in optional combinations:

Encoder only—The model during training makes use of both the encoder neural network and decoder neural network. See bidirectional transformers. At inference time, the model just encodes the input into a vector representation of its semantics using the trained encoder. Examples are BERT [2] and RoBERTa [11].

Decoder only—The decoder just focuses on generating one token at a time, given the preceding tokens. It's a simpler architecture, quicker and cheaper to train, as the focus is only on the decoding neural network. Examples are GPT [16] and Gemini [21].

Encoder/decoder—This family of models make use of the encoder neural network and decoder neural network, both at pre-training and inference time; they involve novel techniques and architecture hybridisation. Examples are BART [6], T5 [18] and modern multi-modal models.

N.B. This nomenclature may be misleading and confusing: all these architectures actually perform encoding/decoding functionalities during pre-training and inference; this is a key mechanism for deep neural networks.

The name "Decoder only" doesn't mean that no encoding happens at all; encoder and decoder are names given to two separate deep neural networks involved in the architecture, so when referring to encoder only/decoder only it means that just one of the two main deep neural networks is present and internally still performs encoding/decoding functionalities of some sort (as any deep neural network).

Generative AI means that algorithms are able to get inspiration from real data to generate new data in various forms, responding to a user request (in natural language).

It's like hiring a copywriter, a poet or a digital painter who is able to perform the tasks you ask and take inspiration from a large portion of Web and historical data to do so.

With one big issue: it's a computer program and not human.

It's already decently complex to assess when a work of a human is far enough from the original inspiration to not be considered copyright infringement.

The scale of generative AI brings this problem to a whole different level.

It's known that the vast majority of these generative models have been trained on publicly accessible data, with no particular attention to the copyright owners of such data.

Many generative models (proprietary or partially open) do not disclose all the details about the training datasets, the model architecture, the training algorithm and the strategies.

This lack of transparency makes it extremely difficult for external entities to assess the exact nature of copyright infringement (if any).

This applies to:

Training—Using content without the permission of the copyright owner may end up in unauthorised copies: exact copies stored during the training phase and copies in the form of deep-learned representations in the model after the training.

Output—The content generated by generative models may create copyright liability if they are exactly the same or too similar to copyrighted work (probably used during the training).

Addressing these issues also depends on where the output work is going to be used.

Many artists and organisations in the creative business (art, film, music, video games, books, comics, etc.) have strongly come out in opposition to these practices.[1]

Some countries have or are working to draft specific laws for these use cases [3, 23].[2]

It's certainly difficult to understand where to draw these lines, and many careers are at stake.

---

[1] https://www.aitrainingstatement.org.

[2] https://www.diligent.com/resources/guides/ai-regulations-around-the-world.

It's true that humans also take inspiration from licensed works of others and create derivative output. When it's dissimilar enough to the original inspiration, it doesn't break any copyright.

Talking about humans, the learning (a parallel to the training of a generative model) part of our brain is opaque enough not to spark a massive outcry.

It's a different story when this happens in the data centres of massive corporations, programmatically and on purpose.

> **Key Takeaways**

- Generative models are mostly deep neural networks trained on huge amounts of data.
- Generative AI systems leverage computational models to generate text, audio, images and videos.
- It's controversial where to set the boundaries to delimit fair usage, respect authorship of the training content and how to prevent cyber criminals from creating fake information.

1.3 What Is a Large Language Model?

Large, because you need a huge quantity of resources and data to train them, and the resulting representation is a complex computational structure.

Language model, because they attempt to encode the syntax and semantics of a language (mostly written but also audio-video multi-modal).

The original idea, the initial implementations and the breakthrough with the development of transformers are key milestones in comprehending how LLMs are designed and implemented.

The training on large-scale data and fine-tuning (on smaller datasets) to perform a specific task completes the picture.

A large language model is a machine learning generative model developed to solve natural language generation and processing tasks.

The term "large" refers to the size in terms of architecture (the parameters of the deep neural network involved) and training/fine-tuning dataset (the amount of data used to learn the language patterns first and then specialise).

Historically, many models were considered "large" at the time of inception and gradually shifted to "not that large anymore" as technology and scales in computer science increased.

What was considered large in 2018, with the first transformers, is now considered to have a modest size, and this trend is expected to continue as technology evolves.

Nowadays, the largest and most interesting LLMs are generative pre-trained transformers.

As seen in the previous section, such models are immensely powerful autocomplete systems that leverage all the input provided to generate successive terms.

The unsupervised pre-training happens on Web-scale textual data (when multi-modality is involved, it's also visual and audio data).

Fine-tuning, on the other hand, has the responsibility of specialising the model on a task, using a supervised approach on a much smaller dataset (ten thousand samples in opposition to the trillions used at pre-training).

> **Key Takeaways**

- Large language models for text are autocomplete on steroids.
- First, the model needs pre-training on large (Internet-scale) datasets to learn the structure of the language.
- Second, the model is fine-tuned on smaller datasets to specialise its ability to solve narrow tasks.
- Multi-modal LLMs work simultaneously on text, video and audio.

1.4 Fine-tuned for…

How can a gigantic representation of a language learn to summarise a news article or write a well-formed code snippet?

It's time to drop the abstraction and read concretely about tasks LLMs proved to be quite good at solving.

Fine-tuning requires a clear definition of the problem you aim to solve, the design of the dataset (content and structure) necessary to learn how to perform the task and an algorithm to use the dataset to modify the internal structure of the base model to tackle the target task better.

Fine-tuning is an approach to refining the parameters of a trained deep neural network to adapt and solve a task.

It's an example of transfer learning: the knowledge gained (the deep neural network architecture and learned weights) from a task (autoregressive text generation) is the starting point to obtain an updated model that is a better fit to solve a new task.

1.4 Fine-tuned for...

Depending on the target task and fine-tuning algorithm, this process may affect the entirety of the neural network or only a subset of the layers, implying smaller or bigger differences from the original pre-trained model and computational footprint.

Fine-tuning generally happens as a supervised learning process, where a labelled dataset is used to learn how to modify the original model.

Generally, it is much smaller than the original pre-training dataset.

The original deep neural network weights are adjusted, iteration after iteration, to minimise a task-specific loss function calculated over the labelled dataset.

Supervised learning is often combined with reinforcement learning from human feedback [16] to fine-tune generative pre-trained models to follow instructions to generate text.

Starting from a model pre-trained on a large corpus of data, to predict terms, let's see how fine-tuning works for different tasks and what type of dataset you need.

1.4.1 Following Instructions

The task of following instructions became hugely popular with the development of chatbots and the release of ChatGPT product in 2022.

It started as a simple textual interaction where the user enters a query prompt with a question and demands text generated in response to the needed information.

With the huge popular adoption, people started to interrogate LLMs to perform any kind of text generation task, and fine-tuning for following instructions became more and more complex.

Nowadays, it's possible to programmatically interact with LLM to solve coding challenges, process and generate multi-modal data, execute third-party functions to increase the model's capabilities and restrict the response in a well-defined and coded format.

So let's start from the basics: what does it mean to supervise fine-tuning a pre-trained large language model for following instructions?

First of all, you need a labelled dataset in which each sample associates a prompt (a natural language request) with a response (in natural language).

The second step consists of identifying the right training objective for the task, and in this instance, it's the same as the pre-training one: predicting the correct next token given the preceding ones.

A loss function is associated with such an objective, and iteration after iteration, the weights in the model are adjusted (using gradient descent or similar optimising techniques) to minimise the loss function, making the model more aligned to the input fine-tuning dataset.

A fundamental breakthrough that opened the door to interesting developments came with reinforcement learning from human feedback [16]:

- A dataset that associates prompts to textual responses is manually produced by humans, with a cardinality in the realm of 10,000 samples
- A first policy model is fine-tuned from the original LLM, using the dataset − > the resulting model is better at generating prompt responses rather than just generating sequences of terms
- The policy model is used to generate many new examples of prompts/responses
- The newly generated responses are labelled by humans with a graded relevance score (from 0 to 5, for example)
- A reward model is trained on such ratings and can be used in a reinforcement learning process to refine the policy model
- Each reinforcement learning episode consists of generating a response for a prompt, measuring the relevance with the reward model and backpropagate with a dedicated algorithm the necessary changes to make more probable such response (if the feedback from the reward model was positive) or less probable (if the feedback from the reward model was negative).

A popular family of algorithms for this is called proximal policy optimisation [20].

The key concept behind this process is that humans are much quicker in labelling a <prompt, response > pair with a rating than answering a prompt with a full text manually written.

In this way, the quality of a model can scale up much quicker.

In addition, once some of these instruction-following models became publicly accessible, a feedback mechanism was added in the user interfaces to additionally collect positive/negative ratings from users (not only from dedicated labellers).

This naturally introduces more noise but also a huge quantity of ratings that can be used to better train the reward model and consequently improve the overall model.

1.4.2 Text Vectorisation

The task of text vectorisation aims to represent textual data in a numerical vector format, preserving its semantic information.

Pieces of text semantically close are mapped to numerical vectors close in the vector space.

Different vector distance metrics can be used to fine-tune a model; generally, cosine distance or dot product are the most used [1].[3]

---

[3] https://www.pinecone.io/learn/vector-similarity.

The fine-tuning dataset may take different shapes (triples, pairs with a relevance label, etc.) but in general associates a sentence with two sentences: one semantically similar and one semantically dissimilar.

The training objective is to reach a vector representation for the sentences that minimises the distance between the vectors of similar sentences and maximises the distance between vectors of dissimilar sentences.

One question that may arise at this point is: How can a neural network trained to predict the next token encode text into a vector?

We've seen the encoder/decoder architecture in Sect. 1.2.

Deep neural networks internally present various hidden layers that encode different stages and aspects of the information (hidden states).

This happens before the information reaches the decoder component and is condensed into the next token prediction.

What does a hidden state represent? Technically, it's a temporary representation of the information, output of the preceding hidden layer and input of the following hidden layer.

In human terms, you can associate a hidden state with the idea you get in your mind of a sentence you just read.

Once you have finished a sequence of sentences, you'll have gathered a clear understanding of the overall semantics of the text, that is, the final hidden state before the decoder.

1.4.3 Summarisation

The task of text summarisation aims to produce a shorter version of input textual data, minimising the loss of information.

The task itself it's similar to following instructions in a prompt and generating text in output: it's still a sequence-to-sequence task where the sequence is a text sequence; this task can be considered as a narrower specialisation of the instruction-based generative task.

Instruction-based LLMs are good at summarising text by default: with the right prompt, you can get quick and valuable results.

But obviously, if you just need to summarise, leveraging the original LLM may be overkill: ideally, you want to distil only the capabilities you care about (in this instance, the ability to summarise text).

If you start from a pre-trained LLM, the dataset to use in the fine-tuning is a list of samples in which each sample associates a text with its summarised version.

Practically all transformer architectures can be fine-tuned for summarisation, starting from encoder-only such as BERT and encoder/decoder models as T5 [10, 26].

The summarisation quality varies from model to model and depends on many factors, including the domain, structure and length of text, but the fine-tuning dataset doesn't change much, allowing decently quick experimentation and an iterative approach.

If you start from an instruction-based model, your dataset needs to be adjusted: the input needs to be changed by prefixing an instruction prompt such as "Summarise the following text"; we are effectively additionally fine-tuning the model to become better at a very specific prompt.

Most recent research in automatic summarisation shifted towards using decoder-only generative models, introducing additional human feedback in the loop [12].

Another interesting fine-tuning approach for summarisation is to fine-tune a compact model using the output of a larger model as a reference using contrastive learning [13].

Contrastive learning, in opposition to supervised learning, performs fine-tuning iteratively, showing the model pairs of summaries with a preference, affecting episode after episode, the way the internal deep neural weights are distributed, and affecting the probability of generating the better summary.

1.4.4 Translation

The task of text translation aims to translate a text from one language to another, minimising the loss of information and keeping both syntactical and semantical integrity: the output text must be grammatically correct and communicate the same meaning as the input text.

Generally, when building a translation system, the focus is on just two languages: a source and a target.

When the translation task involves more than two languages, it's called Multilingual Machine Translation, and more challenges arise.

Similar to text summarisation, also in this case, the task itself is still a sequence-to-sequence task where the sequence in input/output is a text sequence; this task can be considered as a narrower specialisation of the instruction-based generative task.

Instruction-based LLMs are good at translating text by default: with the right prompt, you can build an application that is decently good at translating from many languages to others, but a specialist model, properly fine-tuned, can do better [29].

The key here is the pre-training, where a model must have been exposed to multiple languages already to obtain emergent translation capabilities.

Also, in this case, if you want to focus on translating only, the original LLM won't be the best fit: ideally, you want to distil only translation capabilities.

If you start from a pre-trained LLM, the dataset to use in the fine-tuning is a list of samples in which each sample associates a text in the source language with its translated version in the target language.

Pretty much all transformer architectures can be used as a foundation for fine-tuning for machine translation [27].

If you start from an instruction-based model, your dataset needs to be adjusted: the input needs to be changed by prefixing an instruction prompt such as "Translate the following text from <language1 > to <language2 >": we are effectively additionally fine-tuning the model to become better at a very specific prompt [7,28].

> **Key Takeaways**

- The most popular version of large language models is fine-tuned to follow instructions.
- Instructions following Large Language Models can solve many tasks out of the box with the right prompt.
- Zero-shot prompting can be improved by passing examples in the prompt (few-shot prompting).
- Fine-tuning changes the internals of the model to better serve the task.
- Fine-tuning is cheaper than fully retraining a model.
- A dedicated dataset must be crafted and used to fine-tune a model (supervised), much smaller than the pre-training dataset.

1.5 Limitations and How to Mitigate Them

Large language models are not perfect (yet). They tend to invent plausible lies and generate incorrect information with confidence. They can't be trusted without fact-checking and verification. What can we do to mitigate these risks?

The three main weaknesses of current large language models are:

- Hallucinations
- Outdated information
- Opaque reasoning

A hallucination in the realm of LLMs is when the generated response is syntactically correct, meaningful and credible but not based on any real factual data.

A hallucinating LLM can be very dangerous, as hallucinations look very convincing to a human reader and are very difficult to identify.

Having to double-check all the information generated by an LLM may defeat entirely the benefits of using it in the first place for certain critical tasks.

A preliminary classification of hallucinations:

- **Intrinsic**—When the generated output contradicts the input prompt (easier to identify)
- **Extrinsic**—When the generated output's genuineness can't be verified just using the input information

But why do large language models hallucinate?
Problems can arise at different stages and levels:

- *Data* used for pre-training and fine-tuning
- *Algorithms* used for pertaining, fine-tuning and inference

Incomplete and conflictual information, fake news and biases may be present in the datasets used for training and fine-tuning, which are normally extracted from the Web and not manually curated at a fine-grain level by human reviewers.

Imperfections in learning the information representation and erroneous decoding may end up generating plausible but non-factual text.

According to studies, hallucinations are just inevitable [25].

There are mitigations, though, to both reduce hallucinations and make them more apparent to the reader when they happen, facilitating the task of identifying them.

Polishing the pre-training and fine-tuning dataset and curating the factuality, data quality and readability is the first significant step.

Prompting techniques such as few-shot prompting (adding examples of input/output pairs in the prompt itself) and chain-of-thoughts prompting (adding input/output with reasoning explanation directly in the prompt) can additionally reduce hallucinations.

Also, enriching the context at query time with third-party information has empirically been proven to reduce the phenomenon, but no guarantee of solving it, see Sect. 4.2.

To make hallucinations simpler to identify, many LLMs started adding clickable citations along the generated text, giving the user an additional tool to quickly assess the quality and factuality of the generated text.

Unfortunately, citations are also vulnerable to being completely invented or not related to the generated text at all, so it's still a work in progress and could see major quality improvements over the next few months.

Another aspect that severely limits out-of-the-box large language models is the training date cut-off: the models know information up to a certain point in time (when the dataset for pre-training and fine-tuning was prepared), which means that the more time passes from such date, the more likely the model is to generate outdated answers to the users' prompts.

Pre-training is extremely expensive in time and resources; doing it continuously for a model right now is unthinkable (and with the current energy and carbon footprint of such activity, being self-conscious, we shouldn't even think about it).

On the other hand, fine-tuning is less resource-intensive and can happen more frequently, but in most cases (and for the biggest models) not frequently enough.

To mitigate this problem, large language models can be integrated into retrieval augmented generation pipelines.

External data sources are queried to retrieve additional context for the user prompt and to supply the model with fresher data.

1.5 Limitations and How to Mitigate Them

Empirically, it has been proven that LLMs tend to prefer the newly provided context over the original trained data (see Sect. 4.2).

Depending on the domain, various logics can affect when the external data sources are queried.

Publicly accessible instruction following LLMs tends to run Web queries to enrich the user prompt when an internal classifier detects the need:

- *Timelines*: Does the prompt involve events, trends or data that may have changed or emerged after the cut-off date?
- *Specificity*: Does the prompt depend on detailed, localised or uncommon knowledge not stored in the training data?
- *Explicit user request*: Did the user explicitly ask for a Web query or fresh, real-time information?
- *Ambiguity*: Are there gaps in the model's understanding of the prompt that a Web search could clarify?
- *High-risk of error*: Does the response's reliability depend on precise and up-to-date information?

Such classification logic can be implemented with classifiers of increasing complexity and doesn't guarantee the generation of always up-to-date information, but it's an acceptable mitigation for the large majority of use cases.

Another challenging aspect of current LLMs is the opacity of their reasoning capabilities, which sometimes makes it difficult to understand where certain generated knowledge is coming from, increasing the difficulty of identifying hallucinated or outdated content.

The internals of LLMs are extremely complex and opaque to human understanding. Sure, you can ask the LLM itself to add the reasoning snippet in the prompt, but such a snippet will suffer the same limitations as the original response.

In this regard, available mitigations involve again the usage of citations associated with paragraphs of the generated text and adding explicit instructions in the prompt to add the reasoning in addition to the response.

One final point about prompt engineering: the set of techniques and approaches to write better prompts.

LLMs have been trained and fine-tuned to be able to process as much natural language text as possible without the need to be specialists to interact with them, so it sounds quite counterintuitive that you need special abilities to get the best out of them.

Practically, the models are indeed fine-tuned on prompts and responses, so it's very likely that different models may need slightly different prompts to obtain the same response.

Crafting prompt strategies, unless supplied as documentation by the model owners, is unlikely to be proper engineering: in most cases, it is just trial and error, empirically trying and consolidating prompts that appear to work **probably** well on specific use cases and data.

The key here is the **probably**: at the moment when you need to solve a particular task using a Large Language Model, especially an instruction following LLM, not specifically fine-tuned for the task of your interest, refining the prompt and rewording it will just affect the probability of getting the right response and won't guarantee that you will get a well-formed syntactically and semantically response all the times.

As we increasingly use instruction following LLMs programmatically, we'll have to improve the way we interact with them, adding a programmable interface on top of the natural language prompting.

Interesting developments in this direction are already happening, for example, with the structured output capability of many modern general-purpose models.[4]

This wraps up the introduction!

Now you should have a better basis and tools to digest the main content of the book. I hope you enjoy it!

> **Key Takeaways**

- Large language models' hallucinations are often hard to detect by humans.
- Prompt engineering is more about trial and error than following a structured approach.
- Programming Large Language Models is an emerging area of study.

References

1. Achananuparp, P., Hu, X., Shen, X.: The evaluation of sentence similarity measures. In: Data Warehousing and Knowledge Discovery: 10th International Conference, DaWaK 2008 Turin, Italy, September 2–5, 2008 Proceedings 10, pp. 305–316. Springer, Berlin (2008)
2. Devlin, J., Chang, M.W., Lee, K., Toutanova, K.: Bert: Pre-training of deep bidirectional transformers for language understanding (2019). https://arxiv.org/abs/1810.04805
3. European Union: Regulation (EU) 2024/1689 of the European parliament and of the council (2024). https://eur-lex.europa.eu/eli/reg/2024/1689/oj, official Journal of the European Union
4. Goodfellow, I.J., Pouget-Abadie, J., Mirza, M., Xu, B., Warde-Farley, D., Ozair, S., Courville, A., Bengio, Y.: Generative adversarial networks (2014). https://arxiv.org/abs/1406.2661
5. Knill, K., Young, S.: Hidden Markov Models in Speech and Language Processing, pp. 27–68. Springer Netherlands, Dordrecht (1997). https://doi.org/10.1007/978-94-017-1183-8_2
6. Lewis, M., Liu, Y., Goyal, N., Ghazvininejad, M., Mohamed, A., Levy, O., Stoyanov, V., Zettlemoyer, L.: Bart: denoising sequence-to-sequence pre-training for natural language generation, translation, and comprehension (2019). https://arxiv.org/abs/1910.13461
7. Li, J., Zhou, H., Huang, S., Cheng, S., Chen, J.: Eliciting the translation ability of large language models via multilingual finetuning with translation instructions (2024). https://arxiv.org/abs/2305.15083

---

[4] https://openai.com/index/introducing-structured-outputs-in-the-api.

References

8. Lighthill, J.: Artificial intelligence: a general survey (1973). https://www.chilton-computing.org.uk/inf/literature/reports/lighthill_report/p001.htm, presented to the Science Research Council
9. Lindsay, R.K., Buchanan, B.G., Feigenbaum, E.A., Lederberg, J.: Dendral: a case study of the first expert system for scientific hypothesis formation. Artif. Intell. **61**(2), 209–261 (1993). https://doi.org/10.1016/0004-3702(93)90068-M. https://www.sciencedirect.com/science/article/pii/000437029390068M
10. Liu, Y., Lapata, M.: Text summarization with pretrained encoders. In: Inui, K., Jiang, J., Ng, V., Wan, X. (eds.) Proceedings of the 2019 Conference on Empirical Methods in Natural Language Processing and the 9th International Joint Conference on Natural Language Processing (EMNLP-IJCNLP), pp. 3730–3740. Association for Computational Linguistics, Hong Kong, China (2019). https://doi.org/10.18653/v1/D19-1387. https://aclanthology.org/D19-1387/
11. Liu, Y., Ott, M., Goyal, N., Du, J., Joshi, M., Chen, D., Levy, O., Lewis, M., Zettlemoyer, L., Stoyanov, V.: Roberta: a robustly optimized BERT pretraining approach (2019). https://arxiv.org/abs/1907.11692
12. Liu, Y., Deb, B., Teruel, M., Halfaker, A., Radev, D., Awadallah, A.H.: On improving summarization factual consistency from natural language feedback (2023). https://arxiv.org/abs/2212.09968
13. Liu, Y., Shi, K., He, K.S., Ye, L., Fabbri, A.R., Liu, P., Radev, D., Cohan, A.: On learning to summarize with large language models as references (2024). https://arxiv.org/abs/2305.14239
14. Lowerre, B.T.: The harpy speech recognition system. In: The HARPY Speech Recognition System (1976). https://api.semanticscholar.org/CorpusID:61409851
15. Minsky, M., Papert, S.: Perceptrons: An Introduction to Computational Geometry. MIT Press, Cambridge (1969)
16. Ouyang, L., Wu, J., Jiang, X., Almeida, D., Wainwright, C.L., Mishkin, P., Zhang, C., Agarwal, S., Slama, K., Ray, A., Schulman, J., Hilton, J., Kelton, F., Miller, L., Simens, M., Askell, A., Welinder, P., Christiano, P., Leike, J., Lowe, R.: Training language models to follow instructions with human feedback (2022). https://arxiv.org/abs/2203.02155
17. Radford, A., Narasimhan, K., Salimans, T., Sutskever, I.: Improving language understanding by generative pre-training (2018). https://cdn.openai.com/research-covers/language-unsupervised/language_understanding_paper.pdf, technical report, OpenAI
18. Raffel, C., Shazeer, N., Roberts, A., Lee, K., Narang, S., Matena, M., Zhou, Y., Li, W., Liu, P.J.: Exploring the limits of transfer learning with a unified text-to-text transformer (2023). https://arxiv.org/abs/1910.10683
19. Rosenblatt, F.: The perceptron: a probabilistic model for information storage and organization in the brain. Psychol. Rev. **65**(6), 386–408 (1958). https://doi.org/10.1037/h0042519. https://doi.org/10.1037/h0042519
20. Schulman, J., Wolski, F., Dhariwal, P., Radford, A., Klimov, O.: Proximal policy optimization algorithms (2017). https://arxiv.org/abs/1707.06347
21. Team, G., et al.: Gemini: a family of highly capable multimodal models (2024). https://arxiv.org/abs/2312.11805
22. Turing, A.M.: I.—computing machinery and intelligence. Mind **LIX**(236), 433–460 (1950). https://doi.org/10.1093/mind/LIX.236.433
23. UK Government: Copyright and artificial intelligence: Consultation (2024). https://www.gov.uk/government/consultations/copyright-and-artificial-intelligence/copyright-and-artificial-intelligence
24. Vaswani, A., Shazeer, N., Parmar, N., Uszkoreit, J., Jones, L., Gomez, A.N., Kaiser, L., Polosukhin, I.: Attention is all you need (2023). https://arxiv.org/abs/1706.03762
25. Xu, Z., Jain, S., Kankanhalli, M.: Hallucination is inevitable: an innate limitation of large language models (2024). https://arxiv.org/abs/2401.11817
26. Zhang, H., Yu, P.S., Zhang, J.: A systematic survey of text summarization: from statistical methods to large language models (2024). https://arxiv.org/abs/2406.11289

27. Zhang, X., Rajabi, N., Duh, K., Koehn, P.: Machine translation with large language models: prompting, few-shot learning, and fine-tuning with QLoRA. In: Koehn, P., Haddow, B., Kocmi, T., Monz, C. (eds.) Proceedings of the Eighth Conference on Machine Translation, pp. 468–481. Association for Computational Linguistics, Singapore (2023). https://doi.org/10.18653/v1/2023.wmt-1.43. https://aclanthology.org/2023.wmt-1.43/
28. Zheng, J., Hong, H., Liu, F., Wang, X., Su, J., Liang, Y., Wu, S.: Fine-tuning large language models for domain-specific machine translation (2024). https://arxiv.org/abs/2402.15061
29. Zhu, W., Liu, H., Dong, Q., Xu, J., Huang, S., Kong, L., Chen, J., Li, L.: Multilingual machine translation with large language models: Empirical results and analysis (2024). https://arxiv.org/abs/2304.04675

The Open Source Landscape

2

Abstract

This chapter introduces the reader to what it means for a large language model to be open source, all the aspects involved, the community consensus and stories of false claims. It gives insights on how to recognise when an LLM is truly open and how to be wary of vague marketing. We'll explore notorious examples of modern LLMs that are open in some way or another, highlighting the level of openness each of them is currently at. The chapter closes with popular public repositories and archives to use to navigate the open source landscape of large language models.

2.1 What Does "Open" Mean for a Large Language Model?

For large language models, being fully open source means that:

- You can use the system for any reason without having to ask permission from any entity.
- You can study how the system works internally in all its components.
- You can modify the system for any reason.
- You can share the system for others to use it with or without modifications, for any reason.

This means that the training and fine-tuning datasets, any code used to train and run the system and all the learned parameters, such as the model weights, must be made available under an open-source-approved license.

Since the release of ChatGPT in 2022 and the exponential explosion in LLM adoption and research, there has been a long period where there was no official definition of open source LLM, and this caused quite a lot of havoc and questionable press news releases.

Many companies were releasing large language models, so-called open source, while potentially only the model parameters were accessible (and sometimes with very restrictive licenses).

In the 2020s, open source AI is seen as the benevolent side that fights against the big bad guys of closed software corporations, something more transparent, something you should adopt in opposition to other solutions.

Aside from genuine players, there's a huge economic and reputation interest in positioning yourself in this niche, and with a cloudy definition, many ended up making glorious announcements of openness that were not backed by any real significant fact.

During this uncertain period, the Open Source Initiative[1] brought together global experts and practitioners to establish a shared set of rules and principles that can define what it means for an AI system to be open, similar to that which the Open Source Definition has done for the software ecosystem.

The output of this work was version 1.0 of the Open Source AI Definition[2], released on 28 October 2024.

The definition establishes that to be considered open source, a large language model should make available under an open-source-approved license all its datasets, code, architecture and learned parameter components to guarantee free and unrestricted usage, study, modification and sharing.

If the model doesn't respect this definition, **it can't be considered open source**.

Sometimes, only certain aspects and components are released under open-source-approved licenses.

For example, if the user can access, modify and redistribute only the learned model weights without significant legal or ethical limitations, the model must be called an open-weight model.

Following this interesting survey by Liesenfeld et al. [9], let's dive into the main components of a large language model from an open source perspective.

2.1.1 License

You've read in the previous paragraph that an LLM to be considered open source should release all its components "under an open-source-approved license". What does it mean?

The Open Source Initiative (OSI) is a non-profit organisation that promotes and advocates for open source software by defining what constitutes "open source" and

---

[1] https://opensource.org/.

[2] https://opensource.org/ai/open-source-ai-definition.

by maintaining the Open Source Definition (OSD), a set of criteria that software licenses must meet to be considered open source.

The list of accepted licenses is online and continuously updated.[3]

There are many different variations across all the accepted licenses, and the public OSI review process makes sure that software labelled as open source respects the community standards and expectations.

An approved license ensures that the software can be used, modified and shared freely (without having to ask permission from anybody).

The same applies to datasets and learned weights of LLM; licenses can be applied to any form of digital data, not only to software code.

2.1.2 Datasets: Pre-training and Fine-tuning

As we've seen in the introduction chapter, a lot of data is used to train an LLM.

Such data is organised into different datasets and used in different stages of model training.

At the time of writing, it's quite standardised to have the pre-training dataset, trillions of tokens used to obtain the base model and a fine-tuning dataset, smaller and more curated to specialise on a specific task.

These datasets are an integral part of the model itself as they are fundamental to reproducing it.

At the same time, it's quite rare for a released model to fully disclose these datasets, reason why we'll see later in this chapter that the current available fully open source models are a handful (among the hundreds that call themselves open source).

The reasons that companies and entities behind LLMs are so reluctant to release their datasets are manifold:

- Publicly available doesn't mean you can necessarily do everything you like with it. Many LLMs use data that violates the licensing agreement, making the dataset itself illegal.[4]
- Datasets are often synthesised by accessing directly free/paid services of other LLMs, potentially violating the terms of use, and without asking for special permissions.
- Datasets can contain controversial, biased and unethical data.

Although against open source principles, being datasets expensive to curate, they end up being classed as the "secret sauce" behind successful LLMs: effectively using the same architecture and code, with drastically different training datasets, you will end up with drastically different models.

---

[3] https://opensource.org/licenses.
[4] https://www.theguardian.com/media/2023/dec/27/new-york-times-openai-microsoft-lawsuit.

There's still a long road ahead until all the organisations in the self-called open source AI domain democratise datasets, opening them, removing all illegal and controversial practices and embracing the transparency we are used to with traditional open source software.

2.1.3 Code: Pre-training, Fine-Tuning and Inference

All the code used to train an LLM needs to be fully accessible, readable, modifiable and sharable.

Not only the training code, not only the fine-tuning or inference code: any code base that has been used to produce the model must be released under an open-source-approved license.

As for any other software system, where it to be considered open source, all of its modules must be open; the same applies for LLMs.

Only in this way can we open the doors for reproducibility (which is still immensely expensive nowadays) and community progress.

Many self-proclaimed open source LLMs don't disclose all the code modules that are an integral part of the LLM, but we are starting to see improvements.

2.1.4 Architecture

Starting from the code architecture (how all the software components interact with each other to train and operate the model) and finishing with the neural model architecture itself, it must be fully and openly disclosed.

Only knowing how to connect the dots (all the components and learned parameters), you achieve full transparency and openness.

2.1.5 Weights: Base Model and Fine-Tuned Model

This is the last mandatory component to guarantee a fully open source LLM: all the learned weight parameters for the base and fine-tuned model.

These numbers, along with the model architecture, regulate how the deep neural network works and are fundamental to using the model freely: they are the result of days of expensive training.

They allow you to replicate the black box; it's the bare minimum information you need to operate a model, ignoring its training history and internals.

Most models that claim to be open source only release these learned parameters.

It's still better than nothing and appreciable, given how expensive these numbers are to produce, but you get such an opacity that the usage of them you can do to foster progress in the field is very limited.

2.1.6 Paper

Scientific papers, when well written and peer reviewed properly, are a fantastic resource to better understand a complex system.

LLMs are extremely complex; sometimes they don't innovate much, and their secret is just the training data, but from time to time innovation happens and a clear and exhaustive paper can be a wonderful addition to how open the model is, guaranteeing a better reproducibility, a better understanding of its internals and consequentially an easier adoption and evolution of the ideas presented.

Many LLM producers publish some sort of paper along with their model, which is a great first step, but most of the time, these papers are just marketing white papers that didn't have any third-party or independent peer review.

In general, every claim must be taken with a pinch of salt; not all papers are equal, so make sure to always double-check how and where the paper was published. There's a huge difference between a marketing white paper, a paper published on predatory journals[5] and a solid paper published on an authoritative journal or conference.

Realising a comprehensive paper along with the model is not a requirement for a model being considered open source, but it can be a very positive addition.

2.1.7 Documentation

Associating a well-written documentation with the model to help both the users and potential contributors is not mandatory for an LLM to be open source.

At the same time as for the paper, having it is a great plus for a model: the code architecture, components functionality and interactions will be clearer.

The effort of reproducing and improving the model will diminish, lowering the barrier for additional community engagement, as with any other open source project. Nice documentation is your best calling card to present to future contributors.

2.1.8 APIs

This goes alongside the documentation; having a clear understanding of all the training/fine-tuning and inference APIs offered by an LLM makes it much simpler to adopt.

A clear definition of the expected input/output, both in terms of format and semantics, makes the adoption of the model simpler and its functioning clearer to the public.

---

[5] https://en.wikipedia.org/wiki/Predatory_publishing.

> **Key Takeaways**

- An open source LLM must release all its components, including datasets, code and learned weights, under an open source license.
- Most of the models that claim to be open source are actually only open weight, i.e. they just release the learned model parameters.
- Many components, such as scientific papers, documentation and API details, are not fundamental for being open source, but extremely helpful for a healthy community nonetheless.

2.2 Open Source General Purpose Large Language Models

There are only a handful of models that respect the Open Source AI definition and share openly all their components, including the datasets, the code and the learned weights.

The vast majority of LLMs that claim to be fully open source are actually just open weights and sometimes not even that.

Let's also clarify this, specifying "fully open source" shouldn't be necessary, the model is open source or not.

Practising open washing is becoming an increasingly popular phenomenon: Many corporations in the large language model domain strategically use terms like "open" and "open source" on their Web sites and press releases while, in fact, they hide their models almost entirely from scientific and regulatory scrutiny.

Positioning your model in this niche is done for marketing purposes: there's not actually any intent of providing meaningful insight into source code, training data, fine-tuning data or architecture of systems.

It's a strategy to adverse the notoriously closed models, showing an illusory better ethics to gain public adoption, users and eventually a market share through software as a service approaches.

Most of the time, given the amount of LLMs now present in the market, it's also a way to attempt to go viral and differentiate from the competitor crowd, but the mechanisms won't last long, as now pretty much all models around are advertised as open.

2.2 Open Source General Purpose Large Language Models

Furthermore, a growing community of open source enthusiasts is starting to debunk false open claims.

The reality is that only very few models currently embrace the open source philosophy, and you probably have never heard of them:

OLMo[5] - https://allenai.org/olmo
   Company: Ai2
   License: Apache-2.0 license
   Notable for: Solid model when compared to state of the art, backed by a structured research institute, good quality for all resources, extensive documentation and paper coverage, no controversy to date!

Philanthropist and Microsoft co-founder Paul Allen founded Ai2 in 2014 to develop artificial intelligence solutions for real-world challenges.

Embracing the open source philosophy, the OLMo family of models presents solid performance and competes with closed and open-weight models.

K2[10] - https://www.llm360.ai
   Company: LLM360
   License: Apache-2.0 license
   Notable for: A 65 billion parameter language model trained on 1.4 trillion tokens. It outperforms Llama 2 70B, using less compute to train.

LLM360 believes in a future where artificial general intelligence is reached by a community effort, for the community. Their models may not be the top-performing ones, but they have a decently active blog and a couple of technical reports available.

Aside from the big ones, there's a continuous effort into exploring smaller versions of language models (still decently big but much smaller in comparison to the titans we have explored so far).

TinyLlama [17] is an example of this category: It aims to implement modern cutting-edge standards with a community approach, to train a small model, computationally lighter than traditional large language models but cheaper and with high-quality performance for the small size.

The application of smaller models should not be underestimated: they are valuable to run locally on machines with limited computational and memory capacity (mobile devices) or as a side functionality for other intensive applications (such as video games).

> **Key Takeaways**

- Pretty much all the models you believed to be open source actually are not.
- There are very few open source large language models; OLMo and K2 are some examples.
- There's an effort to explore the small language model landscape embracing full open source.

2.3 Partially Open Large Language Models

Most of the models in this section claim to be fully open source, while they actually share only a little of their internals. There's still value in sharing the learned model weights or a part of the training dataset, but let's call different things by different names. Let's explore the most prominent models in this category with a clear insight into the level of openness of each one.

Starting with the (somewhat fragmented) release of the trained weights of OpenAI GPT-2 in 2019, we've seen plenty of press releases where various corporations embraced the open way for their models.

As expressed multiple times in this chapter, don't get fooled by their claims of full open source-ness; always double-check their statements and verify if they really adhere to the open source initiative.

It could be a surprise, but more often than not, they don't.

This section aims to demystify the jungle of false open source LLMs, carefully verifying the level of partial openness of each of the major players in this category:

Llama[15]—https://www.llama.com/
Company: Meta AI
License: Llama 4 Community License Agreement
(custom, not open source license with several limitations)
  - https://raw.githubusercontent.com/meta-llama/llama-models/refs/heads/main/models/llama4/LICENSE
Notable for: Llama periodically tops the leaderboard on many tasks; it has frequent releases, offers native (pre-trained on textual and visual tokens) multi-modality (text/image support) and a wide context window for long prompts.
How much open?: There's been plenty of controversy around Llama models over the years, as they are one of the biggest examples of open washing in recent

2.3 Partially Open Large Language Models

history.[6] While the "open source" annotation rightly disappeared from Llama 4 press releases, it is still widely present in previous models' Web sites and blogs.

The license slightly changes from model to model, but in general, only open weights are released. There's some vague reference to the datasets used for pre-training and fine-tuning; in general, they say "a mix of publicly available, licensed data and information from Meta's products and services. This includes publicly shared posts from Instagram and Facebook and people's interactions with Meta AI."

Some inference code and tools have been released over time, but only under various versions of their custom license.

Some papers and benchmarks have been published, but mostly on arXiv and GitHub, with a limited peer-review process.

Deepseek[4]—https://www.deepseek.com//
Company: DeepSeek
License: MIT and custom licenses
- https://github.com/deepseek-ai/DeepSeek-V3?tab=License-2-ov-file
Notable for: DeepSeek models made the headlines after it topped the app download charts on the main smartphone markets and caused the US tech stocks to suddenly sink.

Aside geo-political reasons, the main claim that shaked the AI world was the fact that the models performed on par with famous fully closed competitors and the training/inference costed a fraction: the researchers behind it claim it costed $6m to train, a small part of the "over $100m" alluded to by the creators of similarly sized models.

Verifying training costs is difficult, and most competitors don't even share them. What is true at the moment of writing is that the inference prices for the end user are extremely low compared to the competition.

This doesn't necessarily mean the internal costs are lower to the same degree; it is not uncommon for some companies to seek the loss leader strategy (initially selling at a loss for a period of time to dominate the competition and make a profit on other products/increase the prices later on).

At the same time, DeepSeek models are also hosted by independent third-party companies, which are able to offer the service at a decently low cost (but higher than DeepSeek itself generally): the takeaway is that this family of models is quite optimised and allows for lower costs, but also DeepSeek company marketing strategy has a role.

Technically, the main interesting aspects of this family of models are:

- Data type optimisations and quantisation to reduce the memory footprint
- Mixture of experts to only use part of the models at inference time (only a subset of the model parameters are active at a time)

---

[6] https://opensource.org/blog/metas-llama-license-is-still-not-open-source.

How much open?: Although originally advertised as fully open source, the claim is not visible anymore on their Web site.

On their GitHub repositories, there are still references for the models to be open source, even if only the learned weights are released.

There's no reference to the datasets used for pre-training and fine-tuning.

Some papers and benchmarks have been published, but mostly on arXiv and GitHub, with a limited peer review process.

Mistral[7]—https://mistral.ai/
Company: Mistral AI
License: Apache 2.0 and custom licenses
- https://mistral.ai/static/licenses/MRL-0.1.md
Notable for: Mistral made the headlines as one of the first European companies to release an open-weight model with an excellent balance in performance, costs and accessibility (releasing smaller models on par with bigger competitors).
How much open?: Only the learned weights after pre-training, after fine-tuning, and some minimal inference code have been released. Some papers and benchmarks have been published, but mostly on arXiv and GitHub, with a limited peer review process.

Qwen[16]—https://qwenlm.github.io/
Company: Alibaba Cloud
License: Apache-2.0 license
Notable for: Qwen achieves competitive results in benchmark evaluations of coding, math and general capabilities, when compared to other top-tier models.

The Qwen series of models introduces the ability to switch between thinking mode (for slow and deep tasks) and non-thinking mode (for quick and superficial responses).

Additionally, its vast multi-lingual support is promising for use cases that require interaction between many international actors.

How much open?: Only the learned weights have been released.

Gemma[14]—https://ai.google.dev/gemma
Company: Google
License: Custom license
- https://ai.google.dev/gemma/terms
Notable for: Coming from Google, it gained a decent popularity instantaneously, positioning itself as a smaller and faster version of Gemini, with easier accessibility and open weights.
How much open?: The entire training/fine-tuning code has not been shared, but Gemma's developers state they used JAX[7] and ML Pathways.[8]

---

[7] https://github.com/jax-ml/jax.
[8] https://blog.google/technology/ai/introducing-pathways-next-generation-ai-architecture/.

2.4 Domain-Specific Language Models

There is some vague reference on the quantity of data used for pre-training and fine-tuning on the Hugging Face model card, but not much is shared.

The learned weights have been released.

There are some technical reports shared, but in terms of the paper, the authors suggest referring to the Gemini papers (Gemini is another LLM from Google, fully closed).

Falcon[1]—https://falconllm.tii.ae/
Company: TII (Technology Innovation Institute)
License: Custom license
- https://falconllm.tii.ae/falcon-terms-and-conditions.html
Notable for: Falcon made the headlines multiple times for its performance and strong leaderboard presence, gaining decent popularity and adoption at the release date. It's now a little bit less popular but still a solid choice when looking for open-weight models.
How much open?: Although the Falcon family of models is advertised as open source, it has only published some of the datasets used for training [12]: https://huggingface.co/datasets/tiiuae/falcon-refinedweb and the weights of the model. Neither of these components is released under an open-source-approved license; hence, they present some usage limitations.

> **Key Takeaways**

- Most of the models you knew of for being open source are actually just open weight (they only share the learned weights of the model).
- When using open-weight models, pay extra attention to the license.
- Most of the custom licenses covering open-weight models derive from open source licenses + usage limitations.

2.4 Domain-Specific Language Models

Right now, the main focus of the industry and research community is to build general-purpose large language models, but in many applications, bigger doesn't mean better: let's explore some of the most prominent domain-specific language models (nowadays fitting within the small language models circle).

Over the years, in parallel with the development of general-purpose LLM, many researchers focused on specific sub-domains such as bio-medicine, healthcare, finance, etc.

In many instances, these domain-specific models have been superseded by the general-purpose ones, but there are still advantages in fine-tuning and distilling a smaller model with specific competencies.

Especially when running on edge devices (such as your smartphone), having a smaller model that solves the problem is a huge gain in comparison to running bigger models that offer way more than necessary.

Generally speaking, large models require a lot of computing power (both at training and inference time), which translates to higher operational costs and investments.

Domain-specific models, on the other hand, consume way less resources while delivering acceptable accuracy for specific tasks.

This results in a much higher return on investment for businesses and overall better sustainability.

Let's explore some of the major players in the field, assessing their level of openness.

2.4.1 Bioscience and Chemistry

Molformer[13]—https://molformer.res.ibm.com/
Company: IBM
License: Apache 2.0
Notable for: MoLFormer is a chemical language model designed with the intention of learning the structure of small molecules, which are represented as SMILES strings. MoLFormer leverages masked language modelling and employs a linear attention transformer combined with rotary embeddings.

It can infer the structure of molecules from simple representations, making it faster and easier to screen molecules for new applications or create them from scratch.

How much open?: Fully open source[9]

Nucleotide Transformers[3] - https://github.com/instadeepai/nucleotide-transformer
Company: InstaDeep Research
License: Attribution-NonCommercial-ShareAlike 4.0 International
- https://github.com/instadeepai/nucleotide-transformer?tab=License-1-ov-file
Notable for: The models have been developed in collaboration with NVIDIA and TUM to facilitate the study of DNA sequences.

---

[9] https://github.com/IBM/molformer.

2.4 Domain-Specific Language Models

It leverages DNA sequences from over 3,200 diverse human genomes and 850 genomes from a wide range of species. It offers extremely accurate molecular phenotype prediction compared to existing methods.
How much open?:

- Inference code
- Pre-trained weights for all nine NT models and two SegmentNT models
- Instructions for using the code and pre-trained models

2.4.2 Biomedicine and Healthcare

BioGPT[11]—https://github.com/microsoft/BioGPT
Company: Microsoft
License: MIT
Notable for: This model has been pre-trained on large-scale biomedical literature using a GPT-2 architecture and achieves impressive results on most biomedical NLP tasks.
How much open?: The code to reproduce the paper, pre-training and fine-tuning datasets and also the learned weights have been released.

BioMedLM[2]—https://github.com/stanford-crfm/BioMedLM
Company: Stanford Centre for Research on Foundation Models and MosaicML
License: BigScience RAIL License v1.0 - https://huggingface.co/spaces/bigscience/license
Notable for: BioMedLM 2.7B is a language model trained exclusively on biomedical abstracts and papers from The Pile. This GPT-style model can achieve strong results on a variety of biomedical NLP tasks, including a new state-of-the-art performance of 50.3% accuracy on the MedQA biomedical question-answering task.
How much open?: They have released some code for the training and fine-tuning. The dataset used for training and fine-tuning is publicly available (The Pile[10]). The learned weights have been released.

MedAlpaca[6]—https://github.com/kbressem/medAlpaca
Company: Stanford Center for Research on Foundation Models and MosaicML
License: GNU GENERAL PUBLIC LICENSE, Creative Commons license family

---

[10] https://pile.eleuther.ai/.

Notable for: MedAlpaca refines Llama or Stanford Alpaca weights (open-weight LLM) to offer an advanced family of large language models specifically fine-tuned for the medical domain. Their primary objective is to deliver a group of open source language models, building the foundations for the development of medical question/answering applications.

How much open?: The main contribution of this work is the fine-tuning of Llama models, based on a refined and well-curated medical dataset. So, all the aspects of the contribution have been released as open source, but they rely on the open weights of the original Llama model.

BioMistral[8]—https://github.com/BioMistral/BioMistral
  Company: Mistral AI
  License: Apache 2.0
  Notable for: BioMistral is a collection of medical LLMs resulting from additional pre-training Mistral 7B Instruct (another open-weight model from Mistral AI) on high-quality PubMed Central resources.

How much open?: The main contribution of this work is the further pre-training of other open-weight Mistral models. This happens through a dataset that is well detailed in their paper and publicly available, though some "selection" happened to manually curate samples, and the resulting dataset is not easily accessible. Given that, in the paper and online resources, there's a huge misuse of the open source label, which should be corrected. Starting from an open-weight model, even if additional details are shared, it won't be fully reproducible from scratch.

2.4.3 Coding Assistance

In regard to coding assistance, many of the LLMs presented so far have their own coding version.

In general, most of the pre-training and fine-tuning datasets involve a massive quantity of code examples in some form or another, so it's quite natural to see the inherent capabilities of LLM steering towards this direction.

Furthermore, many public assistance Web platforms (such as Stack Overflow[11] have probably been scraped to gain additional Q&A datasets, inclusive of ratings.

Along with the ubiquity of source control repositories and the structured nature of programming languages, this simplifies the building of dedicated small language models.

---

[11] https://stackoverflow.com.

> **Key Takeaways**

- Domain-specific language models got superseded by general-purpose LLMs.
- LLMs are now distilled to become smaller, domain-specific again.
- Vertical domains explored include coding assistance, biomedicine and chemistry.

2.5 Repositories

Where should you look when searching open large language models?
The answer is actually quite simple:

- GitHub for the code and source control
- Hugging Face for the model card and files

This section won't be unnecessarily verbose. When it comes to repositories hosting the code, datasets and learned weights of LLMs, the places to look at are limited and consolidated: Hugging Face for the models and GitHub for their code.

Hugging Face hosts models that are at least open weight, offering the possibility of downloading their files and accessing a first layer of documentation resources well structured in the model card. Their advanced search engine is the best entry point to explore language models by task and many other metadata. You'll find many details about the model itself, from a readme abstract to files and pointers to code repositories.

GitHub, on the other hand, hosts the training/inference code (when available) and instructions to run it.

The pre-training and fine-tuning datasets are generally published on both, while the learned weights are more likely to be found on Hugging Face.

> **Key Takeaways**

- GitHub is the most famous repository platform for open source code.
- Hugging Face is the de facto public repository for model cards and files.

References

1. Almazrouei, E., Alobeidli, H., Alshamsi, A., Cappelli, A., Cojocaru, R., Debbah, M., Étienne Goffinet, Hesslow, D., Launay, J., Malartic, Q., Mazzotta, D., Noune, B., Pannier, B., Penedo, G.: The falcon series of open language models (2023). https://arxiv.org/abs/2311.16867
2. Bolton, E., Venigalla, A., Yasunaga, M., Hall, D., Xiong, B., Lee, T., Daneshjou, R., Frankle, J., Liang, P., Carbin, M., Manning, C.D.: BiomedLM: A 2.7B parameter language model trained on biomedical text (2024). https://arxiv.org/abs/2403.18421
3. Dalla-Torre, H., Gonzalez, L., Mendoza Revilla, J., Lopez Carranza, N., Henryk Grywaczewski, A., Oteri, F., Dallago, C., Trop, E., Sirelkhatim, H., Richard, G., et al.: The nucleotide transformer: Building and evaluating robust foundation models for human genomics. bioRxiv, pp. 2023–01 (2023)
4. DeepSeek-AI, et al.: Deepseek-r1: incentivizing reasoning capability in LLMs via reinforcement learning (2025). https://arxiv.org/abs/2501.12948
5. Groeneveld, D., Beltagy, I., Walsh, P., Bhagia, A., Kinney, R., Tafjord, O., Jha, A.H., Ivison, H., Magnusson, I., Wang, Y., Arora, S., Atkinson, D., Authur, R., Chandu, K.R., Cohan, A., Dumas, J., Elazar, Y., Gu, Y., Hessel, J., Khot, T., Merrill, W., Morrison, J., Muennighoff, N., Naik, A., Nam, C., Peters, M.E., Pyatkin, V., Ravichander, A., Schwenk, D., Shah, S., Smith, W., Strubell, E., Subramani, N., Wortsman, M., Dasigi, P., Lambert, N., Richardson, K., Zettlemoyer, L., Dodge, J., Lo, K., Soldaini, L., Smith, N.A., Hajishirzi, H.: OLMo: accelerating the science of language models (2024). https://arxiv.org/abs/2402.00838
6. Han, T., Adams, L.C., Papaioannou, J.M., Grundmann, P., Oberhauser, T., Löser, A., Truhn, D., Bressem, K.K.: MedAlpaca–an open-source collection of medical conversational AI models and training data. arXiv preprint arXiv:2304.08247 (2023)
7. Jiang, A.Q., Sablayrolles, A., Mensch, A., Bamford, C., Chaplot, D.S., de las Casas, D., Bressand, F., Lengyel, G., Lample, G., Saulnier, L., Lavaud, L.R., Lachaux, M.A., Stock, P., Scao, T.L., Lavril, T., Wang, T., Lacroix, T., Sayed, W.E.: Mistral 7b (2023). https://arxiv.org/abs/2310.06825
8. Labrak, Y., Bazoge, A., Morin, E., Gourraud, P.A., Rouvier, M., Dufour, R.: BioMistral: A collection of open-source pretrained large language models for medical domains (2024). https://arxiv.org/abs/2402.10373
9. Liesenfeld, A., Lopez, A., Dingemanse, M.: Opening up ChatGPT: tracking openness, transparency, and accountability in instruction-tuned text generators. In: Proceedings of the 5th International Conference on Conversational User Interfaces. CUI '23. Association for Computing Machinery, New York (2023). https://doi.org/10.1145/3571884.3604316
10. Liu, Z., Tan, B., Wang, H., Neiswanger, W., Tao, T., Li, H., Koto, F., Wang, Y., Sun, S., Pangarkar, O., Fan, R., Gu, Y., Miller, V., Ma, L., Tang, L., Ranjan, N., Zhuang, Y., He, G., Wang, R., Deng, M., Algayres, R., Li, Y., Shen, Z., Nakov, P., Xing, E.: LLM360 K2: building a 65B 360-open-source large language model from scratch (2025). https://arxiv.org/abs/2501.07124
11. Luo, R., Sun, L., Xia, Y., Qin, T., Zhang, S., Poon, H., Liu, T.Y.: BioGPT: generative pre-trained transformer for biomedical text generation and mining. Brief. Bioinform. **23**(6), bbac409 (2022). https://doi.org/10.1093/bib/bbac409
12. Penedo, G., Malartic, Q., Hesslow, D., Cojocaru, R., Cappelli, A., Alobeidli, H., Pannier, B., Almazrouei, E., Launay, J.: The refinedweb dataset for Falcon LLM: Outperforming curated corpora with web data, and web data only (2023). https://arxiv.org/abs/2306.01116
13. Ross, J., Belgodere, B., Chenthamarakshan, V., Padhi, I., Mroueh, Y., Das, P.: Large-scale chemical language representations capture molecular structure and properties. Nat. Mach. Intell. **4**(12), 1256–1264 (2022). https://doi.org/10.1038/s42256-022-00580-7
14. Team, G.: Gemma 3 (2025). https://goo.gle/Gemma3Report
15. Touvron, H., Lavril, T., Izacard, G., Martinet, X., Lachaux, M.A., Lacroix, T., Rozière, B., Goyal, N., Hambro, E., Azhar, F., Rodriguez, A., Joulin, A., Grave, E., Lample, G.: Llama: open and efficient foundation language models (2023). https://arxiv.org/abs/2302.13971

16. Yang, A., Yang, B., Zhang, B., Hui, B., Zheng, B., Yu, B., Li, C., Liu, D., Huang, F., Wei, H., Lin, H., Yang, J., Tu, J., Zhang, J., Yang, J., Yang, J., Zhou, J., Lin, J., Dang, K., Lu, K., Bao, K., Yang, K., Yu, L., Li, M., Xue, M., Zhang, P., Zhu, Q., Men, R., Lin, R., Li, T., Xia, T., Ren, X., Ren, X., Fan, Y., Su, Y., Zhang, Y., Wan, Y., Liu, Y., Cui, Z., Zhang, Z., Qiu, Z.: Qwen2.5 technical report. arXiv preprint arXiv:2412.15115 (2024)
17. Zhang, P., Zeng, G., Wang, T., Lu, W.: TinyLlama: An open-source small language model (2024). https://arxiv.org/abs/2401.02385

The Commercial Landscape

3

Abstract

This chapter introduces the reader to the biggest and greatest examples of commercial LLM, their real-world application and how to use their products (both programmatically and manually). We'll explore the most interesting features and differentiators and details controversies and problems of such business models, opening the discussion of what the future holds for us in regard to this topic.

3.1 Business Paradigms

> Different corporations are exploring alternative ways of monetising LLMs.
>
> The most common approach is to offer direct products that wrap them, generally chatbots, accessible via APIs or Web UI on the Internet.
>
> Many of these products leverage a freemium business model, where a basic version is available for free and advanced license tiers must be purchased to unlock additional features.
>
> Another popular path is enriching companies' product suite with internal LLM integrations to be offered on more advanced license tiers or to justify price increases.

The first hugely popular example of LLM monetisation has been achieved by OpenAI through the freemium access of their GPT models in the ChatGPT Web application.

The service was released for free to gather global attention and a solid user base to then evolve to a licensing paradigm where you can unlock different tiers of models and services, affecting the monthly fee.

Paying more gives the possibility of sending more requests per minute, of accessing the latest and greatest models and exploring multi-modality such as video and image generation capabilities.

This approach proved to be quite successful: after only two months from the release (October 2022), ChatGPT broke the 100 million users barrier, and it's now among the 10 most visited Web sites globally.

At the time of writing, ChatGPT reaches an average of 400 million weekly active users with more than 10 million paying subscribers; in terms of revenue, it's estimated around $4 billion for 2024 and predicted to increase for 2025 and future years.

These numbers should not fool you, though, as the operating costs for such a tech giant are enormous and the company is far from being profitable.

Many other companies, starting from Google, Microsoft and Amazon, followed the lead in terms of monetisation strategies and are still doing it: being honest, the Software As A Service paradigm dominates our era, it's no surprise it could be applied to LLMs.

Most of the time, a quota is paid per input and output tokens: the longer your input prompt and the model response, the higher the cost for the request.

But that's not the only way LLM companies are doing business; licensing proprietary models to be used in third-party applications and services is quite common, and depending on the type of client, LLM companies can develop custom solutions for large enterprises with specific needs.

Some of the companies in the LLM market are huge corporations doing business across many domains and applications, and it comes naturally to distribute the operational costs of developing and running LLMs among the entire organisation, enhancing their entire product suite with impactful (or sometimes just marketing-driven) integrations.

This allows corporations to recycle old products and ideas, selling them with the new AI shiny coating or just increasing the price of their services with the promise of revolutionary new AI features (practically forcing users to pay for their LLMs even if they didn't want to).

One final consideration regards the training process: it's unclear how much copyrighted content is used without permission to train commercial models, and there have been various lawsuits based on the evidence that the output generated by the model is sometimes an exact copy of scraped material.[1]

---

[1] https://www.wired.com/story/ai-copyright-case-tracker/.

> **Key Takeaways**

- Chatbot products, such as ChatGPT, are the most popular way of monetising LLMs, often through a freemium paradigm.
- Licensing proprietary LLM technology to power custom solutions for clients is quite common.
- Sell derivative products or services that integrate with LLMs is an option.
- Evolve existing products with AI integrations to justify the price increase is another way of seeking a return on investment from investing in LLMs.

3.2 OpenAI: ChatGPT

OpenAI shook the world with the release of ChatGPT in 2022, the first LLM-based product to become widely used by the public.

By January 2023, ChatGPT had become the fastest-growing consumer application in history (at the time). The company emerged from the niche of AI enthusiasts/users to become a giant in the tech industry.

Adopting a freemium business model, OpenAI achieved substantial leadership in the market. They now offer a plethora of models of different sizes and capabilities and have cemented their reputation.

It's early October 2022, and OpenAI as a company is probably known only to experts in the field. Flash forward to the present day, and that's the first company that comes to your mind when thinking about Large Language Models.

Founded in 2015 by a group of tech magnates (including Sam Altman and Elon Musk), OpenAI reached worldwide fame with the release of the ChatGPT product, a chatbot leveraging their proprietary LLM (GPT 3.5 at the time) to power human-like text generation capabilities.

After the ChatGPT event, OpenAI consolidated its presence in the market and its leadership in the field, releasing more products (including multi-modality, image/video generation, agentic modality) and various model iterations.

The models from OpenAI routinely top the leaderboards and are often used as a comparison for competitor benchmarks.

The public intent of the company is to achieve, eventually, Artificial General Intelligence (AGI).

Current model offering ranges over o family models (for complex reasoning tasks), GPT models (for text generation) and visual models (DALL-E and Sora for image/video generation).

3.2.1 o Models

The models identified by the codename "o" refer to deep reasoning models trained to think longer before responding and offering agentic tool use capabilities (such as searching the Web, analysing uploaded files, multi-modality with visual input support and generation).

They are thought to help with complex queries and problem-solving, including coding and math tasks.

There are many variants of increasing quality, response time and costs, and more will come in the future.

In general, they use a process called simulated reasoning, where the model pauses to assess its own internal chain of thought processes before returning the final output.

It mimics human reasoning by identifying patterns useful to solve the task and inferring the output, leveraging those patterns. It's similar to chain of thought prompting, but rather than using the chain of thought to blindly return the output, it's used for an internal analysis.

Reinforcement learning is applied to check whether the model's step-by-step solution is correct or follows a desired pattern.

Better reward is associated with a more accurate chain of thoughts, so the model learns to produce deeper, multi-step reasoning and reflection.

The fine-tuning dataset would likely include examples of multi-step analysis and comprehensive solutions.

The model is also trained with reinforcement learning to use tools appropriately.

The release of o3 (which is actually the second iteration of such a family of models, called with the identifier 3, not to be confused with the British telecommunication provider O2) sparked discussions around the achievement or not of artificial general intelligence.

One of the reasons is the exceptional results of 87.5%[2] of a high compute version of o3 on the ARC-AGI-1[3] evaluation set [2].

Although these results are exceptional, the models fall short on the ARC-AGI-2,[4] a more diverse test, less brute forceable, that checks test-time reasoning with various puzzles.

One note to clarify is that these tests are not a final indicator of AGI achievement or not, but can help put researchers and practitioners in the right direction and better validation routes.

o3's improvement over the GPT series proves that the architecture and algorithmic approaches are fundamental; it's not a matter of throwing increasing computational power to the same family of models and expecting a breakthrough.

Training and fine-tuning a bigger version of LLMs on more data doesn't suffice.

---

[2] https://arcprize.org/blog/oai-o3-pub-breakthrough.
[3] https://github.com/fchollet/ARC-AGI.
[4] https://github.com/arcprize/ARC-AGI-2.

3.2.2 GPT Models

Since the early stages of development, generative pre-trained transformers have shaken the AI world, producing credible and human-like text generation.

Also, these models sparked discussions about signs of artificial general intelligence [1] and proved to be extremely useful in the context of chatbots and natural language generation/interaction.

The overall architecture of the GPT series of models has not changed much over the last few years, but the quantity and quality of training/fine-tuning data, optimisations and computational scale-up brought considerable improvements.

Over the years, progress in the series brought longer context windows for the input prompts, multi-modality and faster responses at feature parity.

3.2.3 Text to Vector

Text-to-vector models (often called Embedding models) are LLMs fine-tuned to encode text to a vector for sentence similarity.

OpenAI also offers these options, but they are not advertised much on their Web site or blog.

If you look into their API specifications and documentation, you can find them.[5]

At the moment of writing, the latest model dates back to the beginning of 2024, showing not much activity in the area.

Just keep an eye on it, in case a new effort is pushed by the company in that direction in the future.

3.2.4 APIs

OpenAI LLMs are also accessible programmatically via APIs, giving high flexibility to integrate their models with third-party applications. These APIs allow for tool usage (through function calling)[6] and JSON schema validation.

Function calling allows us to define and describe external REST endpoints so that the LLM is able to call them at the right time with the right input and parse and use the response.

It's extremely powerful and useful, and there's a lot of research going on in the direction of making agents better at interacting with the outside world (and software services).

The JSON schema support, on the other hand, is extremely handy when using LLMs as tools to interact with programmatically: it's an additional layer that ensures

---

[5] https://platform.openai.com/docs/guides/embeddings/embedding-models.
[6] https://platform.openai.com/docs/guides/function-calling.

structure for input and output of your models, making sure the response you get fits the structure your programmatic access is expecting.

It's vital to make sure the JSON response you want from a specific prompt is not broken, simplifying the parsing activity of the caller.[7]

> **Key Takeaways**

- OpenAI main product is ChatGPT, a user interface to interact with a multi-modal LLM.
- o models focus on reasoning, they are slower but able to solve complex tasks through a multi-step chain of thoughts.
- GPT models focus on text completion; they are decently fast and capable of generating human-like text.
- OpenAI also offers solid text-to-vector models, but the activity there seems to have slowed down recently.
- OpenAI APIs allow for programmatic interaction with LLMs, supporting function calling (tool usage) and structured output.

3.3   Google: Gemini

Google as a company doesn't need any introduction: they've been leading the Web search engine market for decades, and their AI division (DeepMind) has led the path of many breakthroughs in artificial intelligence (such as AlphaGo and AlphaFold).

When ChatGPT was released, a shadow was cast on their established leadership, and since then, there's been a frantic race to come back under the spotlight with the release of PaLM in early 2023 and the Gemini family of models in December 2023.

The release of ChatGPT back in 2022 caught Google off guard and drastically shifted the company's focus towards LLM and chatbot products/integrations.

After some attempts with mixed reception and somehow monumental demo fiascos (see Bard[8]), Google rebranded their product under the Gemini label and is releasing new models periodically, along with image/video/music generation ones.

---

[7] https://platform.openai.com/docs/guides/structured-outputs.

[8] https://edition.cnn.com/2023/02/08/tech/google-ai-bard-demo-error.

3.3 Google: Gemini

Aside from classic human-like text generation capabilities, Gemini models show a focus on Web and front-end development assistance (scoring high on dedicated leaderboards[9]).

Gemini 2.5 Pro consistently demonstrates solid performance across various benchmarks, performing well in reasoning, code generation and multi-modal understanding.

While not the top performer on all the various available public benchmarks, it generally holds a high-scoring profile, although quite far behind the competition in general intelligence tests such as ARC-AGI-1 (this may change in the future).

In terms of marketing, the latest Gemini models are advertised as "thinking models able to solve complex problems", positioning them as direct competitors of OpenAI o-family models (with a better focus on coding).

From the technical perspective, Gemini models are generative pre-trained transformers [6] trained with multi-modality in mind since their inception, following a sparse mixture of experts approach [5].

Over the years, the focus shifted towards chain of thought techniques (it's not clear to what extent they are similar to the ones applied by OpenAI's "o" models), better performance and longer context support.

3.3.1 Text to Vector

Google also offers these options, and in this case, it's not advertised much on their Web site or blog.

If you look into their API specifications and documentation, you can find them.[10]

In opposition to some competitors, the work in the area from the Gemini team is recent [4] and promising, with solid performance across various benchmarks and languages.

3.3.2 APIs

Google LLMs are also accessible programmatically via APIs, giving high flexibility to integrate their models with third-party applications. Like other competitors, these APIs allow for tool usage (through function calling[11] and JSON schema validation.[12]

---

[9] https://web.lmarena.ai/leaderboard.
[10] https://ai.google.dev/gemini-api/docs/models#gemini-embedding.
[11] https://ai.google.dev/gemini-api/docs/function-calling.
[12] https://ai.google.dev/gemini-api/docs/structured-output.

> **Key Takeaways**

- Initial attempts of rivalling OpenAI got mixed reception from the public.
- Latest Gemini models focus on Web/front-end code development and reasoning.
- There's active work happening on the side of text-to-vector models.
- Gemini APIs allow for programmatic interaction with LLMs, supporting function calling (tool usage) and structured output.

3.4 Cohere: Command

> Cohere was founded in 2019 with a focus on artificial intelligence and natural language processing for the enterprise, developing technology that businesses can use to build and deploy chatbots, search engines and general-purpose software enhanced by AI integrations.
>
> They are popular in the information retrieval community for their efforts in dense vector retrieval and reranking, counting in their team fundamental contributors to the sentence transformer open source library.

Cohere positions itself in the market of LLM providers, offering both general-purpose instruction following LLMs and specialist models fine-tuned for sentence similarity vector encoding and reranking.

Their main model family is called Command and targets similar capabilities to the competition: agentic tool usage, text generation, retrieval, augmented generation with citations and multi-language.

The main differentiator for Command is the focus on scalable efficiency and throughput.

It doesn't excel as the top performer across the benchmarks, but it offers fast performance at decent quality.

An important initiative Cohere is leading is Aya:[13] an open science project to create new models and datasets that expand the number of languages covered by AI, involving over 3,000 independent researchers across 119 countries.

As part of the Aya initiative, Cohere has released various open-weight models covering multi-modality and multi-lingual text generation [3].

---

[13] https://cohere.com/research/aya.

3.4.1 Text to Vector

Text-to-vector models are a core business area for Cohere, and this is visible starting from their Web site and homepage.

Supporting multi-lingual and multi-modal capability, the embedded models can be used to encode text and images into vectors.

In opposition to many other embedding models, there's support up to hundreds of thousands of tokens for document encoding (where normally embedding models just embed short texts, such as sentences or short documents, out of the box).

Not many details are published in regard to the internals of such models, so aside from benchmarking them, limited discussion is currently possible.

Also, cross-encoders for rerankers are supported and exposed through dedicated APIs, but the "negligible impact on latency" (marketing claim on their Web site) is questionable.

3.4.2 APIs

Cohere LLMs are mainly accessible programmatically via APIs, with a strong focus on integrating their models with third-party applications.

Like other competitors, these APIs allow for tool usage (through function calling) and JSON schema validation.[14]

> **Key Takeaways**

- Cohere general-purpose LLMs are smaller and less performing in terms of quality, generally compared to bigger competitors.
- The focus is on performance and costs, with strong support for multi-language.
- Text-to-vector embedding and reranking models are core in the Cohere activity.
- Their latest embed models support very long contexts, up to 128k tokens (possibly increasing in the future).
- The Aya project is an open science initiative led by Cohere to foster more inclusive and multilingual AI.

---

[14] https://docs.cohere.com/reference/chat.

3.5 Anthropic: Claude

> Anthropic was founded in 2021 with a focus on AI research and development for safety by ex-employees of OpenAI.
>
> Their major project is Claude, a family of models built for code assistance and reasoning.
>
> A strong effort has been put into aligning the systems with human values, making sure they end up being helpful, harmless and honest.
>
> Another important line of work carried out by the company is about machine learning explainability, especially in the field of GPT models.

Anthropic's main effort is focused on the Claude project: a family of LLMs capable of advanced reasoning, multi-modality, code generation and multi-lingual text processing.

The most recent iteration (Claude 3.7 Sonnet at the time of writing) is a hybrid model that is able to switch between fast responding and a slower "thinking mode" where more reasoning is required.

Claude has historically had a focus on front-end and Web development, excelling in coding tasks and related leaderboards.

In general, it offers solid performances in line with the competition, periodically surpassing them/getting surpassed.

Anthropic does not offer its own embedding model.

3.5.1 APIs

Anthropic LLMs are mainly accessible programmatically via APIs, with a strong focus on integrating their models with third-party applications. Like other competitors, these APIs allow for tool usage (through function calling)[15] and JSON schema validation.[16]

> **Key Takeaways**

- Anthropic started unifying fast responding/slow thinking models, depending on the use case; that's a trend we're going to see more in the industry.

---

[15] https://docs.anthropic.com/en/api/messages#body-tools.
[16] https://docs.anthropic.com/en/docs/test-and-evaluate/strengthen-guardrails/increase-consistency.

- The Claude family of models is a robust choice in line with competitor performances and a focus on coding assistance.

References

1. Bubeck, S., Chandrasekaran, V., Eldan, R., Gehrke, J., Horvitz, E., Kamar, E., Lee, P., Lee, Y.T., Li, Y., Lundberg, S., Nori, H., Palangi, H., Ribeiro, M.T., Zhang, Y.: Sparks of artificial general intelligence: early experiments with GPT-4 (2023). https://arxiv.org/abs/2303.12712
2. Chollet, F.: On the measure of intelligence (2019). https://arxiv.org/abs/1911.01547
3. Dang, J., Singh, S., D'souza, D., Ahmadian, A., Salamanca, A., Smith, M., Peppin, A., Hong, S., Govindassamy, M., Zhao, T., Kublik, S., Amer, M., Aryabumi, V., Campos, J.A., Tan, Y.C., Kocmi, T., Strub, F., Grinsztajn, N., Flet-Berliac, Y., Locatelli, A., Lin, H., Talupuru, D., Venkitesh, B., Cairuz, D., Yang, B., Chung, T., Ko, W.Y., Shi, S.S., Shukayev, A., Bae, S., Piktus, A., Castagné, R., Cruz-Salinas, F., Kim, E., Crawhall-Stein, L., Morisot, A., Roy, S., Blunsom, P., Zhang, I., Gomez, A., Frosst, N., Fadaee, M., Ermis, B., Ütün, A., Hooker, S.: Aya expanse: combining research breakthroughs for a new multilingual frontier (2024). https://arxiv.org/abs/2412.04261
4. Lee, J., Chen, F., Dua, S., Cer, D., Shanbhogue, M., Naim, I., Àbrego, G.H., Li, Z., Chen, K., Vera, H.S., Ren, X., Zhang, S., Salz, D., Boratko, M., Han, J., Chen, B., Huang, S., Rao, V., Suganthan, P., Han, F., Doumanoglou, A., Gupta, N., Moiseev, F., Yip, C., Jain, A., Baumgartner, S., Shahi, S., Gomez, F.P., Mariserla, S., Choi, M., Shah, P., Goenka, S., Chen, K., Xia, Y., Chen, K., Duddu, S.M.K., Chen, Y., Walker, T., Zhou, W., Ghiya, R., Gleicher, Z., Gill, K., Dong, Z., Seyedhosseini, M., Sung, Y., Hoffmann, R., Duerig, T.: Gemini embedding: Generalizable embeddings from Gemini (2025). https://arxiv.org/abs/2503.07891
5. Team, G., et al.: Gemini 1.5: Unlocking multimodal understanding across millions of tokens of context (2024). https://arxiv.org/abs/2403.05530
6. Team, G., et al.: Gemini: a family of highly capable multimodal models (2024). https://arxiv.org/abs/2312.11805

Part II

Large Language Models and Search

- How to integrate large language models with search technologies?
- How to choose the best one for your project?
- What are the most common mistakes in doing so?

The second part of the book delves into the first major area: how to use the technological marvels the reader learned about in Part 1 to enhance their search project.

LLMs are capable of outstanding natural language processing and instruction following.

This means that, generally speaking, a user can ask an LLM to perform any task that can be described via language and expect it to return a relevant textual output.

To be fair, multi-modal models won't stop at written languages and are capable of working with and generating audio, videos and images.

This flexibility opens the door to numerous applications in the domain of information retrieval.

Ever heard of "chatting with your documents"?

Asking for information in natural language and getting back a comprehensive response like a human subject expert would answer is just an example of the many ways LLM can benefit a search application and simplify the lives of users, especially the less tech-savvy ones.

The upcoming chapters traverse the major opportunities, with an eye on the academic state of the art and an eye on pragmatic industry applications.

The narrative won't be limited to success stories but also present and analyse failures, because early adoption and ambitions always come with failures, but they are less cool to advertise: that's not the case for this book, being thought as learning material, there's no best source of learning than from (often our own) mistakes.

Part II is organised as follows:

- Chapter 4 presents the plethora of techniques and strategies to apply large language models to the search domain.

- Chapter 5 explains the factors the reader should pay attention to when choosing an LLM for a project, including a procedural approach to follow to reduce risks.
- Chapter 6 wraps up the second part, exploring typical mistakes in adopting this emerging technology and how to remediate when they happen.

By the end of this part, the reader is expected to learn:

The *LLM applications in search*—how semantic search, retrieval augmented generation and other interesting techniques work and can be applied to the reader's use case.

The *Process of choosing*—the right model for a task, with a careful analysis and a scientific and replicable process.

The *Classic mistakes*—the reader is going to encounter, how to avoid them and reduce the risk of wasting a lot of time and resources in the process.

Applying Large Language Models to Search 4

Abstract

This chapter introduces the reader to ideas, research and practical industry-level applications that use LLMs to improve the user experience of finding the information they need. Encoding the meaning of the text in a numeric vector format, being able to process input/output in natural language, expanding and rephrasing documents and queries to improve their "match-ability" and supporting search across media and language are just the tip of the iceberg. This chapter guides the reader through the state-of-the-art and industry adoptions, highlighting the positive and not-so-positive aspects to give an unbiased and comprehensive perspective.

4.1 Vector Search

> Vector search (also known as neural search or dense retrieval) aims to represent the semantics of text (both the query and the documents) as a numerical vector and perform a nearest neighbour search using a similarity metric based on vector distance.
>
> It can be used as a first-stage retriever to mitigate the vocabulary mismatch problem and in the reranking stage to refine the score of candidates using more expensive vectorisation approaches and similarity metrics.

A traditional tokenised inverted index can be considered to model text as a "sparse" vector, in which each term in the corpus corresponds to one vector dimension.

In such a model, the number of dimensions is generally quite high (corresponding to the term dictionary cardinality), and the vector for any given document contains mostly zeros (hence it is sparse, as only a handful of terms that exist in the overall index will be present in any given document).

Dense vector representation contrasts with term-based sparse vector representation in that it distils approximate semantic meaning into a fixed (and limited) number of dimensions.

The number of dimensions in this approach is generally much lower than the sparse case, and the vector for any given document is dense, as most of its dimensions are populated by non-zero values.

In contrast to the sparse approach (for which tokenisers are used to generate sparse vectors directly from text input), the task of generating vectors must be handled by a dedicated vector embedding model.

The idea of encoding words to vectors (often called embeddings) where the relative similarity between vectors aligns with the semantic similarity between words dates back to the 1950s [18, 59, 66] and 1960s [70].

In the early 2010s, the idea got refreshed hype with the publishing of Word2vec [53].

Word2vec represents each word as a high-dimensional vector of numbers which captures semantic relationships between words.

Word2vec models are shallow neural networks trained on a large corpus of information and use a sliding context window of text to produce these numerical representations.

Two alternative approaches can be used to train a Word2vec model:

Continuous Bag Of Words—CBOW—Estimate a missing word in a window of text, based on the idea that similar words appear in similar contexts. The order of context words does not influence prediction (hence the bag of words).

Continuous Skipgram—The problem is reversed, and the word is used to predict the surrounding window of context. Nearby words are weighted more than far-distant words.

This breakthrough brought renewed excitement in the field and quickly became a dominant trend in academic conferences and soon in the industry landscape.

Word embeddings started to see their application in automatic synonyms generation, document similarity and various classification tasks.

The idea has been extended to embeddings of entire sentences or even documents. A more recent and popular approach for representing sentences is Sentence-BERT, or SentenceTransformers, which modifies pre-trained BERT with the use of Siamese and triplet network structures [64].

Since then, many LLMs have been released to address the text vectorisation problem, often when releasing a new family of general-purpose LLMs, the authors also release the text vectorisation version.

So, how can you use a vectorised text to improve your search engine?

4.1.1 Sparse and Dense First-Stage Retrieval

The vocabulary mismatch problem is evident in traditional keyword search: sometimes the lexicon used by the user to express concepts doesn't align with the lexicon present in the corpus of information to describe the same or related concepts.

Keyword matching won't return those results, causing a recall problem for your search (results coverage).

In general, synonyms (terms with the same meaning), hypernyms (a term with a more general meaning than another) and hyponyms (a term with a more specific meaning than another) are not handled by traditional keyword search out of the box.
e.g.

- Panthera tigris is a synonym of tiger.
- Carnivore is a hypernym of tiger.
- Tiger is a hyponym of big cat.

A lot of research happened in that regard, but even nowadays, most industrial search engines just use manual dictionaries to expand documents and queries, painful to maintain (and rarely updated at all).

First-stage retrieval is the phase of your search when the system matches a set of candidate results to be ranked.

Failing to find results at this stage will impact, in cascade, the overall user experience quality.

In terms of quality measurement it's worth noting that in the realm of vector search, the term "Recall" is often used in slightly different nuance than in general information retrieval: the recall of a top-k approximate nearest neighbour retrieval is the number of ground truth neighbours found in the top-k, divided by the top-k.

A recall of 90% means that within the top-k, 90% of the results are good, true neighbours.

If you come from an information retrieval background, that's basically precision@k, so keep this in mind while working on vector search scenarios, as this can be a cause of confusion.

Vectors can be used to transition from keyword matching into the realm of getting top-k documents closest in meaning to your query.

At indexing time, your documents are vectorised and stored in a dedicated data structure.

At query time, your query is vectorised, producing a vector in the same vector space.

When running the search, the scope is finding the top-k closest vectors to the query one.

What does close mean in the vector space?

Semantic similarity between textual sentences is mapped to a vector similarity metric, at training time: that's encoded in the large language model you are using to encode text to a vector.

The similarity metric can be the cosine distance, the Euclidean distance, the dot product, etc. you name it!

When implementing your vector search pipeline, make sure the similarity metric you use is the one used to train the vectorisation model you use.

How to find top-k results?

The simplest nearest neighbour implementation would involve defining a vector distance metric, such as the cosine distance and doing a distance calculation for your query and all your documents, then ranking them by score and returning the top-k.

This is expensive and even with modern-day hardware, only possible in some scenarios, where you reduce the subset of candidates by applying some sort of filters.

For this reason, researchers started exploring approximate nearest neighbours techniques, compromising on result quality and coverage to get acceptable query time on a big corpus of information.

Modern approximate nearest neighbours approaches involve the usage of clever data structures to minimise the vector space exploration and still return good quality results, close to the exact nearest neighbours strategy.

Hierarchical Navigable Small World Graph [49, 50] (also known as the acronym HNSW) is a prominent example.

This approach has been broadly adopted in the industry and currently powers the majority of vector search systems around, including many open source solutions we'll see in Chap. 8 (Apache Lucene, Apache Solr, OpenSearch, Elasticsearch and Vespa).

HNSW is a proximity graph data structure, where each node is a vector and the arcs connect vectors that are close in the vector space.

The graph is hierarchical as it follows a representation strategy similar to skiplists [78]: there are multiple layers, each of them stores a subset of all vectors, starting from the top layer (less nodes for quick neighbour search) and descending into layers more and more populated (more nodes to refine the best candidate neighbours).

HNSW has been widely explored in the literature, so no need to go into low-level details here, but if you are curious about its internals, this blog proved to be quite interesting.[1]

DiskANN [73] is an interesting alternative focused on handling big datasets efficiently by operating on disk (Solid State Disks) rather than requiring the entire index to be loaded in memory.

The core of DiskANN is the Vamana algorithm, a positional graph approach that builds a flat graph, initially randomly connected and iteratively pruned to optimise query time connections.

The trade-off between slightly slower query time and vastly reduced memory requirements makes DiskANN an attractive option for many real-world applications.

---

[1] https://www.pinecone.io/learn/series/faiss/hnsw/

Open source vector search engines are increasingly exploring DiskANN as an additional option other than HNSW (the Milvus project already implementing it), but pragmatic benefits are debatable, hence it has not seen a big adoption in the open source community yet.[2]

One last approach to mention is Annoy,[3] a random forest tree-based algorithm that splits the vector space into subspaces at each binary tree branching randomly; the process is repeated for k trees (resulting in a forest).

At query time, the vector space is navigated at decision boundaries, so only a subset of the entire space is visited. To simplify, you can think of a vector checking a condition at each branching point and continuing the exploration for nearest neighbours only descending on a tree branch (a vector sub-space).

In general, tree-based approaches such as Annoy proved useful for smaller datasets with smaller dimensionality.

4.1.2 Quantisation and Binary Vectors

A big effort from the research community has been devoted to optimising approximate nearest neighbour algorithms and data structures, with the objective of reducing the query latency and memory footprint, while keeping a competitive level of recall (results quality).

Vector quantisation is a compression technique to reduce the memory footprint of a vector, minimising the information loss. This brings more efficiency in storage (both disk and memory) and faster processing operations (both at indexing and query time). The benefits of quantisation are particularly visible in large datasets or scenarios where indexing/query latency is critical.

Just to give some numbers, imagine a 1,024-dimensional vector: If each element is an uncompressed 32-bit float, you'll need roughly 4 Kilobytes for one vector. Scale it up to 10 million and you'll need 40 gigabytes of memory just to store the vectors.

Not necessarily all of them will be in memory at the same time, but it's definitely a big factor nonetheless.

There are three main families of quantisation approaches:

> **Scalar Quantisation**

Scalar quantisation compresses 32-bit float elements into smaller data types (often 8-bit integers). With the bit reduction, the information needs to be mapped in a narrower space (8 bits, for example, are capable of representing 256 different values, while the original 32 bits are capable of representing more than 2 billion).

---

[2] https://github.com/apache/lucene/issues/12615
[3] https://github.com/spotify/annoy

To do that, a lossy normalisation such as the min-max normalisation will do the job:

Let:

- $x \in \mathbb{R}$: the original 32-bit float
- $q \in \{-128, \ldots, 127\}$: the quantised 8-bit integer
- $s \in \mathbb{R}^+$: the scale factor
- $z \in \mathbb{Z}$: the zero-point

Quantisation:

$$q = \text{round}\left(\frac{x}{s}\right) + z$$

Scale and Zero-point:

$$s = \frac{x_{\max} - x_{\min}}{255}$$

$$z = \text{round}\left(-\frac{x_{\min}}{s}\right)$$

N.B. You may initially get confused by the usage of 255 rather than 256. The possible values we want to scale to are 256, so why use N-1? This is a classic example of Fencepost error[4] when humans mistakenly count the elements in a sequence rather than the intervals between such elements. In the quantisation example, we want to map the min and max, respectively, to the minimum and maximum element in the scale, and then fit the values in the original continuous space in numbered buckets that coincide with the quantised N-1 intervals.

When using scalar quantisation, to maximise the accuracy is worth analysing your data and setting sensible min and max values to drive the quantisation.

Rather than using the float32 general min and max, it is recommended to check the min and max in your dataset.

And not only across your all dataset, it should be beneficial to look at portions of your data: Quantiles specify a percentage of data to look at: for example, a 99% quantile may see a specific min and max that's valid for 99% of your data.

Fine-tuning that hyper-parameter can help in reducing the information loss and use all the quantised buckets as much as possible without wasting them for outliers.

At query time, the vector similarity calculation will run on the quantised vector plus some pre-calculated values to keep the scale, original min and max into account.[5]

---

[4] https://en.wikipedia.org/wiki/Off-by-one_error

[5] https://www.elastic.co/search-labs/blog/scalar-quantization-101

> Binary Quantisation

Binary quantisation consists of compressing the float32 elements in the vector into a single bit representation.

Speed and memory gains are phenomenal, as the storage of each single element goes from 32 bits to 1 (plus a little margin), and search time processing can be performed with blazing fast bitwise operations.

These benefits don't come for free as doing this naively incurs in huge accuracy loss.

An example of naive binarisation is to extract the median value for each of the dimensions of the vector across your dataset and then encode each element of each vector as a 1 or a 0 depending on whether it's greater or smaller than such threshold.

At query time, instead of using traditional vector similarity metrics (such as cosine, dot product, Euclidean, etc.), the Hamming distance comes to the rescue.

The Hamming distance is a simple similarity metric between binary vectors that just calculates how many bits are different between the two vectors using a xor operator: Let $\mathbf{x}, \mathbf{y} \in \{0, 1\}^n$ be binary vectors of length n. The Hamming distance between $\mathbf{x}$ and $\mathbf{y}$ is defined as:

$$d_H(\mathbf{x}, \mathbf{y}) = \sum_{i=1}^{n}(x_i \oplus y_i)$$

Two vectors have a high similarity if their Hamming distance is small (which means that the two vectors share the same binary value for most of their dimensions). The more bits they differ, the higher the distance and consequently the lower the similarity.

There's a huge loss of information, though, so make sure to evaluate carefully your search quality metrics to understand if the speed and memory gains can be enough to justify the degradation (if any in your case).

Unfortunately, in many scenarios, this loss of information is not acceptable, the recall loss is too big, and the performance advantages are not enough: there are many distance collisions between vectors, which make the job of approximate nearest neighbour algorithms quite harder (with an excess of resulting approximation).

RaBitQ [21] improves the situation, delivering massive memory and storage reduction for vectors, maintaining high recall and vastly quicker indexing/query speed.

The algorithm is a bit more complex than the naive one, so I invite you to read the original paper if you want to grasp the full details, but the main advantages are the introduction of a rigorous error bound on the distance estimations (from the original distance to the approximate one), keeping the advantages of fast calculations using bitwise operations.

Empirical results show huge benefits for RaBitQ in comparison to scalar or product quantisation.

The quantisation process is more computationally expensive, but that cost can be mostly addressed offline, so it would be largely acceptable given the huge uplift in storage/latencies and minor impact on result quality.

> Product Quantisation

Product quantisation [32] compresses high-dimensional vectors into a vector with reduced dimensionality and compressed values.

The original vector is first split into a set of vectors with reduced dimensionality.

Then, each of the sub-vectors is clustered and assigned to its nearest centroid (a vector in the same vector space and dimensionality called "reproduction value").

Then the centroid vector is replaced with a unique ID, and the final result is a tiny vector of IDs (with a cardinality equal to the number of sub-vectors).

Going back from the centroid ID to the centroid vector is possible through a mapping data structure called "codebook".

The centroid ID is generally storable in a smaller data type than the original vector elements, requiring fewer bits.

This means that both a dimensionality reduction and a quantisation happen.

Assuming you use 1-byte integers for the centroid IDs and you target a dimensionality reduction of 16, an original vector of 1024 dimensions with 4-byte float elements occupying roughly 4 Kb (4 bytes * 1024) would be compressed to: 64 bytes (1 byte * 1024/16), a 64 times compression.

To initialise the centroids and the codebook, a training must happen at indexing time before we can proceed with the product quantisation (k-means unsupervised clustering would suffice).

This additional time is not negligible and must be taken into consideration when adopting this approach.

What happens at query time?

- *1. Query split*—The query vector is split into the same m sub-vectors (m is the same used at indexing time).
- *2. Lookup tables computation*—For each sub-vector of the query:
  Its distances to all k centroids in that subspace are computed (k is the number of IDs calculated for such a sub-vector at indexing time).
  The temporary results are stored in a distance table: a matrix of shape (m, k).
- *3. Approximate distance computation*—To compute the distance from the query vector to each compressed vector in the corpus, the temporary distance table is accessed, and sums are performed over all the subspaces.

So there is no need to decompress to calculate approximate distances.

An improvement of efficiency and scalability of product quantisation happens with the addition of an inverted file index (IVF)

4.1 Vector Search

IVF adds a preliminary clustering stage at indexing time, so that at query time, we only scan a subset of all vectors (only from close clusters).

The combination of the two approaches, often called IVF+PQ is widely used in high-performance approximate nearest neighbour libraries like FAISS (Facebook AI Similarity Search).

4.1.3 First-Stage Learned Sparse Retrieval

Learned sparse retrieval (sometimes referred to as sparse neural search) is an approach of sparse vector representation for queries and documents inspired by both traditional lexical search and text vectorisation algorithms (sparse because in the vector, most of the values are zeroes).

The main idea is to use deep learning and large language models to learn a sparse representation for queries/documents where each element in the vector is a weight associated with a term, and then use classic retrieval data structures (such as inverted indexes) for fast retrieval and scoring.

The term weight is a learned approximation of the relevance of the term in the query/document.

The most popular approach in this family is called SPLADE [19, 20], introduced for the first time at the 44th International ACM SIGIR Conference in 2021.

SPLADE (stands for **SP**arse **L**exical **A**n**D** **E**xpansion) leverages language models to assign a relevance weight to each term in a sentence and to apply term expansion based on the learned probabilities of words occurring in contexts.

Term expansion is fundamental to solving the vocabulary mismatch problem (the problem that occurs when queries/documents differ in the terms they use to describe similar concepts).

During the training of the model, a masked language modelling approach is followed: in a sentence, a term is masked and the model aims to predict it based on the surrounding terms.

This generates a probability vector over the dictionary, where each term has a certain weight that represents how likely the term is to fit the masked spot.

In this way, a probability distribution is learned and can be associated with each sentence, automatically expanding it.

On paper, this sounds like the best of both worlds approach, but at the time of writing, learned sparse approaches are still rarely used in the industry.

The first limitation that is having a strong impact on a stable industrial adoption is how sparse SPLADE is: learned sparse representations encode information in vectors with way more non-zero values in comparison to traditional methods such as BM25.

This causes a bigger impact on memory, disk and query latency.

The second limitation is the need for training/fine-tuning a SPLADE model: generic SPLADE models rarely perform well across a multitude of datasets and domains, so it's very likely that you end up having the need for a custom one.

Fine-tuning is expensive, not necessarily in terms of resources and hardware, but also in terms of skills: not all teams may be capable of that, and this introduces additional resistance to adopting these types of approach.

The third limitation regards the inference time, which also slows down indexing as the sparse vector needs to be calculated using the model, and potentially, there's going to be some intermediate processing step to adapt the resulting vector into the established inverted index data structures.

The usage of learned sparse retrieval for long documents is still challenging, and further research in the field is necessary.

On top of using the masked language modelling approach as milestone for learned sparse retrieval models, also decoder-only LLMs have been applied to the problem with the idea of combining dense vector representation coming from the LLM with the learned sparse representation coming from the SPLADE model in Mistral [13], or to expand documents with query prediction in DeeperImpact [4].

Additional promising studies are working in the direction of speeding up these learned retrieval models [51].

Given that, it's still uncertain what the future reserves for this approach: modern LLMs are certainly capable of expanding queries and documents with alternative rephrases; certainly they are way bigger than SPLADE models, and the dimension won't be justified just for the query/document expansion task.

A possible route could be to enrich SPLADE models through some form of distillation (that would mean, in practice, to update the internal backbone model).

It's certainly an area I would pay attention to, as query/document expansion is certainly a hot topic nowadays.

4.1.4 Late Interaction Models

Dense retrieval models can be categorised based on the type of interaction that happens between the query and the document while assessing their similarity.

So far, we have explored vectorisation models that encode the query and the documents separately, so no interaction at all happens while encoding them into vectors.

The opposite extreme is full-interaction (also called all-to-all) models, generally called cross-encoders. We'll explore them in the next chapter, talking about reranking. Full-interaction models are the most expensive of the bunch.

No-interaction models are fast but tend to be inaccurate; all-to-all interaction models are better at capturing the semantic relationship between pieces of text, but are slow and expensive; late interaction retrieval models take inspiration from both worlds, achieving an interesting balance between costs and quality.

Late interaction models derive their name from the model's architecture and processing strategy, where the interaction between the query and document representations happens late in the process, after both have been independently encoded.

4.1 Vector Search

Late interaction models encode separately the query and the document, producing a vector for each token. So both the query and the document are encoded to a multi-vector representation, a sort of bag of vectors (similar to a bag of words).

At query time, each query token vector is compared to each document token vector and the resulting similarity is calculated as the sum of each query token vector's max similarity (with each document token vector).

To make it clearer, the algorithm iterates over each query token (encoded to a vector) and calculates the maximum similarity with the list of document tokens (encoded to a vector).

Given a query Q and a document D, let their contextualised token embeddings be:

$$Q = \{\mathbf{q}_1, \mathbf{q}_2, \ldots, \mathbf{q}_m\}, \quad \mathbf{q}_i \in \mathbb{R}^d$$

$$D = \{\mathbf{d}_1, \mathbf{d}_2, \ldots, \mathbf{d}_n\}, \quad \mathbf{d}_j \in \mathbb{R}^d$$

The MaxSim relevance score between Q and D is defined as:

$$\text{Score}(Q, D) = \sum_{i=1}^{m} \max_{j=1,\ldots,n} \langle \mathbf{q}_i, \mathbf{d}_j \rangle$$

where $\langle \cdot, \cdot \rangle$ denotes the dot product between two vectors.

So, for each query token, the algorithm identifies the most relevant document token.

This allows for better explainability in comparison to the traditional approximate nearest neighbours approach of single dense vectors, as it's possible to highlight the most impactful tokens per query and per document (this is the late interaction the title is referring to).

This mechanism was first introduced with ColBERT (Contextualised Late Interaction over BERT) [38] in 2020 as a fine-tuning over BERT models.

Although the approach sounds promising, having to store so many vectors (one for each token) proved to be quite a challenge for both memory and storage.

The second version of ColBERT [67] focused on the issue of improving the situation through distillation from a bigger teacher model and better compression techniques for storage.

More modern versions of ColBERT are released from time to time [34], leveraging the same architecture but different LLM backbone and potential additional optimisations.

Similar ideas have been applied for multi-modal search over documents containing a mix of text and images; we'll see more details in Sect. 4.6.

4.1.5 Reranking

The task of reranking takes in input a ranked list of items, usually the first-stage retrieval candidates and re-orders them.

This happens on a restricted subset of documents from the original corpus, so a more expensive logic can be applied.

Various families of LLMs fine-tuned to encode text to vector can be used in this step:

No interaction (also called Bi-encoders)—Approaches we have seen already: the query and the document are encoded separately into vectors, and then a vector similarity measure is calculated. During reranking, this happens for each query/document pair that needs re-scoring. The new score is used to re-order the elements after the first-stage retrieval. It's pretty much the same as exact nearest neighbour but applied on a subset of documents from the entire corpus.

Late interaction—Multi-vectors per document are pre-calculated at indexing time, and then at reranking time, the max sim algorithm is applied only for the top-k.

All-to-all interaction—(also called cross-encoders) models work differently: the query/document pair that needs rescoring is concatenated and given as input to the model, which returns a similarity score. The process is more expensive than bi-encoding but offers better semantic insight into the relation between the query and the document.

They are based on the transformer architecture and the self-attention mechanism [75] we explored in the introduction of the book 1.2.

This mechanism enables the model to weigh the importance of each word with contextual awareness of the other words from both the query and the document, producing an embedding representation sensitive to their semantic relationship.

Cross-encoders are LLMs fine-tuned for the task of assigning a relevance score to two sentences in input, indicating the grade of relatedness between the two.

Nowadays, with the size of models increasing as you read this chapter, original cross-encoders may not be considered large anymore, but for the sake of this chapter, they are worth exploring as they are capable models, quite effective for reranking (they are way faster than just using a general-purpose LLM to perform the task of reranking).

As of the time of writing, several cross-encoder models have emerged as valid rerankers for text similarity tasks, offering a balance between accuracy and efficiency.

Here's an overview of some of the most recent:

ModernCE-large-sts [54] - https://huggingface.co/collections/dleemiller/modern-cross-encoder-67ba5496e8558463aa1f3dc9
   Architecture: ModernBERT [77]
   Context length: Up to 8192 tokens

4.1 Vector Search

Notable for: Combines high accuracy with extended context handling, making it suitable for evaluating long-form content

NeoCE-sts —https://huggingface.co/dleemiller/NeoCE-sts
Architecture: NeoBERT [6]
Context length: Up to 4096 tokens
Notable for: tailored for the purpose of LLM output evaluation

An interesting development in the domain of cross-encoders happened in 2025 [46] where a cross encoder variant of MiniLM seemed to represent a semantic version of BM25, modelling similar concepts to term frequency, term saturation and document length.

4.1.6 Vector Search in Production

Utilising LLMs fine-tuned to encode text to vector and power vector search solutions has been quite a revolution for the information retrieval world: pretty much all top conferences' papers and talks shifted towards this direction, many new products (open source and not) emerged to solve the new search and marketing exploded.

If you were not talking or doing vector search in the community, you were left behind, you were doing search "still the old way".

Vector search has been advertised by many vector search engine vendors as the silver bullet to finally solve search effortlessly.

Obviously, it's not that simple:

Hard to explain and debug—We are used to search systems based on lexical keyword matches, and even with that, when queries become complicated, it is not that easy to explain why a document is retrieved and why it is ranked above others.

But at least, the foundations are based on keyword matches, so under the hood, everything goes back to some keyword in common between the query and the document.

In vector search, both the queries and documents are encoded in very big (for human standards) vectors of numbers, where each dimension has no particular meaning.

This makes vector search results very hard to explain and even harder to fix: why has the document been returned? What if the returned documents are not relevant?

There's no quick change you can make on the query; sure, you can fine-tune the approximate nearest neighbour hyper-parameters (if any) and play with the top-k size, but if that doesn't work and even exact nearest neighbour doesn't satisfy you, you are left with a big model encoding text to vector embeddings that needs to be changed.

And these models are not easy to be fixed, you don't change one line of code or the configured text analysis and tokenization, you are left with the task of revising the entire model, potentially with additional fine-tuning if you are lucky, or in case you use hosted models, with the necessity of switching model altogether.

Late interaction models go in a better direction for explainability and are capable of showing the most significant terms for the query and each document. This is brilliant when it works, but if your use case ends up with weird keywords highlighted as important, also in this case there's no easy fix, the highlighted tokens come from the underlying resulting vector similarity, and again, such vectors are encoded by big models, difficult to explain and quickly change.

Weak for low-resource languages—The vast majority of LLM research has English as the top priority, and that reflects in the quality of vector embeddings. Outside English and shifting towards low-resource languages, the quality degrades swiftly up to the point that the models won't be usable unless additionally fine-tuned. The more research and industrial applications happen, the better this situation will evolve, but it's hard to predict when good models will be available for your language of interest.

Computational and storage demand—In comparison to traditional keyword search, when switching to vector search, you may be better off with different hardware, specifically moving from CPU-intensive tasks to GPU-intensive.

Generally speaking, this complicates migrations, in case you aim to obtain the best performance, and these hardware solutions may be subject to shortages in certain periods of time and regions, given their utilisation has gone through the roof with the current AI spring.

Also, depending on the type of model you use, you may have memory and storage problems. If you have a big dataset, approaches such as ColBERT will end up generating many vectors per document, and the impact shouldn't be underestimated.

Not well suited for long documents—Most text-to-vector models are fine-tuned for sentence similarity, which means they work best with short text. This makes them good for queries (although sometimes, if the queries are too short, you may end up with the opposite problem), but not very good at handling long textual documents.

This means you'll end up needing pre-processing steps where you split your documents into chunks (and this brings additional complexity and problems), summarisation or techniques to enrich your document with new sentences that capture the main aspects of the document itself, before proceeding with vectorisation.

Not well suited for structured data—Pure vector search doesn't handle exact filters and doesn't work well with many search systems scenarios where you calculate aggregations over the search results and then apply filtering on click. For this reason, many vector search solutions nowadays integrate a hybrid approach where you can combine semantic search with a pre/post-filter of the search results using lexical matching.

Taking all of this into account, as you can imagine, bringing vector search to production is not a breeze; it requires deep analysis, many iterations of experimen-

4.1 Vector Search

tation and the acceptance of the possibility of having to do many back and forths on the different levels involved in the loop (embedding model, chunking strategy, approximate nearest neighbour strategy and hyper-parameters).

Mixing up traditional keyword search with vectors is not as easy as well; there are many strategies, such as Reciprocal Rank Fusion [10] and similar, but they lay their foundations on having good vector search results with consistent intersection between the two.

Most of the time, what we experienced as the ideal solution in production environments is to expose vector search as an alternative to traditional one, enriching the result page through a different visual section or triggered when traditional search hits 0 results (or a specific threshold).

Obviously, given the vast amount of pluggable components, it's not a binary situation where vector search works or not; there are many shades, and the overall process must be carefully assessed, ignoring the seducing fascination of the final silver bullet.

In general, if your use case allows for more tolerance in regard to latency, it's recommended to experiment with first-stage retrieval algorithms (testing both dense and sparse retrieval approaches) + various layers of reranking.

We are not yet at the point that only one approach is "the one"; mixing different solutions depending on different use cases and query intents should be accepted and not seen as a failure.

> **Key Takeaways**

- LLMs can be fine-tuned to encode text to a vector that summarises its semantics.
- Bi-encoders or traditional vector embedding models encode text to a vector, separately for the query and the document; at query time, exact/approximate nearest neighbour search is performed to find relevant results.
- These approaches can be used to identify a first candidate set of relevant documents (first-stage retrieval) and refine the order of the results through advanced reranking.
- Quantisation can be used to speed up the system and alleviate the memory/storage costs.
- Late interaction models improve accuracy at the cost of major memory/storage costs as they encode queries and documents to multiple vectors (one per token).
- Cross-encoders take in input the query and a document to assess a relevance score; they are expensive and best suited for reranking a subset of the results.
- Vector search is not a silver bullet; it has many downsides and must be carefully assessed when implementing modern search system solutions.

4.2 Retrieval Augmented Generation

> The holy grail of information retrieval has always been to be able to satisfy the user's information need in the shortest amount of time possible. Not talking only about query response time, but the actual time the user needs to access the information, read it and connect the dots.
>
> Retrieval augmented generation aims to revolutionise traditional information retrieval by leveraging large language models to generate the information needed by the user, in natural language and the optimal format (including citations) so that the user quickly satisfies their needs without having to scan through multiple documents.

LLMs are capable of wonders but suffer from well-known limitations: hallucinations, outdated training data and opaque reasoning, among others, see Sect. 1.5.

Retrieval augmented generation (RAG from now on) has emerged as a solution to mitigate such problems by leveraging corpora of information external to the LLM itself (such as databases, search engines and document repositories).

Research in this field started after observing that large language models present emerging capabilities at scale.

Emergent capabilities refer to functionalities that LLMs demonstrated to have, that were not explicitly designed and implemented; these capabilities are not visible on small models but started to become apparent on larger models at scale.

The massive interactions with users and tasks sparked by the ChatGPT boom in 2022 had a role in this, and since then, more research has focused on analysing the phenomenon [68].

Among other skills, LLMs proved to be able to leverage additional context in the prompt to refine the answer and craft a response within the contextual reference data. It has been empirically observed that LLMs tend to give higher precedence to the additional information provided in the prompt at inference time above past data derived from the pre-training and fine-tuning.

This means that models can update their knowledge base, at least temporarily, during a request and mitigate the problem of outdated information frozen at the training time cut-off date.

We said temporarily because, in opposition to fine-tuning, this happens at inference time, and each request presents a different context, which means that the LLM won't change internally nor learn the new information; it's only able to use it when supplied in the user prompt.

Refining the prompt with the addition of well-crafted, relevant context can also help dramatically reduce hallucinations.

Many studies have proven this empirically [17,40], but there remains a gap in the literature regarding how and why the addition of context in the prompts can reduce hallucination and how this additional external information should be presented to the LLM to guarantee a hallucination-free response.

At the moment, the best we can do is to inject in the prompt contextual information which is cohesive and noise-free, perfectly aligned to the instructions, complete and well formatted: this means we need the perfect information retrieval system, and that's challenging nonetheless.

The denomination retrieval augmented generation (RAG) comes from 2020 [40], but it roots its principles from way back in time.

- Retrieval—Information relevant to the user query is retrieved from external data sources.
- Augmented—The retrieved information augments the prompt and it's sent to the LLM.
- Generation—The LLM leverages the user query and the augmented context to generate an answer.

It's common to divide RAG implementations into three main groups:

- Naive RAG—An external source of data is queried to gather relevant context to pass in the LLM prompt request.
- Advanced RAG—Additional techniques are applied to improve the pipeline at various stages (pre-retrieval, retrieval, post-retrieval).
- Modular RAG—The additional techniques are modularised and switched on/off on demand.

4.2.1 Naive

To satisfy the following query:

> ? $q = I$ Would Like a List of Pizza Restaurants in Tarquinia City Centre

- Index time—A search engine is populated with up-to-date restaurant documents; each document represents a restaurant, including metadata for the type of restaurant and the location.
- Query time—A query is executed against the restaurant search engine, and "top-K" relevant pizza restaurants are retrieved.
- Query time—The original query "q" and the "top-K" restaurants are used to build the LLM prompt.

> I would like a list of pizza restaurants in Tarquinia city centre. To respond, only use the following data:
>
> - Restaurant Il Falchetto - Pizzeria - Tarquinia, Italy
> - Restaurant Fronte al porto - Pizzeria - Tarquinia, Italy
> - Restaurant 500 gradi - Pizzeria - Tarquinia, Italy

A Naive RAG approach consists of:

Indexing—The external source of knowledge is cleaned and processed to be plain textual data. Each document is encoded in a dense/sparse vector space and indexed in dedicated data structures optimised for fast and accurate retrieval.

Retrieval—The user query is encoded in the same dense/sparse vector space used at indexing time, and the indexed data structures are queried to return the top-k most similar documents.

Generation—Both the original user query and the retrieved top-k documents are used to build the final prompt submitted to the large language model. This prompt has the responsibility of providing additional context to the LLM and getting back a natural language response that leverages both the external data and the ability of the LLM.

The phases involved in a naive RAG approach all present challenges:

Retrieval—Information retrieval is not a solved problem: garbage in, garbage out. If your retrieval system performs poorly, the top-k irrelevant documents passed to the LLM won't help in generating better answers.

Augmentation—It's not easy to formulate a coherent prompt that seamlessly enriches the answer. It's common to get back disjoint or poorly rendered answers from the LLM's inability to integrate the dual information provided in the input.

Generation—Even explicitly asking the LLM to use a restricted context doesn't guarantee the model will only use such context. Hallucinations are still possible, and it's common to see the model derail.

4.2.2 Advanced

We can call advanced RAG anything that builds on top of the simple lexical/vector retrieval we have seen so far, with strategies aiming to improve:

Pre-retrieval—Corpus, indexing data structures, metadata addition and query rewriting/expansion

Retrieval—Hybrid search (mixing lexical and vector results), query routing/federation

Post-retrieval—Reranking, results summarisation

If you are familiar with information retrieval, the list above won't sound any new: these techniques have been used for ages to improve information retrieval systems and have seen thousands of iterations and improvements over the years.

The fact is that RAG under the hood is just a way to get better answers from LLM providing better queries and contexts, as we've mentioned already, garbage in, garbage out, so the more you improve the retrieval process, the more you make it "advanced", the better your chances of seeing an improved response.

4.2.2.1 Pre-retrieval

> **Knowledge Curation**

The curation of your corpus of information (your external knowledge base) should be your first stop:

- Is it human-readable? Are sentences written with correct syntax, using a well-defined single language, plainly and coherently?
- Are there many acronyms and ambiguities?
- Is the text clean of HTML tags or other coding expressions?
- Are single documents easily digestible, short enough, but conveying unambiguous information?

Your external knowledge source must be easily consumable by humans: LLMs mimic the human language and its patterns; this means that the easier the content is usable by a human, the better it will be for the LLM.

One of the main problems of many corpora of information I've experienced in the many years of service as a search consultant is that many organisations prefer to have uncurated, dirty, non-homogeneous text and try to solve this down the pipeline with complicated retrieval solutions.

Reasons are manifold: the information is generated by disjointed departments or sub-organisations following different standards, the content was created for a different scope and then adapted as a source of information, the content owners left the company and new owners preferred to add stuff and leave the old as it is, etc.

The advent of RAG brings new energy and funds for such activities: in the past, such requests were normally made by the search department, but even if bearer of promising improvements, often they were seen as trivial, in opposition to the shiny AI model that could be added on top with the hope of silver-bulleting everything.

Now the cleanup is an AI requirement; what's cleaner for a human is cleaner for an LLM. This is a game-changer that rewards the organisations that already spent effort in a sustainable, clean source of information; others now have to follow if they want to jump on the AI train. Furthermore, content curation can now be done automatically, using the same LLMs we use for RAG: fixing the syntax and using the language correctly in a huge corpus of information is cheaper than ever, both in time and money.

▷ Indexing Data Structures

Indexing data structures encode information in a way that's quickly accessible at query time and fit for the purpose of matching the user's information needs.

Information is represented in a vector format and then stored in dedicated data structures.

If each term of your dictionary corresponds to one vector dimension, you are using a "sparse vector" representation.

In such a model, the number of dimensions is generally quite high (corresponding to the term dictionary cardinality), and the vector for any given document contains mostly zeros (hence it is sparse, as only a handful of terms that exist in the overall index will be present in any given document).

A "dense vector" representation contrasts with a term-based sparse vector representation in that it distils approximate semantic meaning into a fixed (and limited) number of dimensions.

The number of dimensions in this approach is generally much lower than in the sparse case, and the vector for any given document is dense, as most of its dimensions are populated by non-zero values.

Examples of indexing data structures used to store and access the information vector representation are inverted indexes [88] (vastly used for sparse retrieval approaches) and hierarchical navigable small world graphs [49, 50] (very popular for dense retrieval).

Depending on whether you go with a traditional sparse retrieval (based on keyword match), dense vector retrieval (based on encoding text to vector) or a hybrid approach (a mix of the two), there are going to be indexing time decisions that affect how precise, recall-oriented and fast your retrieval is going to be.

Designing the correct data model is fundamental; your information may be structured or unstructured, and when structured, you have an additional tool at your disposal as information is already divided into separate fields that retain a specific syntax and semantics, and this simplifies the job of identifying the correct data processing strategy to build the appropriate data structures.

When working with a sparse representation and textual information, it's extremely important to split your content into units of information (tokens) that retain a meaningful semantic value to be used to match the user's information needs.

This requires a deep understanding of the language, syntax and semantics of the information involved. Tokenisation is a complex topic on its own, my recommendation is to not underestimate this phase of your RAG implementation and carefully study your information and expected user interactions, test your text analysis pipeline and validate what ends up in the index: languages' nuances are manifold and extra testing care is needed if you want to identify edge cases to cover.

Depending on the query time algorithm you plan to use, you may need to attach additional payloads to such tokens, such as the term frequency (how many times the token appears in your document) or the inverse document frequency (inverse of how many times the token appears in the corpus) [71].

With the development of dense retrieval, strategies to store such vectors in optimised graph representations have boomed, approximate nearest neighbour data structures offer a multitude of tuning knobs [1], and it's outside the scope of this book to look at their intricate internal implementations to suggest what to change and where depending on the scenario.

The most important (and probably obvious) takeaway is to carefully assess if your favourite technology offers a choice in terms of data structure selection, read as much as possible about the configurable parameters and when not enough, the original papers are a powerful resource to fully grasp the functioning of such hyperparameters.

> **Chunking**

Chunking is the process of splitting textual information into concise paragraphs that retain a cohesive semantic meaning, offering a useful unit of information.

Large language models in RAG scenarios have been empirically proven to work better with short passages rather than full noisy documents, as it happens with humans, diluted knowledge is more difficult to manage.

Additionally, most text vectorisation models are fine-tuned on sentences of limited length (10–15 words). When working with dense vector representations that leverage such models, it's important to align your input documents so that the encoded vectors express their best potential.

The first step when designing your chunking approach is to study the model you used to encode text to vector, starting from its fine-tuning dataset.

Exploring the structure, length and semantics of the passages used during the fine-tuning step can help design a chunking approach that produces the same results or is as close as possible.

Once identified the ideal length of your chunks, how can you process your text to produce meaningful passages?

The easiest approach is to split on fixed characters, but a strong recommendation is to consider the appropriate tokenisation algorithm and punctuation to avoid breaking words. Using this approach is common to create chunks with a bit of characters overlapping with the preceding one, so that the probability of splitting mid-sentence is covered by the following chunk.

This doesn't guarantee that all chunks to be meaningful or that relevant paragraphs will not be split. So, additional chunking algorithms have been developed to use machine learning and text segmentation or sentence boundary disambiguation.

More complicated approaches attempt to find a paragraph delimiter by building a sliding window of chunks, calculating a vector representation for each produced and then finalising the delimiter choice when it produces two chunks with a vector similarity below a defined threshold. This is computationally very expensive, and studies have yet to confirm if the benefits overweight the computational burden [62].

▷ Metadata Addition

This is strictly coupled with the way you designed the data model: adding structure to your documents enhances the retrieval possibilities beyond the full-text search, giving additional filtering capabilities.

This aligns very well with established user experience patterns for results set navigation such as faceting or autocompletion, where the user provides additional context on top of the full-text query and the search engine can combine these new filters with the main search query to reduce the results further and help the user find a narrow scope for their information need.

Document enrichment can also happen automatically: natural language processing techniques can be used to extract named entities and populate dedicated fields (people, locations, companies, etc.), and machine learning can be used to extend the document content with new text (queries) the document is relevant to [25].

▷ Query Rewriting/Expansion

In this architecture, we have a *Rewriter*, a *Retriever* and a *Reader*.

The *Rewriter* is the component that has the responsibility of rewriting the query, potentially multiple times, to help both the *Retriever* and the *Reader* perform their best.

The *Retriever* is the system that queries the external knowledge source and returns relevant passages (the context for the LLM).

The *Reader* is the large language model responsible for reading the query and the context to formulate the final answer.

Not all queries are written the same: some users pay more attention to the way the query is formulated, and others just input a short sequence of cryptic keywords.

Being able to expand such queries to better, unambiguous natural language expressions is extremely important to help the *Retriever* in providing a better context for the *Reader* and to facilitate the *Reader* task of associating the context with the query itself.

Depending on the style of *Retriever* chosen, query rewriting could be as easy as introducing manually curated synonyms or as complex as using machine learning (potentially another small or large language model) to rephrase the query with a different lexicon but keeping unaltered semantics.

How can a query be rewritten or expanded? [58]

Ontology based—A dictionary containing synonyms or in general word relations (hypernyms, hyponyms, etc.) is manually or automatically crafted [55]. Then, at query time is used to expand the query to cover an augmented lexicon.

4.2 Retrieval Augmented Generation

Relevance feedback based—Documents retrieved by the system for the query and documents rated to be relevant for the query (implicitly or explicitly) by users are used to extract additional keywords that can be used to enrich the original query.

Language model based—A language model is used to estimate, for each query term/s, alternative candidates that preserve the same meaning, with a probability associated [47].

The latter approach became prominent in recent years, and it's worth some additional discussion.

The *Rewriter* can be a small language model trained by reinforcement learning using the *Retriever* and *Reader* performance as a reward: it learns the best sequence of terms to rewrite the query to maximise the downstream tasks.

This process needs some preparation steps to build a training set that associates queries with reformulations and the final generated answer.

This means that the initial model is pre-trained on a training set where an original query is associated with a predicted rewritten query that produces a golden generated answer from the *Retriever* and *Reader*.

After this pre-training, we have a modest policy model, able to predict query reformulations.

Then reinforcement learning happens: Training episodes are repeated, and the policy model evolves. At each episode, a reward is calculated, and depending on the result (positive or negative), changes to the policy models are back-propagated, and a new episode begins.

The reward function in our instance passes the newly formulated query to the *Retriever* and *Reader* and assesses how far the generated answer is from the golden, manually curated answer.

These are just a few out of many different rewriting approaches.

In conclusion, query rewriting and expansion have an impact on both the precision and recall of the retrieval system and should be carefully evaluated.

4.2.2.2 Retrieval

> **Federated Search**

The best information to satisfy the user's needs could be fragmented across different systems and data sources, and it may be necessary to interrogate multiple of them and reconcile the resulting result sets.

Applying federated search strategies means:

Data Source Selection—Identifying the best candidate data sources to satisfy the user's information need may require a query intent classification algorithm to make sure the selection is appropriate.

Query Federation—Each candidate data source is queried, and a number of results are retrieved from each to guarantee we get enough for the final top-k to be returned.

The relevance function that assigns the score to each result document and regulates the ranking of the items in the result set must use features that are consistent across the data sources.

Whenever a feature takes into account corpus statistics that are meant to be global (considering the individual data sources as part of a single corpus of information), an exercise of aggregation is needed:

e.g.

Document frequency is a feature used in TF-IDF-based algorithms [71]; it represents how rare a term is in a corpus and the rarer the higher the impact on the score.

If this feature is used to calculate the relevance score in a federated search environment, extra care is necessary to make sure that a global Document Frequency is calculated for the terms, and this can happen at indexing time or, more likely, at query time (when the candidate data sources are selected).

In general, scores coming from different sources must be comparable, and this requires attention and a full understanding of the relevance function used.

Results aggregation—After query federation, we end up with N top-k result sets (one from each data source). They need to become a single ranked list of items to be passed to the LLM, and these items must be ordered by relevance. The easiest approach is to just aggregate all of them and rank them by score. The score needs to be comparable.

But score, it's not the only way, what happens if different data sources may return the same item multiple times?

What if you want to retrieve information from the same data source, but in different modalities?

⊳ Hybrid Search

Hybrid search is the denomination used for an approach where you run some sort of lexical (keyword-based) search and vector search and merge the results.

You may apply this on top of federated search across multiple data sources, and potentially you may want to combine more than two retrieval models (e.g. keyword search on a metadata field of a document, vector search on a vectorised metadata field of a document, keyword search on another metadata field and so on and so forth).

As in federated search, we are dealing with an N results set that needs to be merged to produce a final top-K of results to be passed to the LLM.

Different retrieval models may return items in their ranked lists with a score that's potentially not comparable across.

4.2 Retrieval Augmented Generation

In the literature, we can identify two main strategies (with various implementations, variations and mixes):

Score based—The ranking of an item in the final top-K depends on a linear/non-linear combination of the scores the item had in each separate ranked list.

This means the score for an item is a ranking feature and can be manually combined (e.g. the final score is the sum of each score) or machine learned [42].

Scores must be normalised in most scenarios, and it's quite common to work with probabilistic scores:

$$0 < score < 1 \qquad (4.1)$$

where possible or approximate to such boundaries.

Ranking based—The ranking of an item in the final top-K depends on a linear/non-linear combination of the ranking the item had in each separate ranked list.

Reciprocal Rank Fusion is the most popular [10] and consists of assigning the final score for a result as the sum of the reciprocal of the rank it had in each ranked list.

Given a set D of documents to be ranked and a set of ranked lists R, each a permutation on the items in D, we compute

$$\text{Score}(d \in D) = \sum_{r \in R} \frac{1}{k + r(d)} \qquad (4.2)$$

where $k = 60$ was fixed during a pilot investigation in the original paper, and not altered during subsequent validation (most search engines offer this as a parameter).

4.2.2.3 Post-retrieval

Research shows that LLMs' capacity to use the additional context for RAG degrades as context length grows bigger [43].

If a top-k set of results is provided in the context in descending order of score, it is not necessarily used with decreasing importance by the large language model ... ... Is this counterintuitive? Humans, when presented with a list of items, tend to remember better the first element of a list and the most recent element (the last in the ranking). This behaviour is reflected in LLM in a similar flavour, with an intensity that depends on the model architecture.

This means we need to carefully limit and order the context data to information that is as useful as possible.

This can happen in two phases non-mutually exclusive:

Reranking—A cut-off K is identified, and only the top-K retrieved documents are passed to the LLM. The original ordering can be updated using expensive algorithms that are applied to a subset of the original retrieved data to find the new top-k.

Results summarisation—The textual content of the retrieved documents is compressed, minimising the information loss.

Furthermore, it may be worth experimenting with re-positioning the ranked items after to make sure the top relevant items are rendered at the beginning and the end of the context in the prompt, while the less relevant ones are left in the middle.

> Reranking

The task of reranking K elements consists of taking in input a ranked list of items, coming from the retrieval phase and reordering the top-k elements.

Happening on a subset of the retrieved documents means that more expensive algorithms can be used to re-score and re-order such items.

Once you have identified a good set of candidate results to be used for RAG, you may end up having to decide on a top-k cut-off, as the retrieved documents may be too numerous. This means that you'll leave some of your results out of your scope:

They won't be part of the LLM request, so the LLM won't be able to use them to enrich its knowledge.

Establishing a good reranking strategy can be crucial in many use cases to recalculate the best candidate ordering and identify the most effective top-k to use with the LLM.

Information retrieval has been studying and implementing reranking strategies for many years, and books have been written on the topic, so we'll highlight here only two approaches:

- Cross-encoders [11]
- Learning To Rank [42]

Cross-encoders are LLMs that take as input both the user query and the passage/document concatenated and return as output a single score that represents the probability of relatedness between the two. We described them in 4.1.5.

Learning to rank is the application of machine learning to learn a relevance ranking function based on an implicit (user interactions with the system) or explicit (ratings explicitly provided by domain experts) training set.

When approaching a learning to rank problem, the first activity to carry on is the feature selection and engineering: identifying the factors that should affect the new ranking score for the item.

4.2 Retrieval Augmented Generation

Features describe various aspects of the query-document pair and can be of different types:

Quantitative—Describe a property for which the possible values are a measurable quantity, e.g. the price of an e-commerce product

Ordinal—Describe a property for which the possible values are ordered, e.g. the educational level of a student

Categorical—Describe an exact category of a document, such as the MIME type of a file

Features can be extracted from:

Document metadata—Including business-related factors such as how profitable an e-commerce product is.

Text—Based on the terms distribution in the document and/or the query, such as how many times a specific term appears in a metadata field for a certain document, e.g. The term "Vegeta" appears twice in the field title "Vegeta is the prince of all saiyans and was born on the Vegeta planet".

Semantic—Based on a query-document similarity score, potentially cross-encoders.

Once your query-document pair is sufficiently described as a feature vector, it's time to build your training set: a list of samples where the query-document feature vector is associated with a relevance rating that establishes how good the document is for the query in terms of relevance. You need thousands of samples, and to produce them, you can resort to:

Implicit feedback—Users' interactions with your system (clicks, views, downloads, sales, etc.) are used to estimate how relevant documents are for queries.

Explicit feedback—Human domain experts are interviewed to assign how relevant documents are for queries (on a certain scale, for example, from 0 to 4).

LLM as a judge—LLMs (instruct following models or potentially fine-tuned for the task) are used to estimate how relevant documents are for queries [26, 87].

Training data is used to learn a relevance function (model) that takes in the query-document feature vector and returns a score that is used to rank documents for a given query.

Such a model [39] can be used at query time to assign a score to each query-document candidate and rerank the results.

► Prompt Compression

As a last step to improve the generation and mitigate the risk of losing sight of key elements of the context, it's important to select the most essential information and reduce the length of the prompt to be processed: as it would happen with humans it's better to concentrate the information rather than diluting it.

Natural language appears to contain redundancy [69] that is useful in human communication and comprehension but not necessary to LLMs.

As discussed in the reranking section, redundant or long contexts are challenging for current LLMs [43].

The RAG task becomes more difficult due to positional bias in the context, the computational cost is higher, and the generation is slower.

Let's start from the basics: the task of text summarisation is the process of condensing textual data to obtain a shorter version (a summary) that preserves the most crucial information from the original content.

There are two general approaches for doing this automatically: extraction and abstraction.

Extraction—The content is extracted from the original data and not modified in any way.

Terms and/or sentences are selected to be returned as part of the summary according to a dedicated classification algorithm.

Abstraction—New text is generated, such text didn't exist in the original textual data.

Abstractive approaches are generally more computationally expensive than extractive ones.

Building on top of this long-standing research, similar ideas have been applied to context and prompt summarisation for RAG.

One of the most interesting ideas to compress the prompt comes from Microsoft research [35, 36, 60]. Published as open source, the approach of LLMLingua follows these principles:

- Language models (large or small, fine-tuned) are good at identifying pieces of information that are not useful to them.
- Leveraging the full bidirectional context is beneficial.
- To avoid hallucinations and slowness, extracting gives better results than abstracting.

Each term in the original prompt is classified to be preserved or discarded, keeping in consideration the terms preceding and following it.

Doing this with a dedicated small language model improves both latency and costs before we interact with a Large Language Model.

4.2 Retrieval Augmented Generation

Initial iterations of LLMLingua [35] followed a task-aware strategy: the downstream task, for example, the task of satisfying a user's information need (RAG), is used to better estimate what to preserve and what to discard.

Extending and improving the approach, LLMLingua2 [60] follows a task-agnostic pattern to be able to better adapt to many use cases and LLMs.

ReComp [80] also follows a task-aware strategy and proposes both an extractive compressor (that extracts sentences from the original context) and an abstractive compressor (that generates a shorter version of the context).

Extractive compressor—A dual encoder model is trained to encode both a sentence and the original query into two distinct vectors; their similarity, for example, a dot product, represents how useful the sentence is to be appended to the original query to obtain the final answer from the LLM.

This encoder is used to encode all the sentences of the original prompt, and the resulting compressed prompt is a concatenation of the top K sentences, ordered by the vector similarity metric.

Abstractive compressor—An encoder-decoder is trained to take in the original query and the concatenated list of documents from the context to generate the compressed prompt.

When prompted carefully, generic LLMs proved to be quite effective in summarising text, but they are obviously expensive.

So, distillation happens to obtain a lightweight compressor [28].

Distillation is the process of taking in input a large model after training and transferring the knowledge to a small model that is suitable for deployment and fast real-time inference.

You can consider the small model as an approximation of the first one, losing all the aspects learned by the original that are not useful for the target task.

The abstractive compressor preserves the capacity of the original LLM for summarising text but forgets many other abilities that are not necessary for the target task.

According to the experimental part of the research, both compressors proved to be interesting on various datasets, definitely something to experiment with when setting up your RAG architecture.

Also, generic summarisation algorithms may be used for the task, but the risk of discarding important elements of the prompt is higher, so it's recommended to invest in prompt compression approaches specifically designed for the task.

4.2.3 Modular

Modularity is a key principle in software development, and RAG architectures are no exception:

All the strategies we've seen so far can be switched on/off depending on the use cases and necessity; they are not mandatory, and clearly, you can customise them/interchange and concatenate them in pipelines according to your requirements.

Each stage (pre-retrieval, retrieval and post-retrieval) can be a pipeline as complex as you like, where you enable the components when and if you need them.

4.2.4 Evaluation

When evaluating a RAG system, you need to quantify the precision and recall of the retrieval phase and the faithfulness to facts of the generated answer.

Regarding classic information retrieval metrics, there's plenty of literature that goes deep on the topic [3].[6]

For the sake of this book, it's important to know that an evaluation metric takes in input relevance-labelled query-document pairs and calculates a score that measures how well the information retrieval system performs from a specific angle.

What are the different perspectives we care about when evaluating an information retrieval system?

Precision—How many of the results returned are relevant to the query.

Recall—How many of all the relevant results from the corpus of information are returned in the results.

Once this main distinction is clear, we can complicate the evaluation as much as we like:

Binary/graded relevance—Is a document relevant or irrelevant to a query? Or should we map various levels of relevance? Such as irrelevant, vaguely relevant, relevant, perfectly relevant, etc.

Ranking aware—Does it matter if a relevant document appears higher or lower in the ranked result set?

This is just for the retrieval stage; to evaluate a full RAG architecture, you also need to assess the generated end-to-end answer, verifying how much of the information needed is covered and how much is hallucination-free.

---

[6] https://www.pinecone.io/learn/series/vector-databases-in-production-for-busy-engineers/rag-evaluation/

4.2 Retrieval Augmented Generation

There are plenty of proprietary and open source solutions to do that, let's list them by popularity and explore their main peculiarities:

RAGAS [15]—https://www.ragas.io/
GitHub Stars: 9,500
License: Apache-2.0 license
Language: Python
Best for: Experimenting, proof of concepts, initial RAG explorations

RAGAS is a library that offers evaluation metrics, synthetic evaluation data generation and online monitoring. In terms of metrics, it covers both the context retrieval (precision, recall) and the response (noise sensitivity, relevance and faithfulness). **N.B.** Most of the metrics rely on LLMs to work and are not deterministic. This has many implications, including costs and a certain level of unpredictability, so it's highly recommended to perform the due diligence before going all in with the tool. As with many other open source tools, there are always concerns in terms of code quality, so make sure to double-check if it's up to your organisation's standard (as you may need to debug such code). On the other hand, the faithfulness metric demonstrated robust performance in certain datasets [24].

DeepEval [44]—https://docs.confident-ai.com/
GitHub Stars: 7,300
License: Apache-2.0 license
Language: Python
Best for: Metrics variety support

DeepEval includes support for various metrics (from various frameworks), it's integrated with various LLM pipeline frameworks, and it's backed by a good-sized community. In terms of metrics, it covers both the context (precision/recall) and the response (relevance and faithfulness).

ARES [65]—https://ares-ai.vercel.app/
GitHub Stars: 600
License: Apache-2.0 license
Language: Python
Best for: Systems with continuous upgrades

ARES leverages synthetic training data and uses it to fine-tune small language models to act as judges for the evaluations. Human annotators can be optionally used in the process. In terms of metrics, it covers both the context (relevance) and the response (relevance and faithfulness). For each metric, a separate judge (small language model) with a binary classifier is fine-tuned to classify positive and negative examples. This brings interesting cost reductions and performance improvements in comparison to other solutions.

In general, nowadays, many products try to solve the RAG (and in general, LLMs) evaluation challenge, but overall, pretty much all of them end up with the same problems:

- To measure factual correctness, you need access to ground truth. Unless you provide ground truth manually, you need to generate it, and if an evaluation system is able to generate it perfectly, then RAG would be solved in the very first place.
- They use an LLM to evaluate the response of an LLM (most of the time it is exactly the same LLM). Identifying incorrectly generated responses can only work if the evaluation framework writes better prompts for the model, but it's not guaranteed.
- The frameworks that introduce humans in the loop are the most reliable. It's obviously more expensive and less scalable, but it still feels like the best way to tackle this challenge (up to this point).

4.2.5 Current Limitations

Retrieval augmented generation systems are becoming more and more popular, but there is room for improvement (this should be pretty much valid independently of when you read the book, as there is always room for improvement).

First and foremost, RAG has only been empirically proven to work, but we lack a comprehensive understanding of why an LLM should prefer contextual information in the prompt over the knowledge it was trained on.

There is no guarantee it will happen, but we are decently confident thanks to the plethora of empirical evidence we have mentioned in the chapter.

That brings unpredictability, which is generally an unpleasant surprise.

Now that you have read the chapter, you may have observed that RAG is pretty much information retrieval under cover: there is very little you can do aside from improving the contextual information you pass in the prompt. The better and more compressed the context, the better the generation.

Someone may argue that if we need to reach almost a perfect retrieval to have a nice working RAG, do we need RAG in the first place?

I do believe that there is value in formulating the response in natural language and gathering information from different data sources in a concise representation, but this critique is reasonable and up for discussion.

Another point of friction is the evaluation aspect: at the moment, most frameworks rely on additional LLMs to evaluate RAG systems, and we know that LLMs are probabilistic machines.

I'm not saying that humans are reliable evaluators; sometimes I even find myself in disagreement with a version of myself from the past, but I kind of feel uncomfortable in having evaluation systems that are not deterministic by design.

Finally, when building RAG systems, we end up with long trial-and-error sessions, and this is an engineering practice I dislike entirely: we should aim to programmatically interact with LLM to perform specific tasks rather than asking them (with polite manners of course!).

In this regard, encouraging progress is happening, and we may soon observe interesting breakthroughs.

> **Key Takeaways**

- RAG satisfies the user's information need, in natural language, including citations from external sources of knowledge.
- Pre-retrieval strategies optimise and polish the external data source.
- Retrieval strategies fetch relevant information from the external data sources.
- Post-retrieval strategies improve the prompt to better interact with the LLM.
- RAG is not a silver bullet to magically improve existing mediocre search solutions.
- RAG is the cherry on top of your information retrieval cake: give some love to your search before you embark on the RAG journey.
- RAG has been empirically proven to help; more studies are needed.

4.3 Query/Document Expansion

> Large language models can be used to expand queries with additional reformulations, to generate synonyms on the fly and mitigate the vocabulary mismatch problem with no need to change the underlying index and available data structures. With a specular approach also documents can also be enriched with summaries or hypothetical queries they answer. This introduces additional latency both at query and index time, so it may not be an acceptable solution for your use case.

Query expansion has been studied in information retrieval for decades [2, 8] with many iterations of dedicated specialist models.

With the development of LLMs, expanding a query to different reformulations becomes as easy as asking it via a prompt, with no need to collect user query logs and study/train on users' query rephrases.

This naive approach proves to be quite effective and requires minimal effort to be implemented.

The task definition is the following:

"Given a query q, generate an expanded new query $q1$ with additional query terms useful to retrieve relevant documents".

The task can be expressed in the prompt just as a:

- *Zero shot* request (literally copying and pasting the task definition above)
- *Few shots* adding examples of query expansion
- *Chain of thought* adding examples of query expansion and including a step-by-step reasoning on how the examples are generated

Different prompts yield different results (all of them quite good given the simplicity of the approach), and chain of thought prompts proved to behave better than few-shot or zero-shot prompting in the paper study [31] (results also depend on the LLM model used).

Modern LLMs are all based on similar architectures but have different nuances across their capabilities and trained data, so it's recommended to experiment with the above and evaluate the results to identify the best way of defining the task for the model of your interest. This approach is extremely useful for traditional lexical search, but when applied to vector-based search (which already aims to solve the vocabulary mismatch problem) loses a bit of its benefits.

Alternative approaches such as query2doc [76] and HyDE [22] consist of generating pseudo documents (hypothetical document generation) supposedly relevant for the query and use them (potentially along the original query) to perform traditional keyword search or encoding them to vector(s) and run vector search.

This approach presents its utility also in the context of vector search: most of the time, there's a discrepancy between the query and document length, and this causes non-negligible challenges in modelling them in the same vector space.

By generating a pseudo-document that expands the information needed expressed in the query, the gap is mitigated, and also vector search can be applied with reduced friction.

The results shown experimentally for such approaches are promising, but it's debatable how well they can adapt to real-world usages.

A recent study [82] highlights that the datasets used in the benchmarks to evaluate some of the query expansion methods potentially leaked in the pre-training of the LLM used to expand the query itself.

This may cause overfitting to a certain degree and present less generalisation ability. Given that the LLM to use to expand the query is a pluggable component, the approaches mentioned remain valuable, but extra care and testing are needed to make sure they work well with your use case.

The approaches mentioned so far happen at query time: this means query latency is directly affected, and additional time is added. If using a general-purpose LLM as a service, this latency may be significant.

4.3 Query/Document Expansion

Mitigations involve building intermediate caches, potentially pre-populated with expansions of popular queries, extracted from query logs. This can happen at startup and periodically, reducing the query times and LLM requests.

Distillation has been shown to be an effective way to transfer the abilities of a large model to a smaller one. So another option to reduce costs and query times is to distil the query expansion capability into a smaller (faster and cheaper) model: this has been explored in the e-commerce domain [57] but can also be applied to other domains.

Document expansion on the other side aims to enrich documents with a summary or hypothetical queries related to the document.

The task definition is the following:

"Given a document d, generate an expanded document $d1$ including hypothetical queries for whom the document is relevant".

This moves the expansion at indexing time, increasing the time necessary to process the input documents but reducing to a minimum the impact on the query latency.

In structured documents, the enriched content can be stored in separate fields and used at retrieval time in a different way than the original content:

Once the generated content is in a separate attribute, it can be used at matching time to improve the recall (results coverage) of the system, but also at ranking time, assigning a different weight to query matches that happen in the generated field rather than the original content of the document.

For example, a learning to rank model may learn to weight the generated text matches as less/more important than matches in other fields (generated or not).

Like many other indexing time approaches in information retrieval, the main benefit of doing this offline at the document level is hiding the expansion processing time from the final user: there's still a minimum impact at query time, due to the increased index size and additional document content (this impact can be limited if only dense vector search is performed and only a fixed size vector per document is stored).

The negative side is that the expansion is static, and in case we want to enrich the documents with new generated text, we need to re-index.

There's also another extreme that presents problems: near real-time search.

In this scenario, you want your incoming documents to be indexed as fast as possible, to serve the final user, but adding more processing at indexing time means more latency between pushing a document to the system and seeing it searchable.

The takeaway is that you need to carefully assess your latency tolerance both at query and index time and how often your expansion should be refreshed: when you answer these questions, you'll be ready to choose the ideal query/document expansion approach for your use case.

> **Key Takeaways**

- Naive approaches for query expansion with LLMs proved to be quite promising.
- Using full-scale LLM for query expansion brings a significant query latency impact.
- LLMs can also be used for document expansion at indexing time, to reduce the query time impact.

4.4 Semantic Neural Highlighting

> The traditional highlighting feature in a search engine offers a layer of explainability of the search results to the end user, identifying what portions of each search result matched the user query, in a human-readable snippet.
>
> With the introduction of LLMs, this functionality can expand its horizon beyond keyword matching and highlight document snippets that are semantically related to the user's information needs, with no need to share the same lexical terms.

Highlighting snippets in a search results page is a common expectation since Google introduced them back in the late 1990s.

They are useful to the end users to quickly identify the relevant portion of a document, have a better idea if the search result could answer their information need and potentially answer it directly with no need of expanding the document.

For many years, the snippet has been based on lexical keyword matching: after retrieval, a lookup happens for the query terms, all matches are located and the position extracted, and a surrounding window of text is returned to make the snippet more readable.

This happens algorithmically and still has value nowadays, but what happens with the vocabulary mismatch problem?

What if your search is not only lexical anymore, and relevant documents are returned even if they have nothing in common lexically with the original query terms?

In case your search implements some sort of query expansion to then run a lexical search, you still have control over running traditional highlighting.

You could keep track of the expanded query terms and potentially pass them as a special parameter for your highlighter to differentiate their matches in the resulting document.

4.4 Semantic Neural Highlighting

This can be extremely useful when presenting the snippet to the end user, as they can have a visual, quick confirmation of what exactly matched their query and what matched from a semantic expansion.

What happens if your search is vector-based or hybrid?

If your matching and ranking pipeline involves late interaction models at any point, you get a powerful semantic highlighting for free, when processing the score for the query-document pair: for each query token, you get the most semantically close token for each document (see 4.1.4).

If you are in the dense retrieval scenario with a pure approximate nearest neighbour with each query/document encoded to a single vector, you may have no clue about the semantic expansion that happens behind the scenes.

A first approach is to split your documents into chunks and vectorise them separately. When returning a document, you keep track of the best chunk, the highest in similarity for the returned document, and that chunk is used as a semantic highlighting snippet.

If the chunk size is decently small, your problem is solved, but you may want to additionally refine the snippet, especially if the chunks are not short enough and fit for your purpose.

LLMs are generally quite good at identifying the semantic relatedness between pieces of text, and the highlighting task is a natural fit.

The task definition is the following:

"Given a document d and a query q, return a snippet of text from the original document that best responds to the query".

This task can be easily described in a prompt, and even this naive implementation brings generally high-quality results with modern instruction-based LLMs.

Highlighting happens post-retrieval and takes in input a small amount of documents, as normally search engines offer paginated results, where each page consists of a human-manageable list of items (generally 10–20 elements).

This makes even the naive implementation quite sustainable as the latency added to each search result page rendering depends on a fixed page size and can happen after retrieval, with a minimal impact on the user experience.

Potentially quick traditional highlighting is returned with the search results, and the additional semantic layer of LLM-powered highlighting is added a few hundred of ms later with no harm or on demand.

More advanced use cases may require the LLM to also extract positional offsets for the extracted snippet, depending on the kind of integration you are building.

Pay attention to these situations as the more you complicate the task for the LLM, the more likely to misinterpret it and in programmatic interactions, this can end up with errors and unpredictable situations.

The recommendation here is to keep the interaction as simple as possible, so as to minimise the probability of misunderstanding the task.

> **Key Takeaways**

- Traditional highlighting identifies matching query keywords in each search result.
- Semantic highlighting identifies relevant snippets in each search result independently of the exact query keyword match.
- Naive LLM integration is enough to get quick and surprisingly good results out of the box.
- Given that highlighting happens per search result page, on limited search results, the added query latency is generally acceptable.

4.5 Spellchecking and Autocompletion

> Spellchecking is an auxiliary task that aims to provide spelling suggestions in case of typos or misspellings and has been traditionally implemented with string similarity algorithms.
>
> Autocompletion is also an auxiliary tool that aims to speed up users' query formulation, autocompleting terms and sentences based on their probability of fulfilling the users' intent.
>
> Large language models' deep context modelling and text generation capabilities make them a good fit for the tasks, but their benefits at the cost of latency are debatable.

Spellchecking and autocomplete are fundamental aspects of any modern search engine.

Users expect them and expect them to work correctly and quickly, especially for the autocompletion that by definition is meant to speed up the user query formulation.

Spellchecking is a little bit more tolerant in terms of latency, as it normally happens during the query processing (although it can be implemented alongside the autocompletion to predict the user's intention and fix the typos at the same time).

Traditional techniques solve these problems with string distance-based algorithms and solutions based on finite state automata/transducers that are fast, decently cheap in memory and can use data structures pre-computed at indexing time [7, 29].

Additional studies have applied deep learning to the problem, ending up with models that were considered large at the time, but nowadays fit better into the small language models category [83–85].

4.5 Spellchecking and Autocompletion

By design, LLMs seem a perfect fit to supercharge both, but let's see the pros and cons, with a critical analysis.

4.5.1 Spellchecking

Let's start simple, for query time spellchecking is unlikely you'll get much benefit from deploying a large-scale general-purpose LLM for the task, especially if your user queries tend to be quite short and involve few keywords, the traditional method will be more than enough, and an LLM is just overkill.

The situation changes slightly if your query tends to be very long or you want to use the spellchecker at indexing time as a preprocessing step to clean up your content: for this use case you may need both typo and grammar corrections, and an LLM is a better fit, although a dedicated small language model is likely to perform the task quicker and cheaper.

The latency and costs introduced by using general-purpose LLM for spellchecking are hard to justify, but if your use case is ok with them, the recommendation is to measure the level of improvement that the approach brings over the traditional methods.

For certain languages where the traditional spellchecking methods are not functioning very well (like logographic languages), there have been recent studies in integrating modern LLM in the spellchecking pipeline [12]: this happens through few-shot prompting, where examples are given to enhance the LLM spellchecking capabilities with ad hoc input context.

Latency is not taken into consideration in the study, so keep that in mind if you want to experiment in that direction.

At this point, you may think of distilling a spellchecker from a general-purpose LLM to create a smaller, faster model that mirrors only the spellchecking performance of a larger LLM, but with significantly reduced computational resources and faster processing times.

This process, known as knowledge distillation, teaches a "student" model to mimic the predictions of a "teacher" LLM (in this case, the larger, general-purpose model spellchecker).

Although the idea of applying distillation to separate different abilities from models to deploy only the ones you need is becoming more and more popular, research in the spellchecking field is still a work in progress.

Another aspect to consider is the ranking of spellchecking suggestions. Once a set of candidates is identified, the user normally expects to see just one fixed query, so this means that, behind the scenes, it's needed to score the candidates to identify the most likely best one to show to the user.

This ranking phase may involve factors external to the spellchecking model entirely, combining multiple query term suggestions and testing different phrase searches on your collection of data.

The ordering may depend on the number of results the corrected query produces (the more, the better or the opposite, depending on your business case, with a minimum requirement of the spellcheck fixing the zero result problem).

Sometimes, the spellchecking correction score is completely independent of how many results it matches in your data or how far it is from the original user query, and some business logic and commercial rules must affect the score.

4.5.2 Autocompletion

LLMs were born as powerful autocomplete services and slowly transitioned to bigger text generation, multi-modal and task-solving systems.

Are they still good for their initial purpose, or is it now overkill and smaller models should be preferred?

In search, autocompletion needs to be fast, complete query terms and potentially entire sentences to speed up the user experience with flexible ranking capabilities (as the user input could be completed by more than one option).

In many other fields, such as coding suggestions or documents/e-mail writing suggestions, there's more tolerance for latency, and both general-purpose and specialist LLMs are widely used.

But what about the classic autocompletion you experience in the search bar of your favourite search engine?

When extreme requirements in terms of latency come up, a big and slow general-purpose LLM quickly loses its charm.

Once fine-tuned for following instructions, autocompletion capabilities are still latent but less accessible with fast performance and limited by tokenisation (so partial terms are unlikely to be completed, depending on the model).

General-purpose LLMs are not good for quick query completion anymore; they have evolved to a much more complex direction.

Also, the problem of autocompletion is not only fetching quickly a list of candidates but also scoring them, and many factors may come up as business rules to rank the suggestions.

In many scenarios, instant search is also implemented, so the autocompletion candidate is not free text anymore but could be entities in a specific domain with complex (potentially machine learned) relevance ranking rules.

There is still value in using LLMs offline to enrich your autocompletion dictionary and feed your traditional data structures to then provide classic suggestions to your user.

To do that, you may leverage your query autocompletion logs, especially the ones tracking zero result autocompletions: they can be the most valuable inputs to enrich your dictionary as they indicate situations where your current dictionary failed to offer a completion option to the user.

This is particularly helpful in case your system is implemented through some sort of semantic search (vector or at least hybrid) approach: in traditional keyword search, there's little value in suggesting query terms that are not present in your original corpus of information, as they will produce zero matching results.

On the contrary, semantic search is much more fuzzy in nature, so it may be useful to autocomplete your query via LLM pre-generated content.

The autocomplete query is then vectorised, so the fact that the suggested term doesn't appear lexically in your original data is less of a problem thanks to the abstraction layer offered by vectorisation (which aims to solve the vocabulary mismatch problem).

> **Key Takeaways**

- Large Language Models are generally an overkill for spellchecking and auto-completion due to their query latency.
- LLMs can be used offline to enrich the spellchecking and autocompletion dictionaries.
- There are studies around distillation to produce smaller language models from big teacher models to solve these tasks.

4.6 Multi-modal Search

Multi-modality allows searching for an information need expressed through text, audio, images or video in a corpus that can potentially contain information in any of the data modes above.

This means that you can potentially search via textual queries a dataset of images with no metadata attached.

LLMs achieve this by encoding the information from different media in the same vector space, allowing them to perform vector search or data enrichment seamlessly across.

A key approach to multi-modality consists of leveraging a model fine-tuned for cross-media similarity, which means a model capable of encoding information from different formats (text, audio, video, images, etc.) to the same vector space.

The vector distance between points captures the semantic similarity between the data (this is often called a modality encoder).

This can happen between text and image, text and audio, audio and image and so on and so forth.

To keep it simple, the text "a tiger roaring in the jungle", a picture of a tiger roaring in the jungle, the sound of a tiger roaring in the jungle and a video capturing a tiger roaring in the jungle will all be encoded to very similar vectors, independently of their media format.

Aside from the internal architecture, various factors affect how good a modality encoder could be:

- *Resolution*—The quantity of information per data point.
- *Parameter size*—How complex is the neural network used to represent the model?
- *Pre-training and fine-tuning corpus*—The data used to learn the similarity between modalities.

The model can be fine-tuned to generate a single vector or multiple vectors per data point, or for related generative tasks such as adding a textual description to an image, audio or video or the other way around [81].

A first important breakthrough in the field happened with CLIP [63] (Contrastive Language-Image Pre-training) in 2021.

In short, CLIP is a joint image and text embedding model trained using 400 million image and text pairs in a self-supervised way.

This means that it encodes both text and images into the same vector space.

So, the picture of a tiger in the jungle and the text "a tiger in the jungle" would be encoded to very similar vectors and be close to each other in the vector space.

Fast-forward to 2025, and you have many text-image CLIP models, and they can be used to encode text/images to vectors.

Honourable mention to OpenCLIP [9] that re-implements the original CLIP idea using open source software and datasets.[7]

Similar concepts have been applied to videos [79] and audio [14, 27].

Once you have pre-computed the vector embeddings for your documents, it won't matter much at query time if they were originally text or images and applying nearest neighbour techniques, you can implement multi-modal search.

So far, so good, we now have a good understanding of how multi-modality can be achieved for first-stage retrieval through top-k nearest neighbours.

This is pretty much what we've seen with bi-encoders and vector search for text only in 4.1.1.

What about late interaction models or rerankers? Can we apply the same ideas and concepts to multi-modality?

ColPali [16] targets image/text multi-modality with a focus on rich documents (such as PDF with both images, tables, diagrams and text.

---

[7] https://github.com/mlfoundations/open_clip

The result is a multi-vector representation of the input data that can be used to calculate late interaction via max similarity between the information need and the target document.

The original idea behind ColPali is to improve the standard indexing pipelines for rich documents, which involve most of the times running optical character recognition (OCR [30,72]) systems on scanned documents (that becomes effectively images after scanning) and reconstruction techniques to identify the reading order of the page, extract paragraphs, tables and images.

The approach leverages a vision language model, PaliGemma [5] and multi-vector retrieval through the late interaction mechanisms as proposed in ColBERT.

A Vision LLM (PaliGemma-3B in the original paper) encodes the document into multiple vectors:

- *Patches embeddings*—The image is divided into patches, and each patch is encoded to a vector by a vision encoder, also positional encoding is added to preserve the spatial layout.
- *Cross attention fusion*—A decoder-only GPT model (based on Gemma in the PaliGemma architecture) takes in input a prompt asking what the document says and the visual embeddings (with position) from the patches as context.
- *Multiple vectors generation*—The output is a sequence of tokens (each of them already encoded as a vector) that answer the question, considering both image and textual regions.
- *Projection layer*—Finally, a projection layer is added to map the multiple embedding vectors to a vector space of reduced dimension (128) for efficient storage and to keep the representations lightweight.

At query time, the query is encoded to multiple vectors and a max similarity is calculated between them and the pre-computed multiple vectors for each document.

The approach proved to be quite good on public benchmarks, surpassing many state-of-the-art optical character recognition systems, even if limited by the PaliGemma resolution and embedding dimensions (but both can be improved in future iterations, given the pluggability of the system architecture).

One interesting aspect is how high-resolution inputs are handled: The original ColPali model leveraged a PaliGemma version supporting 448x448 pixel resolution, which may seem quite small in our current times (where full HD or 4k monitors are the norm).

Documents in the industry and in public benchmarks (such as Vidore[8] contributed as part of the ColPali paper) tend to be in much higher resolutions, so they need to be downscaled, minimising the information loss (Fig. 4.1).

As you can see from the example image, even if the resolution reduction brings fuzziness in certain areas of the page, the text is still generally readable and the headers/structure are preserved.

---

[8] https://huggingface.co/vidore

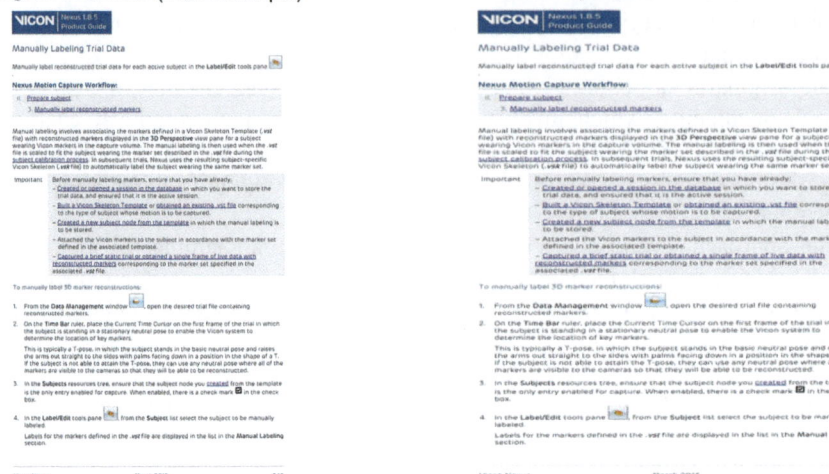

Fig. 4.1 On the left, the original resolution, on the right, the downscaled one

ColQwen[9] shares the same architecture, but instead it uses Qwen as its backbone model (both vision and cross-media decoder).

Once multi-modal documents are retrieved, you may need to rerank across modality.

The considerations we've seen about reranking in Sect. 4.1.5 still apply here; in addition, the reranking problem for multi-modality is generally approached with ad hoc fine-tuned vision language models (or similar for other media types) capable of assigning a score given an input query (also multi-modal) and a document [23].

> **Key Takeaways**

- Data from different modalities can be encoded into the same vector space.
- Once the data is encoded to vectors, you can run approximate nearest neighbour search (or exact).
- ColPali introduces an interesting architecture to process rich documents (like PDFs) with no need for optical character recognition, leveraging vision language models.
- Cross-modal rerankers can help in unifying the scores better after the first-stage retrieval.

---

[9] https://huggingface.co/vidore/colqwen2-v1.0

4.7 Multi-lingual Search

> Multi-lingual search allows searching for an information need expressed in a language and retrieving information from the corpus in other languages.
> Initial attempts involved introducing translation models in the process, capable of translating the information needed and the corpus of information, at query time (to reduce storage costs) or at indexing time (to speed up the query latency).
> LLMs facilitate this, encoding the information from different languages to the same vector space, allowing to perform vector search or data enrichment seamlessly across languages, with a decent compromise in terms of storage/query latency.

Use cases in the field of multi-language information retrieval can go from cross-lingual (query and documents in different languages) to multi-lingual (searching across documents in many languages).

Back in the days, implementing multi-lingual search involved the utilisation of some sort of translation service/translation machine learning model to be applied at query or index time:

- *Query time translation*—Your corpus of information is on a single language, at query time, language identification is applied to the user query, and in case the language is not aligned, a translation happens, and then the query is executed.
- *Query time language routing*—Your corpus of information is on multiple languages, each document presents the information across multiple fields, each of them localised in one language, at query time, language identification is applied to the user query, and the query is routed to the relevant field.
- *Index time translation*—At indexing time, the content of the document that requires internationalisation is translated to all the languages needed to be supported. At query time, language identification is applied to the user query and the query is routed to the relevant field.

Many other approaches can be applied to solve the problem, potentially separating languages on isolated different systems and offering the user experience through separate Web applications or Web sites, but in general the approaches above, among others, introduce additional query/indexing latency and increase the storage needed (when storing multiple translations per document).

Modern LLMs are pre-trained on multiple languages and fine-tuned for cross-language sentence similarity: sentences from different languages are encoded to the same vector space and retain their semantic relation.

As seen in single language vector search or multi-modal, the information is encoded in a way that sentences close in meaning (even if expressed in different languages) are encoded to vectors close in the same vector space.

This brings excellent storage benefits as you don't need to store various translations but only the resulting encoded vectors.

At query time, first-stage retrieval won't look much different from the rest of the use cases observed so far: the query is encoded using the same multi-lingual model and then an approximate nearest neighbour (or exact) is performed.

There's really a plethora of multi-lingual embedding models out there, many of them open weight and each of them supporting a set of languages.

The recommendations is the following: when approaching the model, double-check its internal details as much as possible to get a glimpse of the level of multi-lingual support, and where possible, explore the pre-training (a rough idea of the percentage distribution for languages is probably enough) and fine-tuning datasets to check on the quality and quantity of the training sample for the languages of your interest.

Don't forget to always check updated public leaderboards[10] and benchmarking datasets, as they are very useful to evaluate multi-lingual capabilities of models [52, 56].

Especially if the languages of your interest are low-resource languages, extra care is needed, as it may be more challenging to find adequate embedding models. Falling back to traditional methods may be an option, but bear in mind that modern machine learning translation models may suffer from the same problem.

Section 5.3 further elaborates on the topic.

> **Key Takeaways**

- Plenty of general-purpose and embedding LLMs support multiple languages.
- Common practice is to encode the query/documents to vectors, then perform approximate nearest neighbour, which becomes language independent.
- There are still issues with low-resource languages.

4.8 From Natural Language to Structured Queries

When a user presents an unstructured information need (natural language query) but the corpus of information is made of structured documents (a map of fields, each containing semantically distinct information), we enter the realm of multi-field search. Searching across multiple fields in documents

(continued)

---

[10] https://huggingface.co/spaces/mteb/leaderboard

4.8 From Natural Language to Structured Queries

is a common use case, but also quite hard at the same time: it's difficult to map which part of the query (terms and concepts) refers to which part of the document (the fields). LLMs proved to be quite good in disambiguating entities and concepts based on a specified structure, making them valuable allies when parsing unstructured queries.

If you are working in Information Retrieval or you have at least been exposed to the internals of a decently recent search engine is highly likely you encountered the problem of multi-field search.

This happens because many documents in the real world are actually structured, and the information is categorised under multiple fields.

For example, a document from a corpus of information describing events may look like:

```
{
  "type of event": "concert",
  "location": "Las Vegas",
  "date": 2025-05-29T21:05:53Z,
  "leading person": "Lady Gaga",
  "description": "the last date of the 2025 world tour"
}
```

Each field may be free text (description), an element from a taxonomy (type of event={"concert", "sport game", "theatre play", "movie"}) or typed metadata (like the date in the example).

Lexically, each field may have a different term dictionary for the information it contains across all documents: depending on its type, this dictionary may be quite extended or as small as an enumeration of well-defined items.

Semantically, each field should represent a well-defined angle of the information, described by a comprehensible field name (in the example, a human reader may have an intuition of possible values for the fields based on their name).

Building a search engine on this kind of data is not simple, as this structure and the related term dictionaries are not necessarily known to the end user.

Most of the time, in terms of user experience, search on this sort of corpora is offered to the user with a search box able to process free text queries (then it's up to the user to use natural language or keyword search).

It's also common to support this with an alternative "advanced search" that offers a better view over the document structure and allow the user to search by field, potentially with select lists over enumerations and other user experiences gimmick to facilitate the job, but let's be honest, users want to satisfy their information need as fast and as easy as possible and rarely go the hard way with the "boring" advanced search.

So we are back to the free text search box now, which needs to process a free text input but match structured documents.

Given an example query: "2025 singing performances by Stefani Joanne Angelina Germanotta in the US".

This poses multiple challenges:

Query Segmentation

The query covers different concepts, which need to be segmented:

2025 <u>singing performances</u> **by Stefani Joanne Angelina Germanotta** <u>in the US</u>

This task is hard as it requires an understanding of the language, of the domain and of the dictionary involved.

Field Mapping

Each query segment may refer to a specific field or multiple:

2025 → date
singing performances → type of event
by Stefani Joanne Angelina Germanotta → leading person
in the US → location

This task is also hard as it requires an understanding of the language, of the domain and of the dictionary to identify the best candidate for each segment in the document structure.

Vocabulary Mismatch

The terms used by the user may not align with the taxonomies used in the corpus of information.

2025 → 2025-05-29T21:05:53Z
singing performances → concert
by Stefani Joanne Angelina Germanotta → Lady Gaga
in the US → Las Vegas

Normalising the entity labels requires an advanced knowledge base, potentially proprietary.

Each of these challenging problems has been studied for many years in the fields of natural language processing [33], but solutions have seen rapid improvement with the integration with LLMs.

4.8.1 Query Parsing Approach

A first idea to solve the problem via LLMs is to define a prompt template that takes as parameters the user query and the domain structure in JSON (or any other data-interchange format).

The scope of the prompt is to request the large language model to render the user query following the domain structure and generate the structured version of the query in the response.

A naive example of request and response may look like this:

Request
```
Given a domain specified by this structure:
{
"type of event": "the type of the event",
"location": "the location of the event",
"date": "the date of the event",
"leading person": "the main actor in the event",
"description": "a free text description of the event"
}

How would a query=
"2025 singing performances by Stefani Joanne Angelina
Germanotta in the US" look like?
```

Response
```
The corresponding structured representation would be:

{
  "type of event": "singing performance",
  "location": "US",
  "date": "2025",
  "leading person": "Stefani Joanne Angelina Germanotta",
  "description": "Singing performances by Stefani Joanne
  Angelina Germanotta in the US in 2025"
}


Notes:
"type of event": "singing performance" is extracted directly.

"location": "US" (interpreted as the country).

"date": "2025" (interpreted as a year).

"leading person": Full name of the performer.

"description": A natural language summary of the query
```

As you can see from the naive example, modern LLMs (the above example is from GPT-4-turbo) handle solving the first two challenges quite well, with a decent rationale in case we want to show it to the end user.

To complete our query parser, we still need to solve the vocabulary mismatch problem, generate a structured output that can be used programmatically consistently and potentially some speed up to have decent performance and use it at runtime.

- *Vocabulary mismatch problem*—In the naive example, we didn't pass any dictionary-related context to the LLM, so the generated structured query may not align with the lexical terms present in the corpus of information.

  We talked about this problem extensively in the vector search Sect. 4.1. To solve it, you may leverage external solutions such as implementing vector search on top of the query parsing above or manual synonyms.

  An alternative, we have experimented with and that proved to work extremely well, is to directly rely on the LLM to solve it, passing in the context not only the structure with the description but also the possible values for each field to choose from.

- *Structured output*—The response shown in the naive example is out of the box, surprisingly good, but integrating it in a query parsing pipeline requires a structured output that can be plugged programmatically into the pipeline.

  It's ok to get back from the LLM both the structured query and the rationale, but they need to be encapsulated in a well-defined and predictable format.

  This can be done outside the LLM, adding a response parsing layer that takes in the unstructured response from the LLM and wraps it in a well-defined JSON, for example.

  Although doable, this adds additional post-processing, potentially quite complicated to write and to test. Modern LLMs support structured output out of the box, most of them through an additional parameter containing the JSON schema[11] to comply with.

  How it's implemented internally in the LLM APIs is up to the vendor, but from a user perspective, it's a way to constrain the response from the LLM to be always consistent with a well-defined programmatic expectation.

- *Latency speedups*—Parsing each query with a call to a general-purpose LLM is slow.

  You can act at the application level, reducing the number of calls you make to the LLM and act at the LLM level, to speed up the inference.

  A basic application optimisation would be to add a caching layer in your query parsing pipeline, so already parsed queries will skip the LLM call entirely and fetch the structured query from the cache.

  The cache key can be naively the exact query, or some simple pre-processing text analysis may output a simplified version of the query (maybe removing

---

[11] https://json-schema.org

plurals or some token variation, good enough for your use case), similar enough to make the cached entry useful and not requiring a new LLM call.

In regard to the LLM call, you can choose a smaller model, compromising on the quality for faster responses. The suggestion here is to support this decision with offline quality benchmarking that validates the performance of your parser across a test set of realistic queries and expected structures.

An additional option, where feasible, would be to self-host an open-weight LLM to speed up the networking and inference part, with optimised hardware and networking designs.

When self-hosting is not an option, there's still a chance to find a vendor that does that for you, possibly on an optimised application-specific integrated circuit, rather than general-purpose GPUs.

Another alternative, that would require much more technical effort from your team, could be to distil a bigger model into a smaller one specialised in the task of query parsing.

The feasibility is debatable, and more studies in this direction are necessary to make it a well-established and repeatable process.

4.8.2 Filtering Suggestions Approach

The query parser approach has the benefits of hiding from the users the complexities of the generated structured query and running it transparently: the user will just get results to their natural language query, and the experience will be pretty much aligned with their general expectation.

But as we know, LLMs are not perfect and hallucinate from time to time.

Implementing a structured output drastically improves the situation, but there may be debatable choices made by the LLM in your specific domain, so extra care is needed, and potentially, a human in the loop would mitigate the situation.

Especially for search engines that deal with a lot of enumerations (rather than free text fields), faceting ended up as an interesting way of exploring search results: field values are aggregated with counts and offered visually to the user to further refine a search result list.

If that's your case, you may integrate the capability of LLMs to build a structure out of your natural language queries as enhanced faceting: The LLM call to generate a structured query happens in parallel to the main query execution and generates a structured response with a rationale snippet explaining why the query has been structured that way (as seen in the naive example).

The structure and snippet are offered to the users as recommended filters to further refine the search results or potentially expand them.

In certain scenarios, for example, zero results queries, the recommended filters can be applied automatically to expand the empty result set, still presenting the user with the rationale so they are aware of what their query has become and why.

In this approach, the user may accept only partially the LLM suggestions, introducing implicit feedback through their action that can be leveraged to further improve the assistant.

In terms of latency, it's also going to be potentially more acceptable as the call now happens in parallel and supplies only a part of the search result page. This means that the loading can be separated and the delay less noticeable, as the user will have information to assess in the meantime and then explore the LLM filter suggestions.

4.8.3 Document Enrichment Approach

Both the ideas mentioned so far target a query runtime phase, and this inevitably has an impact on the latency; it can be optimised but not removed entirely.

An alternative approach could follow a similar principle to what we've seen in the document expansion Sect. 4.3.

For each structured document, a list of natural language queries can be generated by an LLM and added into a dedicated field.

At query time all natural language queries will target the new field to retrieve results, speeding up the query that now has only to look at a single "catch all" field and matching documents with a compatible structure (being the field generated out of the original structure) mimicking the behaviour obtained by the query time approaches.

The idea of collapsing multiple fields into one is an idea that we've seen multiple time across the industry with keyword-based lexical search: it's fast and simple but brings also downsides such as term frequencies pollution (as term occurrences are artificially inflated) with an impact on the scoring mechanism and consequentially on the precision of the system as a whole.

Furthermore, in scenarios where the document structure presents many multi-valued fields, generating the query variance to take into consideration all the values of interest may be quite expensive and impractical.

This approach helps with the recall of the system (enhancing the retrieval coverage of documents), so it may be worth considering and experimenting with.

4.8.4 Conclusions and Evaluation

Using LLMs to parse/give structure to natural language queries is promising; a few years ago, to build similar prototypes would have taken months, and now they are doable in a few days.

Bringing the solution to production has its challenges, but it's doable: it's important not to oversimplify things and set the right expectations.

There are fundamental aspects you should pay attention to if you want to maximise the probability of success:

- *Human readable fields*—The more the structure is self-explicit in natural language, the easier the integration with LLMs. To be honest, independently of using LLMs or not, choosing human readable names for your fields and field values has a huge impact to the maintainability of your system: humans work better with readable and explicit code and configurations, using cryptic names or abbreviations may sound cool and usable in small like-minded teams, but as soon as you open your system to new employees or external consultants you'll pay the consequences. So don't use acronyms, weird codes or abbreviations for both your field names and values, and the probability of a successful integration with LLM will grow exponentially (and also humans in your team will be grateful to not have to decipher what a field called "lisa_rtx_5090_tms" means.
- *Offline validation*—There are various moving parts in this integration, and you may want to change the prompt, the way you pass the document structure and the underlying LLM model, for example.

  Setting up a testing framework to assess the impact of changes is vital, and you should aim to set it up offline and online.

  Offline speeds up experimentation and has no impact on the production system, while online is key to keep track of how your real users experience the new functionality.

  An offline evaluation framework for such an integration should assess how well the system is able to give structure to natural language queries.

  This means you need a test dataset that associates queries with their expected structure.

  Then you need to define a metric that reflects the value this approach can bring to your system, for example, for each query, a score from 0 to 1 that assesses how the LLL-generated structure for the query matches the expected one.

  An example of a useful metric could be to calculate the Jaccard index of the two sets of fields and then the Jaccard index of the values for each field that the actual and expected structures have in common.

  Let's elaborate:

  Jaccard Index (Intersection Over Union)

  Given two sets A and B, the **Jaccard Index** is a statistic used for comparing the similarity and diversity of the two sets. It is defined as the size of the intersection divided by the size of the union of the sets:

  $$J(A, B) = \frac{|A \cap B|}{|A \cup B|}$$

  where
  - $|A \cap B|$ is the number of elements in both A and B.
  - $|A \cup B|$ is the number of elements in either A, B, or both.

Properties

- $0 \leq J(A, B) \leq 1$
- $J(A, B) = 1$ if and only if $A = B$
- $J(A, B) = 0$ if $A \cap B = \emptyset$

Example

Given the query from the naive example:
"2025 singing performances by Stefani Joanne Angelina Germanotta in the US".
and the expected structure:

```
{
  "type of event": "concert",
  "location": "US",
  "date": 2025,
  "leading person": "Lady Gaga"
}
```

Let's see an example of the Jaccard Index metric applied to an actual generated structured query from an LLM:

```
{
  "type of event": "singing performance",
  "location": "US",
  "date": 2025,
  "leading person": "Lady Gaga",
  "description": "2025 singing performances"
}
```

Let

$$expectedFields(A) = \{\text{``typeofevent''}, \text{``location''}, \text{``date''},$$
$$\text{``leadingperson''}\},$$
$$actualFields(B) = \{\text{``typeofevent''}, \text{``location''}, \text{``date''},$$
$$\text{``leadingperson''}, \text{``description''}\}$$

$$A \cap B = \{\text{``typeofevent''}, \text{``location''}, \text{``date''}, \text{``leadingperson''}\},$$
$$A \cup B = \{\text{``typeofevent''}, \text{``location''}, \text{``date''}, \text{``leadingperson''},$$
$$\text{``description''}\}$$

$$J(A, B) = \frac{4}{5} = 0.8$$

4.8 From Natural Language to Structured Queries

We can further refine the score and apply the Jaccard Index for each field in the intersection, so, being the example structures single valued, we get a 0 (when the actual values are different from the expected one) or a 1 (when the actual and expected values match).

```
{
  "type of event": "singing performance", → 0
  "location": "US", → 1
  "date": 2025, → 1
  "leading person": "Lady Gaga", → 1
  "description": "2025 singing performances" →
  outside intersection
}
```

So the metric can be adjusted to:

$$Similarity(A, B) = \frac{0+1+1+1}{5} = 0.6$$

We can calculate the similarity between what's expected and what's returned by the LLM for each query in the test set and then do an average over the query set.

Being LLMs, probabilistic machines, it's a good idea to repeat each test execution a certain number of times to get a better view of the consistency of the results.

- *Context*—It's important to pay attention to the size of your document structure and dictionaries as they end up directly in the prompt or in the request via the structured output parameter.

Generally speaking, the longer the context, the more expensive and slow the inference time, so be careful with that and double-check that it's compatible with the LLM-supported length and your budget.

Pay also attention to the privacy and data policies at your company: document structures and dictionaries may be sensitive and shouldn't be openly shared in prompts, even for prototyping.

Make sure you choose a compatible LLM with your legal department's requirements, or potentially self-host one, making sure no data leak happens.

> **Key Takeaways**

- Large language models can be used to give structure to natural language queries.
- The structure of the documents in your corpus is passed along with the user query as context for the LLM.
- Query time approaches are intuitive and decently simple to implement at the cost of increased query latency.

- Indexing time approaches may give similar benefits, introducing less latency, but are not compatible with all use cases (see long multi-valued fields scenarios).
- LLMs work best with document structures that are self-explanatory; the more human-readable the structure, the better the expected results.
- Always validate the work done through offline quality benchmarking.
- Jaccard Index-based metrics can help measure the quality of the generated structured queries.
- Pay attention to your document structures and dictionaries as they inflate the LLM context, causing additional latency and costs.

4.9 Reranking

> Late interaction models such as ColBERT and cross-encoders proved to be quite good to rerank the list of documents after the first-stage retrieval (or down the road in case of multi-stage reranking).
> But what about general-purpose LLMs?
> Reranking a list of items via a prompt is possible but presents challenges and a substantial latency impact.

In common modern search engines, retrieval and ranking are not an atomic block anymore. It's quite common to proceed with a cheap first-stage retrieval strategy and then process the top-k candidates with more expensive algorithms to provide an increasingly better ranking.

This doesn't necessarily mean you rerank just once; you may want to add a cascade of rerankers, each of them with an increasing cost and running on a smaller and smaller list of top-k candidates.

Sometimes your reranking criteria go beyond the pure semantics of the document and need to include business logic optimised on users' interactions and commercial online metrics.

This is out of scope here, but feel free to read about learning to rank [37] techniques if you are curious to learn how machine learning can help you with that.

Coming back to using LLMs for reranking, we had an overview on using ad hoc fine-tuned models for the task in 4.1.5, but also general-purpose LLMs can be used for the task, and that will be the focus here.

A naive way of attempting reranking with an instruction-based LLM would be to send a prompt with the user query, a list of candidate documents, and explicitly ask to rerank the list based on their relevance with the query:

Prompt

```
Given the query: "genus panthera"
and the list:
[lion, cheetah, cat, dog, tiger, leopard, elephant,
 snow leopard].
Can you rerank the items based on their relevance to the
 query?
```

Response

```
The query "genus panthera" refers to a specific genus
within the family Felidae (cats), which includes large
wild cats.

Given that, let's rerank the list:

Reranked List (Most to Least Relevant):
Lion → Panthera leo

Tiger → Panthera tigris

Leopard → Panthera pardus

Snow leopard → Panthera uncia

Cheetah → Not in Panthera; but still a large cat

Cat → Domestic cat (Felis catus), in a different
 genus (Felis)

Dog → Not in the cat family; genus Canis

Elephant → Not related; entirely different order
(Proboscidea)
```

The results are already extremely good, both in terms of the order and explainability, but they lack in structure to be used programmatically as a reranker. The prompt can be refined by adding another naive instruction:

Prompt

```
structure the response in JSON, with a label and
 explainability snippet
```

Response

```
[
  {
    "label": "Lion",
    "explanation": "A member of the genus Panthera,
    specifically Panthera leo."
  },
  {
```

```
    "label": "Tiger",
    "explanation": "Belongs to the genus Panthera;
    its scientific name is Panthera tigris."
  },
  {
    "label": "Leopard",
    "explanation": "A species in the genus Panthera,
    known as Panthera pardus."
  },
  {
    "label": "Snow leopard",
    "explanation": "Part of the genus Panthera;
    its scientific name is Panthera uncia."
  },
  {
    "label": "Cheetah",
    "explanation": "A large cat but not in the genus Panthera;
    belongs to the genus Acinonyx."
  },
  {
    "label": "Cat",
    "explanation": "Refers to the domestic cat,
    which is in the genus Felis, not Panthera."
  },
  {
    "label": "Dog",
    "explanation": "Not a felid."
  },
  {
    "label": "Elephant",
    "explanation": "Unrelated to felids;
    belongs to a completely different order, Proboscidea."
  }
]
```

That's much better, and the response can be consolidated using the structured output feature of many modern LLMs.

The results appear to be generally in sync with human expectations, and also explainability is top-notch. Have we solved semantic reranking, then?

Not quite yet...

First of all, reranking via general-purpose LLMs is slow; how much slower depends on the type of model, the inference hardware and the network latency, but in general is way slower than dedicated rerankers such as late interaction models or cross-encoders.

Slower and more expensive: this means you can use it nowadays on a limited size of top-k candidates, as the longer the context (up to the supported limit), the slower and more expensive the response.

4.9 Reranking

4.9.1 Top-k and Context

Reranking top-k candidates higher than the maximum supported context length can still be done, but multiple calls would be necessary (involving additional costs and latency).

A possible approach involves proceeding in reranking sliding windows of candidates, involving a call to an LLM for each subset of candidates.

Depending on the supported size for the context, this approach becomes similar to pairwise, and potentially in the extreme of a single item per call, you'll end up with a pointwise approach.

Luckily, nowadays more and more LLMs support larger contexts, making it easier to approach this sort of problem with a reduced number of calls and the original listwise intent.

The inference cost may not be that dissimilar, though, as many LLM services charge for input/output tokens.

Let's assume you have a context that supports a maximum of 4 items per call, and you want to rerank topk=10 documents, but you only care about a final first page of 2 items, you could run 4 calls, with a sliding window [74].

The top-2 include the best two paragraphs, but you had to run many reranking calls.

Furthermore, the rest of the list is just locally reranked, so in case of pagination needs, you will end up with additional calls (something clunky, not recommended and probably unfeasible).

Let's see what this looks like to have a better understanding:

```
Initial list (positions 1 to 10):
Pos 1 2 3 4 5 6 7 8 9 10
ID  10 9 8 7 6 5 4 3 2 1

Step 1: Window 7 to 10 on initial list
Window: [4, 3, 2, 1]

Re-rank ascending → [1, 2, 3, 4]

Updated list after Step 1:

Pos 1 2 3 4 5 6 7 8 9 10
ID  10 9 8 7 6 5 1 2 3 4

Step 2: Window 5 to 8 on updated list
Window: [6, 5, 1, 2]

Re-rank ascending → [1, 2, 5, 6]

Updated list after Step 2:

Pos 1 2 3 4 5 6 7 8 9 10
ID  10 9 8 7 1 2 5 6 3 4
```

```
Step 3: Window 3 to 6 on updated list
Window: [8, 7, 1, 2]

Re-rank ascending → [1, 2, 7, 8]

Updated list after Step 3:

Pos 1 2 3 4 5 6 7 8 9 10
ID 10 9 1 2 7 8 5 6 3 4

Step 4: Window 1 to 4 on updated list
Window: [10, 9, 1, 2]

Re-rank ascending → [1, 2, 9, 10]

Final updated list after Step 4:

Pos 1 2 3 4 5 6 7 8 9 10
ID  1 2 9 10 7 8 5 6 3 4
```

LLMs are probabilistic in nature, so you won't necessarily get the same reranking order if you repeat the same calls (depending on the domain, it can or cannot be a big deal).

As usual, some of these limits can be overcome via caching (to speed up the reranking and avoid inconsistencies across calls), so depending on your use case, you may be able to use general-purpose LLMs as rerankers right now with acceptable costs and latency.

Moving past the naive example, leveraging large language models for document reranking has been a popular and promising research direction in recent years, and many studies are dedicated to improving the performance and efficiency of the approach.

In general, there are three main reranking paradigms studied (inherited from learning to rank approaches): pointwise, pairwise and listwise.

The pointwise approach aims to estimate the relevance score of a single ⟨ query, document ⟩ pair at a time [41].

The pairwise approach aims to select the most relevant document for a query given two input documents. Basically aims to give an order of relevance to a list of two items [61].

The listwise approach aims to order a list of documents based on their relevance to the query [48].

In traditional learning to rank the literature and state of the art moved towards the listwise direction and in general it remains the simplest approach to build a single call to the LLM, although pointwise and pairwise can be useful to simplify the job of understanding the task and can also be used in related tasks such as using LLMs as judges (that we'll see in Sect. 4.10).

Notable improvement directions target the frontier of distillation [74, 86] to reduce the size of the model, keeping good reranking performance (but "forgetting" unnecessary abilities) and context compression techniques [45], to reduce costs and speed up inference.

> **Key Takeaways**

- Large language models are good at reranking and explaining the rationale behind it.
- Even a naive approach can bring good results, but structured output is necessary to obtain a predictable structure to interact with.
- They are slow and expensive for the task, recommended on the short list of documents.
- Research is happening in many directions, mainly to optimise the costs, keeping the quality (smaller models, context compression).

4.10 Search Quality Evaluation

Search quality evaluation is a fundamental auxiliary tool for any search-focused engineer: measuring how well your system is performing is a foundational milestone on the road towards improvement.

If this is basic in any academic research activity, most often in the industry, the lack of ad hoc test datasets for proprietary data makes it easy to neglect evaluation.

LLMs can finally fill this gap, helping with the process of building test datasets and ratings to facilitate the process of evaluation.

When evaluating the quality of an information retrieval system, you need:

- A framework that allows you to run evaluation processes targeting your system and using a test dataset to calculate quality metrics
- A test dataset, with as many samples as possible, where each sample is a query associated with a document with a numeric relevance rating, stating how well the document satisfies the information need in the query

In terms of frameworks there are plenty around, including academic ones like Trec Eval[12] and open source implementations with an industrial focus such as Rated Ranked Evaluator[13] (creation of my colleague Andrea Gazzarini) and Quepid.[14]

---

[12] https://github.com/usnistgov/trec_eval
[13] https://github.com/SeaseLtd/rated-ranking-evaluator
[14] https://quepidapp.com

These tools allow you to evaluate the quality of your search engine in terms of metrics (precision, recall, NDCG, ERR, etc.) with a caveat: you need a test dataset that tells the framework which documents in your search engine are good for what queries.

This is elementary to the eyes of any reasonable academic researcher: experimental evidence is a needed foundation to verify how solid any theoretical idea is, and in one form or another, any researcher has done some evaluation using well-known public datasets, specifically meant to be used for research benchmarks and comparisons.

In the industry, the situation is extremely different; most of the time, you are dealing with proprietary data, queries and documents that change all the time, and no test dataset is available.

Building datasets manually is expensive: queries can be extracted decently easy from production logs (and they should, as your evaluation aims to improve the queries that are the most used) but relate queries to documents with a reliable relevance rating is hard, requires a lot of time to human experts, agreement between them and it's extremely boring, so it's likely that a human expert after a while will lose interest and ratings become more approximate.

This challenge over the years made offline search quality evaluation a chimaera in the industry; everyone is talking about it, recognising its importance, but for many teams, it remained just a utopia.

4.10.1 Queries

Queries are normally available in the industry if your system has been online for a while: users are interacting with it, and logs keep track of all queries.

Also, the query distribution can be used to estimate some sort of query importance, allowing the team to focus on the queries that have more impact on the user base.

But what about a system that's not in production yet?

During the first phases of a project, you may still be interested in estimating a baseline quality of the system, before going live, and at that point, finding probable queries is just guesswork.

Similar search engines around may have a public list of queries to take inspiration from, but most of the time, you are left in the dark.

LLMs can be very helpful in this phase, and you can use the corpus of information itself to generate plausible queries.

Keep in mind that generating is much more expensive than reviewing, so it's recommended to keep humans in the loop.

How would the process look?

An iterative software will scan the documents in your corpus of information you want to generate queries, and for each document, a request will be sent to an LLM to generate related queries.

4.10 Search Quality Evaluation

The association between the generated queries and the document is kept; being generated from the document means the document is relevant for such queries, and this rating will be handy when talking about rating and rationale generation.

Let's see a naive example:

Prompt

```
Given a document:
"Panthera is a genus of the family Felidae.
The tiger is the largest Panthera species, and the largest
 of all cats.
The leopard is the smallest Panthera species.
After a genetic analysis also the snow leopard
was classified as Panthera by IUCN assessors in 2008.
Lion, Panthera leo
Jaguar, Panthera onca
Leopard, Panthera pardus
Tiger, Panthera tigris
Snow leopard, Panthera uncia "

generate 10 relevant queries for it
```

Queries

```
Which species is the largest member of the Panthera genus?

Which species is the smallest member of the Panthera genus?

Does the snow leopard belong to the Panthera genus?

What are the names of all living Panthera species?

When was the snow leopard classified under the Panthera
genus by IUCN?

What is the scientific name of the lion?

What is the scientific name of the tiger?

What is the scientific name of the jaguar?

What is the scientific name of the leopard?

What is the scientific name of the snow leopard?
```

Depending on your domain and use case the human feedback in the loop may be more or less important, but the key point is that reviewing is much faster than generating, so using the LLM for the generation part and involving humans only for the quality assessment for the queries can immensely boost up the query dataset generation process.

Don't get me wrong, when involving humans in the loop for repetitive tasks, care is always needed, and the team should always make sure to reduce as much as possible the possibility of loss of attention, fragmenting the amount of work and mixing it with other activities.

4.10.2 Ratings and Rationale

Once the queries are collected and the documents in the corpus of information of your system are available, the next step is to assign a relevance rating for each query-document pair.

This rating should respond to the question: How relevant is document D for the query Q?

The scale is up to your use case; the simpler the better, so starting with a binary rating is a good idea.

But many metrics take into consideration a graded relevance scale, so you may opt for different grades of relevance:

- 0 → The document is not relevant at all.
- 1 → The document is vaguely relevant to the information need.
- 2 → The document is relevant to the information need, but it doesn't satisfy it completely.
- 3 → The document fully satisfies the user's information needs.

Be careful with the grain of the scale; the finer the grain, the more difficult it is to assign a rating to a document (also for humans).

Going back to the Panthera document example, a naive example would be:

Prompt

```
Given the relevance scale:
0 → The document is not relevant at all
1 → The document is vaguely relevant to the information need
2 → The document is relevant to the information need, but it
doesn't satisfy it completely
3 → The document fully satisfies the user's information needs

Given the query: $Q
How relevant is the document:
"Panthera is a genus of the family Felidae...
"
Structure the response in a simple JSON object
containing only the numerical rating and the rationale
```

Rating for Q="How many living species are in the Panthera genus?"

```
{
  "rating": 3,
  "rationale": "The document clearly states
  that there are five living species in the Panthera genus
```

```
        and lists all of them by name, fully satisfying
        the information need."
}
```

Rating for Q="What is a tiger?"

```
{
  "rating": 2,
  "rationale": "The document mentions that the tiger
   is the largest Panthera species and provides
   its scientific name, but it does not provide
   a full definition or description of what a tiger is,
   such as its habitat, behavior, or appearance."
}
```

Rating for Q="How fast does a tiger run?"

```
{
  "rating": 0,
  "rationale": "The document does not mention anything
   about the speed or running ability of a tiger,
   making it completely irrelevant to the query."
}
```

Having the ratings and the rationale can help massively any human expert reviewer, and the ratings can be enriched with implicit estimations (such as click-through rates, download rates, etc.).

This is a game-changer and can dramatically facilitate the adoption of offline search quality evaluation frameworks in the industry.

Another bonus aspect not to underestimate is the utility of the dataset, not only for evaluation tasks but also to actively improve the relevance of the system.

The dataset can also be used to train Learning To Rank models, distilling a similarity function from the generated dataset (potentially enriched with additional samples).

> **Key Takeaways**

- LLMs can be used to generate queries out of documents to build an evaluation test set.
- LLMs can be used to evaluate a document for a query, assigning a relevance label with a rationale.
- Reviewing is much cheaper than generating; humans should be involved in the loop as reviewers.
- The generated dataset can be used to train Learning To Rank models.

References

1. Aumüller, M., Bernhardsson, E., Faithfull, A.: Ann-benchmarks: a benchmarking tool for approximate nearest neighbor algorithms. Inf. Syst. **87**, 101374 (2020). https://doi.org/10.1016/j.is.2019.02.006, https://www.sciencedirect.com/science/article/pii/S0306437918303685
2. Azad, H.K., Deepak, A.: Query expansion techniques for information retrieval: a survey. Inf. Process. Manag. **56**(5), 1698–1735 (2019). https://doi.org/10.1016/j.ipm.2019.05.009
3. Bama, S.S., Ahmed, M., Saravanan, A.: A survey on performance evaluation measures for information retrieval system. Int. Res. J. Eng. Technol. **2**(2), 1015–1020 (2015)
4. Basnet, S., Gou, J., Mallia, A., Suel, T.: DeeperImpact: optimizing sparse learned index structures (2024). https://arxiv.org/abs/2405.17093
5. Beyer, L., Steiner, A., Pinto, A.S., Kolesnikov, A., Wang, X., Salz, D., Neumann, M., Alabdulmohsin, I., Tschannen, M., Bugliarello, E., Unterthiner, T., Keysers, D., Koppula, S., Liu, F., Grycner, A., Gritsenko, A., Houlsby, N., Kumar, M., Rong, K., Eisenschlos, J., Kabra, R., Bauer, M., Bošnjak, M., Chen, X., Minderer, M., Voigtlaender, P., Bica, I., Balazevic, I., Puigcerver, J., Papalampidi, P., Henaff, O., Xiong, X., Soricut, R., Harmsen, J., Zhai, X.: PaliGemma: a versatile 3B VLM for transfer (2024). https://arxiv.org/abs/2407.07726
6. Breton, L.L., Fournier, Q., Mezouar, M.E., Chandar, S.: Neobert: a next-generation bert (2025). https://arxiv.org/abs/2502.19587
7. Cai, F., De Rijke, M., et al.: A survey of query auto completion in information retrieval. Found. Trends Inf. Retr. **10**(4), 273–363 (2016)
8. Carpineto, C., Romano, G.: A survey of automatic query expansion in information retrieval. ACM Comput. Surv. **44**(1) (2012). https://doi.org/10.1145/2071389.2071390
9. Cherti, M., Beaumont, R., Wightman, R., Wortsman, M., Ilharco, G., Gordon, C., Schuhmann, C., Schmidt, L., Jitsev, J.: Reproducible scaling laws for contrastive language-image learning. In: Proceedings of the IEEE/CVF Conference on Computer Vision and Pattern Recognition, pp. 2818–2829 (2023)
10. Cormack, G.V., Clarke, C.L.A., Buettcher, S.: Reciprocal rank fusion outperforms condorcet and individual rank learning methods. In: Proceedings of the 32nd International ACM SIGIR Conference on Research and Development in Information Retrieval, pp. 758–759. SIGIR '09. Association for Computing Machinery, New York (2009). https://doi.org/10.1145/1571941.1572114
11. de Souza P. Moreira, G., Ak, R., Schifferer, B., Xu, M., Osmulski, R., Oldridge, E.: Enhancing q&a text retrieval with ranking models: benchmarking, fine-tuning and deploying rerankers for rag (2024). https://arxiv.org/abs/2409.07691
12. Dong, M., Chen, Y., Zhang, M., Sun, H., He, T.: Rich semantic knowledge enhanced large language models for few-shot Chinese spell checking (2024). https://arxiv.org/abs/2403.08492
13. Doshi, M., Kumar, V., Murthy, R., P, V., Sen, J.: Mistral-SPLADE: LLMs for better learned sparse retrieval (2024). https://arxiv.org/abs/2408.11119
14. Elizalde, B., Deshmukh, S., Ismail, M.A., Wang, H.: Clap: learning audio concepts from natural language supervision (2022). https://arxiv.org/abs/2206.04769
15. Es, S., James, J., Espinosa Anke, L., Schockaert, S.: RAGAs: automated evaluation of retrieval augmented generation. In: Aletras, N., De Clercq, O. (eds.) Proceedings of the 18th Conference of the European Chapter of the Association for Computational Linguistics: System Demonstrations, pp. 150–158. Association for Computational Linguistics, St. Julians (2024). https://aclanthology.org/2024.eacl-demo.16
16. Faysse, M., Sibille, H., Wu, T., Omrani, B., Viaud, G., Hudelot, C., Colombo, P.: ColPali: Efficient document retrieval with vision language models (2025). https://arxiv.org/abs/2407.01449
17. Feldman, P., Foulds, J.R., Pan, S.: Ragged edges: the double-edged sword of retrieval-augmented chatbots (2024). https://arxiv.org/abs/2403.01193

18. Firth, J.: A synopsis of linguistic theory 1930–1955. In: Studies in Linguistic Analysis. Philological Society, Oxford (1957). Reprinted in Palmer, F. (ed. 1968) Selected Papers of J. R. Firth, Longman, Harlow
19. Formal, T., Lassance, C., Piwowarski, B., Clinchant, S.: Splade v2: sparse lexical and expansion model for information retrieval (2021). https://arxiv.org/abs/2109.10086
20. Formal, T., Piwowarski, B., Clinchant, S.: SPLADE: sparse lexical and expansion model for first stage ranking (2021). https://arxiv.org/abs/2107.05720
21. Gao, J., Long, C.: RaBitQ: quantizing high-dimensional vectors with a theoretical error bound for approximate nearest neighbor search (2024). https://arxiv.org/abs/2405.12497
22. Gao, L., Ma, X., Lin, J., Callan, J.: Precise zero-shot dense retrieval without relevance labels (2022). https://arxiv.org/abs/2212.10496
23. Geigle, G., Pfeiffer, J., Reimers, N., Vulić, I., Gurevych, I.: Retrieve fast, rerank smart: cooperative and joint approaches for improved cross-modal retrieval (2022). https://arxiv.org/abs/2103.11920
24. Goh, H.W.: Benchmarking hallucination detection methods in rag (2024). https://towardsdatascience.com/benchmarking-hallucination-detection-methods-in-rag-6a03c555f063
25. Gospodinov, M., MacAvaney, S., Macdonald, C.: Doc2query–: When less is more (2023). https://arxiv.org/abs/2301.03266
26. Gu, J., Jiang, X., Shi, Z., Tan, H., Zhai, X., Xu, C., Li, W., Shen, Y., Ma, S., Liu, H., Wang, Y., Guo, J.: A survey on LLM-as-a-judge (2024). https://arxiv.org/abs/2411.15594
27. Guzhov, A., Raue, F., Hees, J., Dengel, A.: Audioclip: extending clip to image, text and audio (2021). https://arxiv.org/abs/2106.13043
28. Hinton, G.E., Vinyals, O., Dean, J.: Distilling the knowledge in a neural network. ArXiv abs/1503.02531 (2015). https://api.semanticscholar.org/CorpusID:7200347
29. Hládek, D., Staš, J., Pleva, M.: Survey of automatic spelling correction. Electronics **9**(10) (2020). https://doi.org/10.3390/electronics9101670, https://www.mdpi.com/2079-9292/9/10/1670
30. Islam, N., Islam, Z., Noor, N.: A survey on optical character recognition system (2017). https://arxiv.org/abs/1710.05703
31. Jagerman, R., Zhuang, H., Qin, Z., Wang, X., Bendersky, M.: Query expansion by prompting large language models (2023). https://arxiv.org/abs/2305.03653
32. Jégou, H., Douze, M., Schmid, C.: Product quantization for nearest neighbor search. IEEE Trans. Pattern Anal. Mach. Intell. **33**, 117–28 (01 2011). https://doi.org/10.1109/TPAMI.2010.57
33. Jehangir, B., Radhakrishnan, S., Agarwal, R.: A survey on named entity recognition – datasets, tools, and methodologies. Nat. Lang. Process. J. **3**, 100017 (2023). https://doi.org/10.1016/j.nlp.2023.100017, https://www.sciencedirect.com/science/article/pii/S2949719123000146
34. Jha, R., Wang, B., Günther, M., Mastrapas, G., Sturua, S., Mohr, I., Koukounas, A., Akram, M.K., Wang, N., Xiao, H.: Jina-ColBERT-v2: a general-purpose multilingual late interaction retriever (2024). https://arxiv.org/abs/2408.16672
35. Jiang, H., Wu, Q., Lin, C.Y., Yang, Y., Qiu, L.: LLMLingua: compressing prompts for accelerated inference of large language models. In: Bouamor, H., Pino, J., Bali, K. (eds.) Proceedings of the 2023 Conference on Empirical Methods in Natural Language Processing, pp. 13358–13376. Association for Computational Linguistics, Singapore (2023). https://doi.org/10.18653/v1/2023.emnlp-main.825, https://aclanthology.org/2023.emnlp-main.825
36. Jiang, H., Wu, Q., Luo, X., Li, D., Lin, C.Y., Yang, Y., Qiu, L.: Longllmlingua: accelerating and enhancing LLMs in long context scenarios via prompt compression (2024). https://arxiv.org/abs/2310.06839
37. Kabir, M.A., Hasan, M.A., Mandal, A., Tunkelang, D., Wu, Z.: A survey on e-commerce learning to rank (2024). https://arxiv.org/abs/2412.03581
38. Khattab, O., Zaharia, M.: Colbert: efficient and effective passage search via contextualized late interaction over BERT (2020). https://arxiv.org/abs/2004.12832

39. Lee, J., Bernier-Colborne, G., Maharaj, T., Vajjala, S.: Methods, applications, and directions of learning-to-rank in NLP research. In: Findings of the Association for Computational Linguistics: NAACL 2024, pp. 1900–1917 (2024)
40. Lewis, P., Perez, E., Piktus, A., Petroni, F., Karpukhin, V., Goyal, N., Küttler, H., Lewis, M., tau Yih, W., Rocktäschel, T., Riedel, S., Kiela, D.: Retrieval-augmented generation for knowledge-intensive NLP tasks (2021). https://arxiv.org/abs/2005.11401
41. Liang, P., Bommasani, R., Lee, T., Tsipras, D., Soylu, D., Yasunaga, M., Zhang, Y., Narayanan, D., Wu, Y., Kumar, A., Newman, B., Yuan, B., Yan, B., Zhang, C., Cosgrove, C., Manning, C.D., Ré, C., Acosta-Navas, D., Hudson, D.A., Zelikman, E., Durmus, E., Ladhak, F., Rong, F., Ren, H., Yao, H., Wang, J., Santhanam, K., Orr, L., Zheng, L., Yuksekgonul, M., Suzgun, M., Kim, N., Guha, N., Chatterji, N., Khattab, O., Henderson, P., Huang, Q., Chi, R., Xie, S.M., Santurkar, S., Ganguli, S., Hashimoto, T., Icard, T., Zhang, T., Chaudhary, V., Wang, W., Li, X., Mai, Y., Zhang, Y., Koreeda, Y.: Holistic evaluation of language models (2023). https://arxiv.org/abs/2211.09110
42. Liu, T.Y.: Learning to rank for information retrieval. Found. Trends Inf. Retr. **3**(3), 225–331 (2009). https://doi.org/10.1561/1500000016
43. Liu, N.F., Lin, K., Hewitt, J., Paranjape, A., Bevilacqua, M., Petroni, F., Liang, P.: Lost in the middle: how language models use long contexts (2023). https://arxiv.org/abs/2307.03172
44. Liu, Y., Iter, D., Xu, Y., Wang, S., Xu, R., Zhu, C.: G-Eval: NLG evaluation using GPT-4 with better human alignment (2023). https://arxiv.org/abs/2303.16634
45. Liu, Q., Wang, B., Wang, N., Mao, J.: Leveraging passage embeddings for efficient listwise reranking with large language models (2025). https://arxiv.org/abs/2406.14848
46. Lu, M., Chen, C., Eickhoff, C.: Cross-encoder rediscovers a semantic variant of bm25 (2025). https://arxiv.org/abs/2502.04645
47. Ma, X., Gong, Y., He, P., Zhao, H., Duan, N.: Query rewriting for retrieval-augmented large language models (2023). https://arxiv.org/abs/2305.14283
48. Ma, X., Zhang, X., Pradeep, R., Lin, J.: Zero-shot listwise document reranking with a large language model (2023). https://arxiv.org/abs/2305.02156
49. Malkov, Y.A., Yashunin, D.A.: Efficient and robust approximate nearest neighbor search using hierarchical navigable small world graphs (2018). https://arxiv.org/abs/1603.09320
50. Malkov, Y., Ponomarenko, A., Logvinov, A., Krylov, V.: Approximate nearest neighbor algorithm based on navigable small world graphs. Inf. Syst. **45**, 61–68 (2014). https://doi.org/10.1016/j.is.2013.10.006, https://www.sciencedirect.com/science/article/pii/S0306437913001300
51. Mallia, A., Suel, T., Tonellotto, N.: Faster learned sparse retrieval with block-max pruning (2024). https://arxiv.org/abs/2405.01117
52. Michail, A., Clematide, S., Sennrich, R.: Examining multilingual embedding models cross-lingually through LLM-generated adversarial examples (2025). https://arxiv.org/abs/2502.08638
53. Mikolov, T., Chen, K., Corrado, G., Dean, J.: Efficient estimation of word representations in vector space (2013). https://arxiv.org/abs/1301.3781
54. Miller, D.L.: ModernCE STS: An STS cross encoder model (2025). https://huggingface.co/dleemiller/ModernCE-large-sts
55. Miller, G.A., Beckwith, R., Fellbaum, C., Gross, D., Miller, K.J.: Introduction to wordnet: An on-line lexical database*. Int. J. Lexicogr. **3**(4), 235–244 (1990). https://doi.org/10.1093/ijl/3.4.235
56. Muennighoff, N., Tazi, N., Magne, L., Reimers, N.: MTEB: massive text embedding benchmark (2023). https://arxiv.org/abs/2210.07316
57. Nguyen, D.A., Mohan, R.K., Yang, V., Akash, P.S., Chang, K.C.C.: RL-based query rewriting with distilled LLM for online e-commerce systems (2025). https://arxiv.org/abs/2501.18056
58. Ooi, J., Ma, X., Qin, H., Liew, S.C.: A survey of query expansion, query suggestion and query refinement techniques (2015). https://doi.org/10.1109/ICSECS.2015.7333094

References

59. Osgood, C., Suci, G., Tannenbaum, P.: The Measurement of Meaning. Illini book, IB 47. University of Illinois Press, Champaign (1957). https://books.google.co.uk/books?id=qk5qAAAAMAAJ
60. Pan, Z., Wu, Q., Jiang, H., Xia, M., Luo, X., Zhang, J., Lin, Q., Rühle, V., Yang, Y., Lin, C.Y., Zhao, H.V., Qiu, L., Zhang, D.: LLMLingua-2: data distillation for efficient and faithful task-agnostic prompt compression. In: Ku, L.W., Martins, A., Srikumar, V. (eds.) Findings of the Association for Computational Linguistics: ACL 2024, pp. 963–981. Association for Computational Linguistics, Bangkok (2024). https://doi.org/10.18653/v1/2024.findings-acl.57, https://aclanthology.org/2024.findings-acl.57
61. Qin, Z., Jagerman, R., Hui, K., Zhuang, H., Wu, J., Yan, L., Shen, J., Liu, T., Liu, J., Metzler, D., Wang, X., Bendersky, M.: Large language models are effective text rankers with pairwise ranking prompting (2024). https://arxiv.org/abs/2306.17563
62. Qu, R., Tu, R., Bao, F.: Is semantic chunking worth the computational cost? (2024). https://arxiv.org/abs/2410.13070
63. Radford, A., Kim, J.W., Hallacy, C., Ramesh, A., Goh, G., Agarwal, S., Sastry, G., Askell, A., Mishkin, P., Clark, J., Krueger, G., Sutskever, I.: Learning transferable visual models from natural language supervision (2021). https://arxiv.org/abs/2103.00020
64. Reimers, N., Gurevych, I.: Sentence-BERT: sentence embeddings using Siamese BERT-networks (2019). https://arxiv.org/abs/1908.10084
65. Saad-Falcon, J., Khattab, O., Potts, C., Zaharia, M.: ARES: An automated evaluation framework for retrieval-augmented generation systems (2024). https://arxiv.org/abs/2311.09476
66. Sahlgren, M.: Distributional legacy: the unreasonable effectiveness of Harris's distributional program. WORD **70**(4), 246–257 (2024)
67. Santhanam, K., Khattab, O., Saad-Falcon, J., Potts, C., Zaharia, M.: Colbertv2: effective and efficient retrieval via lightweight late interaction (2022). https://arxiv.org/abs/2112.01488
68. Schaeffer, R., Miranda, B., Koyejo, S.: Are emergent abilities of large language models a mirage? In: Oh, A., Naumann, T., Globerson, A., Saenko, K., Hardt, M., Levine, S. (eds.) Advances in Neural Information Processing Systems. vol. 36, pp. 55565–55581. Curran Associates, Inc., Red Hook (2023). https://proceedings.neurips.cc/paper_files/paper/2023/file/adc98a266f45005c403b8311ca7e8bd7-Paper-Conference.pdf
69. Shannon, C.E.: Prediction and Entropy of Printed English. Wiley-IEEE Press, Piscataway, pp. 194–208 (1993). https://doi.org/10.1109/9780470544242.ch12
70. Snider, J., Osgood, C.: Semantic Differential Technique; a Sourcebook. Aldine Publishing Company, New York (1969). https://books.google.co.uk/books?id=TMC7zQEACAAJ
71. Sparck Jones, K.: A Statistical Interpretation of Term Specificity and Its Application in Retrieval, pp. 132–142. Taylor Graham Publishing, GBR, Stamford (1988)
72. Subramani, N., Matton, A., Greaves, M., Lam, A.: A survey of deep learning approaches for OCR and document understanding (2021). https://arxiv.org/abs/2011.13534
73. Subramanya, S.J., Devvrit, Kadekodi, R., Krishaswamy, R., Simhadri, H.V.: DiskANN: Fast Accurate Billion-Point Nearest Neighbor Search on a Single Node. Curran Associates Inc., Red Hook (2019)
74. Sun, W., Yan, L., Ma, X., Wang, S., Ren, P., Chen, Z., Yin, D., Ren, Z.: Is ChatGPT good at search? Investigating large language models as re-ranking agents (2024). https://arxiv.org/abs/2304.09542
75. Vaswani, A., Shazeer, N., Parmar, N., Uszkoreit, J., Jones, L., Gomez, A.N., Kaiser, L., Polosukhin, I.: Attention is all you need (2023). https://arxiv.org/abs/1706.03762
76. Wang, L., Yang, N., Wei, F.: Query2doc: query expansion with large language models (2023). https://arxiv.org/abs/2303.07678
77. Warner, B., Chaffin, A., Clavié, B., Weller, O., Hallström, O., Taghadouini, S., Gallagher, A., Biswas, R., Ladhak, F., Aarsen, T., Cooper, N., Adams, G., Howard, J., Poli, I.: Smarter, better, faster, longer: a modern bidirectional encoder for fast, memory efficient, and long context finetuning and inference (2024). https://arxiv.org/abs/2412.13663

78. Xing, L., Vadrevu, V.S.P.K., Aref, W.G.: The ubiquitous skiplist: a survey of what cannot be skipped about the skiplist and its applications in big data systems (2025). https://arxiv.org/abs/2403.04582
79. Xu, H., Ghosh, G., Huang, P.Y., Okhonko, D., Aghajanyan, A., Metze, F., Zettlemoyer, L., Feichtenhofer, C.: Videoclip: contrastive pre-training for zero-shot video-text understanding (2021). https://arxiv.org/abs/2109.14084
80. Xu, F., Shi, W., Choi, E.: RECOMP: improving retrieval-augmented LMs with context compression and selective augmentation. In: The Twelfth International Conference on Learning Representations (2024). https://openreview.net/forum?id=mlJLVigNHp
81. Yin, S., Fu, C., Zhao, S., Li, K., Sun, X., Xu, T., Chen, E.: A survey on multimodal large language models. Natl. Sci. Rev. **11**(12), nwae403 (2024). https://doi.org/10.1093/nsr/nwae403
82. Yoon, Y., Jung, J., Yoon, S., Park, K.: Hypothetical documents or knowledge leakage? Rethinking LLM-based query expansion (2025). https://arxiv.org/abs/2504.14175
83. Zhang, S., Huang, H., Liu, J., Li, H.: Spelling error correction with soft-masked BERT (2020). https://arxiv.org/abs/2005.07421
84. Zhang, X., Yan, H., Sun, Y., Qiu, X.: SDCL: Self-distillation contrastive learning for Chinese spell checking (2022). https://arxiv.org/abs/2210.17168
85. Zhang, J., Guo, X., Bodapati, S., Potts, C.: Multi-teacher distillation for multilingual spelling correction (2023). https://arxiv.org/abs/2311.11518
86. Zhang, X., Hofstätter, S., Lewis, P., Tang, R., Lin, J.: Rank-without-GPT: building GPT-independent listwise rerankers on open-source large language models (2023). https://arxiv.org/abs/2312.02969
87. Zheng, L., Chiang, W.L., Sheng, Y., Zhuang, S., Wu, Z., Zhuang, Y., Lin, Z., Li, Z., Li, D., Xing, E.P., Zhang, H., Gonzalez, J.E., Stoica, I.: Judging LLM-as-a-judge with MT-bench and chatbot arena (2023). https://arxiv.org/abs/2306.05685
88. Zobel, J., Moffat, A.: Inverted files for text search engines. ACM Comput. Surv. **38**(2), 6–es (2006). https://doi.org/10.1145/1132956.1132959

What Large Language Model Is the Best for You?

5

Abstract

This chapter introduces the reader to a procedural strategy that should be followed to approach the model selection phase in an effective and organised manner. The starting point is a clear understanding of the task we want to perform and how integrating LLMs with the search solution should benefit the system. After an initial selection based on task-solving capabilities, the set of candidates must be filtered by the type of license to guarantee legal compatibility with the intended usage. Finally, the training data should be evaluated both in terms of form, domain and language, to be as close as possible to the domain of interest. The chapter closes by exploring useful platforms to compare LLMs side by side and help users and developers with such a daunting decision that's key to the success of a project.

5.1 Start from the Task You Need to Solve

You may be tempted to just use general-purpose instructions following LLMs to solve any problem or task at hand.

This feels like the general trend with such gigantic and capable models, but you may be better off with a model that has been fine-tuned or distilled for your specific need. So the first question you need to ask yourself is:

What is the problem I'm trying to solve?

Large language models can help you implement a search project from many angles, and depending on the area of integration, you may prefer one type of model over another.

That's not the end of the story, as nowadays, you have a huge number of alternative models that belong to the same category, so let's proceed iteratively, starting from the basics and focusing on identifying a subset of candidate models based on the specific problem you need to solve.

Identifying the task you face may seem an obvious activity, but it hides many challenges:

Many times, humans tend to cut corners, make assumptions and unconsciously transform their problems into others. It's an ability that helped our evolution and survival, but that can be harmful to designing an analytical approach to interact with machine learning models.

The XY problem[1] is your first enemy:

- The task you need to perform is X.
- You don't know how to achieve X, but thinking about possible solutions, you end up thinking that doing Y would help.
- You don't know how to achieve Y either.
- You invest your energies into solving Y.
- You "forget" your real problem is X.

This sounds possibly unusual, but trust me, having personally interacted with open source software mailing lists for a couple of decades, I can confirm that this happens all the time, to tech-savvy or non-tech-savvy people alike.

Actually, if you feel decently confident in the problem domain, it may happen even more often.

Don't jump to conclusions; do your homework and carefully scope the real problem you need an LLM to solve.

Do you need to reduce the length of a text, keeping the semantics of it as complete as possible? Summarisation problem.

Do you need to enrich your query with a tag that categorises the query? Classification problem.

Do you need to parse your query, recognising the concepts in it and correlating them with a knowledge base? Named entity recognition and linking problem.

Sure, there may be situations where you need to dissect your main problem into smaller ones and coordinate a solution (divide et impera), but make sure that your original problem is not covered already by the literature (and in our use case, by a fine-tuned LLM).

---

[1] https://xyproblem.info

A good exercise is to get familiar with the known tasks LLMs are fine-tuned for, and public repositories such as HuggingFace[2] are extremely valuable to get an idea of the multitude of different large language models out there, grouped by tasks.

Spend time exploring the tasks more than the models: understand the main taxonomies (multi-modal, computer vision, natural language processing, audio, etc.) and then focus on each task to better understand the expected inputs and outputs with examples.

Once you have a good overview of what's out there, it's more likely that you'll be able to make connections and match your problem with well-known tasks.

This allows you to focus your attention on specific models that are optimal in helping you, massively reducing the scope of your exploration and facilitating the next steps.

To complicate the situation even more, there is a trend of just using instructions following LLM to solve any type of problem.

A note on that: at the time of writing, this approach is extremely useful to quickly spin up prototypes and explore routes in your project, but when building production-grade solutions, make sure to do the due diligence and explore models that are specifically fine-tuned for your problem.

Obviously obsolescence is a problem as well, so make sure to assess how competitive the models you have filtered are on the specific task of your interest.

Luckily, leaderboards that compare the performance of models on tasks are publicly available online for the vast majority of situations.

> **Key Takeaways**

- XY problem: Focus on your original problem X rather than your attempted solutions Y.
- Get familiar with the tasks LLMs are capable of: there are not only instructions following LLMs.
- Match your problem with existing tasks to reduce the scope of your models' exploration.

5.2 Validate the License

Licensing in LLMs is a complex matter: there are a plethora of different licenses that affect how and in what circumstances you can use or modify

(continued)

---

[2] https://huggingface.co/models

> a model. Additionally, each component and aspect of the model may be regulated by a different one. It's important to identify your expected usage and match only the models whose licenses comply.
>
> Be prepared to dedicate to this activity the time it deserves, as licenses are full-length contracts!

Exploring what it means for an LLM to be fully open source in all its components is a deep topic on its own, big enough to deserve a dedicated section: Sect. 2.1.

On the other hand, the focus of this chapter is to guide the reader into better understanding how they plan to use a licensed LLM and if the license is compatible with their needs.

First of all, most modern LLMs will require you to share your information (name, affiliation, country, etc.) and accept their license even just for accessing their code repository, independently of the usage you are planning for it.

The first differentiation you will incur is the distinction between commercial and non-commercial usage.

Commercial means that the usage of the model brings a commercial advantage or monetary compensation to the user.

In a company context, it means that the integration of the LLM in your project or product is intended to bring direct economic benefits to the company.

Everything else pretty much ends up in the non-commercial bucket: personal private usage for entertainment, research and exploration, etc.

Sometimes, custom licenses can be ok in terms of commercial usage but present limitations nonetheless, for example, from the LLAMA 3.2 COMMUNITY LICENSE AGREEMENT:[3]

"If the monthly active users of the products or services made available by or for Licensee, or Licensee's affiliates, are greater than 700 million monthly active users in the preceding calendar month, you must request a license from Meta."

There are grey areas, though, so the recommendation is to evaluate extra carefully if your intended usage resides in one realm or the other and consult with a lawyer specialist in case of need.

Once it's clear whether your intended usage is commercial or not, you should ask yourself what you intend to do with the LLM itself:

- Are you just going to use it (inference time) or modify it?
- Are you going to distribute a modified version?
- Are you going to self-host it somewhere privately/publicly?
- Are you going to leverage a service provider to access it?

---

[3] https://huggingface.co/meta-llama/Llama-3.2-3B-Instruct

5.2 Validate the License

Depending on how you answer these questions, you will need to focus on different areas of the license.

As a rule of thumb, even if you plan to access an LLM just at inference time, potentially shielded by an intermediary service provider, make sure to fully read and understand the underlying license:

There are many providers that make it extra easy to switch the model behind the scenes, so it's vital not to use this flexible feature lightly.

In the end, you will end up being bound to the underlying license anyway, so it's important to fully comprehend it.

Taking again as an example the LLAMA 3.2 COMMUNITY LICENSE AGREEMENT:

"If you distribute or make available the Llama Materials (or any derivative works thereof), or a product or service (including another AI model) that contains any of them, you shall (A) provide a copy of this Agreement with any such Llama Materials; and (B) prominently display **"Built with Llama"** on a related website, user interface, blogpost, about page, or product documentation."

And this applies also if you interact with the model through intermediaries.

Actually, to be fair, the more indirections you use, the more likely additional intermediary licenses apply, so please be extra careful with that.

So, what are the most famous licenses, and how do they apply to LLMs?

Apache 2.0 License—Under this very permissive license, users can do pretty much anything they want with the model but must give credit to the original authors, include a copy of the license and state any changes made to the software. Using the trademarks or logos associated with the software requires permission.

MIT License—This license is also very permissive and allows the user to use, modify and distribute the software for any purpose as long as they include a copy of the license and a notice of the original authors.

GPL-3.0 License—This license allows the user to use, modify and distribute the software for any purpose as long as they share any modifications to the code under the same license. This means that users cannot create proprietary versions of the software or incorporate it into closed-source software without disclosing their code.

> **Key Takeaways**

- Commercial usage means you aim to get direct monetary benefits out of the model.
- Licenses are full contracts; make sure to grasp all the details of them or refer to a specialist.
- Licenses also apply if you access a model through a service provider.

5.3   Analyse the Training Data

> Large language models are pre-trained on a huge quantity of data; given the scale, it's unlikely you can double-check all the data manually.
> If the model is open enough, you should aim to grasp a high-level understanding of where the data is coming from, its structure and languages covered.
> This gives you a first intuition if the model you are looking at could be a good fit to work in your domain.
> Your main focus should be on the fine-tuning dataset: smaller in scale and focused on a specific task.

You filtered down the list of candidates for the perfect LLM for your use case based on the task and licensing compatibility, but your selection is still quite crowded: it's time to get serious and dig into the data used to train the models.

First of all, this exercise is limited to the models that make their datasets fully or at least partially accessible.

This is a requirement for full transparency, but it's still rare to find models that openly and genuinely give you a full excursus of their pre-training and fine-tuning data.

Sometimes the datasets are only described at a high level in a vague manner, sometimes aggregations over the datasets are revealed (percentages of languages, text categories, domains, etc.), and in some open scenarios, the full data is readable.

But is that easy to navigate such information even when available?

Starting from the pre-training, we are talking about trillions of tokens and publicly available sources: a data volume that's not manageable by humans.

Furthermore, the scope of pre-training is to be as generic as possible, so it's very likely you end up having a huge quantity of data that contains a bit of everything. So, what considerations can you draw from the pre-training dataset itself? Can you make any decision based on it?

Effectively considering or discarding a model, based on its pre-training dataset, is a hard task, but there is some information that you could leverage to aid your decision: data aggregations.

It should be decently easy to find out the language distribution across the dataset, and that should be a first valuable discriminant: many models are multi-language nowadays, but the percentage distribution can help you differentiate a model that has been specifically pre-trained on the language(s) of your interest from models that marginally cover them.

That's the most important observation you can make out of the pre-training; then, having an understanding of the distribution of content categories and type of

5.3 Analyse the Training Data

textual data can bring additional value: the key takeaway is that you won't be able to evaluate such data manually.

The fine-tuning dataset is a different story as it's smaller in nature, most of the time humanly curated and coupled to a specific task.

All these factors make it much more readable and manageable, helping you understand how close it is to your domain and data.

Let's remember that the more the fine-tuning dataset is aligned with your domain in terms of meaning and lexicon, the more successful the usage of the model at inference time.

On top of the language checks, the fine-tuning dataset allows for more advanced analysis:

- Is the language aligned with your expectations? dialects? ways of saying? Thanks to the smaller numbers, you don't have to rely on aggregations and sampling; you and your team can potentially double-check the quality directly.
- What about the domain? Is the dataset aligned with your use case domain? Both in lexicon and semantics?
- What is the structure of the input/output of the model? This can be extra helpful in crafting the format of the data you will use to interact with the model.

Especially when dealing with specialist tasks, such as encoding text to vector, understanding the fine-tuning dataset will boost dramatically the integration with your system: knowing the type, structure, domain and language of the text the model is expecting will frame the way you interact with it at inference time.

Also, if the journey of model selection ends up with the best candidate, that is decently good but requires additional fine-tuning, knowing what the dataset looks like will make it easier to refine it and extend it.

> **Key Takeaways**

- You cannot evaluate pre-training data manually; your focus should be on data aggregations, statistics and languages covered.
- Most of your energy should be channelled into the study of the fine-tuning dataset, as it's generally smaller and human-readable.
- Understanding the structure and content of the fine-tuning dataset will make it easier to build one of your own.

5.4 How to Compare Large Language Models

> When dealing with a set of candidates, it can be challenging to select and justify the best one. Why select and justify?
>
> Aside from the scientific nature of the activity that strongly encourages not only a selection of the best candidate but also a rationale that motivates it, most of the times you and your team are making this decision for a project, and it's fundamental to back it with solid evidence to present to colleagues or business owners.
>
> Public benchmarks and manual checks can be valuable to ballpark the expectation, but the final answer is one and only: a benchmark with your data in a reproducible framework.

Once you have reached the point where you have a handful of LLM candidates, the first comparison you should make is through public benchmarks.

Ideally, you want to target benchmarks that are as close as possible to your use case and data, reproducible, unbiased and hopefully carried over by third-party entities rather than the creators of the models themselves.

Don't get me wrong, I'm not saying that model creators are dishonest, but it happens quite often that they end up cherry-picking the results, and that's quite normal when you aim to show how good your model is to the world.

Luckily, nowadays there are plenty of third-party leaderboards, divided by task, languages and additional metadata.[4]

Independent and unbiased reviewers are your best bet for an initial comparison.

Make sure the leaderboard of your interest is fully understood and evaluated, specifically spend the necessary time to understand the dataset's format, content and the metrics used in the benchmark.

This will be extremely helpful when you have to design the benchmarking solution on your data, as you can re-use some of the public logic, as most of the time, the code used is shared for reproducibility.

The second comparison step you can carry out is through a manual check: you experiment with the LLMs, manually, doing several side-by-side comparisons.[5]

This is visually appealing, and these platforms present a lot of useful tools to help with it: it's definitely useful for some experimentation, debugging and identifying candidates that are definitely not up to your standards, but it should be used with parsimony, and you shouldn't abuse it.

---

[4] https://huggingface.co/spaces/open-llm-leaderboard/open_llm_leaderboard

[5] https://lmarena.ai/?leaderboard

5.4 How to Compare Large Language Models

Because a small number of manual tests will inevitably offer a biased comparison, and if not done with the right level of consciousness, it may cause sub-optimal choices, you should not get fascinated by the illusion that an hour of quick comparisons and debugging can match a proper benchmark.

Unfortunately, the user-friendliness of such tools and frameworks is the first cause of stopping the comparisons there, it's so easy to compare models on the fly that the "look good to me" phenomenon could win the lazy minds.

Why am I mentioning this practice if I'm not a huge fan of it?

The reason is that each use case is different; these tools are well done, and there are situations where they can be beneficial, so it's good to share them.

Don't want to leave you vague here, so here is a list of possible scenarios where some manual side-by-side comparison is useful:

- Prototyping stage to run a quick comparison between model candidates and highlight unfit models quickly
- To reproduce specific edge cases reported by users and check how such edge cases react to the prompt/model
- Checking how models react to the same prompt, for prototyping a migration

But you shouldn't stop there, and a comprehensive benchmark on your real data should be your focus when comparing candidate models.

The biggest deal here is the data gathering and preparation: the software to run the benchmark, the data format and metrics to use are probably already available in the public; the biggest effort is to comply with such formats and prepare a comprehensive and realistic dataset to run the benchmark on.

That is expensive and requires human labour; I've seen many instances where this activity is neglected, and trust me, you'll pay for that down the road, so it's a good idea to dedicate a good amount of time and human effort to make sure that your use cases, domain data and language are carefully covered.

It's also true that new models are released all the time, so your benchmarks should be flexible, easy to reproduce and model-agnostic as much as possible.

This will guarantee a minimal cost if you need to re-do them periodically.

> **Key Takeaways**

- Public benchmarks are fundamental for an initial comparison.
- Side-by-side arenas and tools can help in having a sense of how LLMs perform live.
- Performing a comprehensive benchmark on your data should be your real focus.

Rabbit Holes

6

Abstract

This chapter educates the reader on the importance of measuring the quality of their system through standard metrics that capture different aspects of its performance. It gives an overview on what happens if the wrong technology stack is chosen due to hype or marketing and how we should avoid doing that. The chapter closes by describing the consequences of choosing the wrong LLM for the task, how to reduce such risk and how to recover when this happens.

6.1 Not Measuring Search Quality Metrics

> Setting up a search quality evaluation framework for your project takes time and effort. To the uneducated eye, it's time wasted: why should you spend a lot of energy building something that measures your target system rather than focusing on building the target system in the first place as soon as possible?
>
> In many startup ecosystems (and not only), time to market is vital, and the first areas that don't get the love they deserve are always the testing and quality evaluation frameworks.
>
> The main issue is that it all happens so quickly that you realise you are now 2 years into the project and have no idea about the search quality of your system. The only info you have is that your boss feels the search doesn't work as it should (with exactly this level of detail).

How can you improve something if you don't know the current quality status of your system?

How can you know how much you improved the system without measuring?

How can you systematically show unambiguous progress without factual and exhaustive evaluation?

What I've heard countless times in my search consultant career is "My search system doesn't work as it should".

An immediate question I tend to have in these scenarios is "Well, how should it work? Are you measuring aspects that interest you, and they are not up to your expected standards?"

A normal answer would be "Well, no, but you see, I tried these 3 random queries and the results are terrible".

This happens way more than you can imagine, also in big, well-known tech corporations.

And where's the rabbit hole here?

If the search team is condescending, they will study the boss's feedback, do some ad hoc bugfix and go back to the boss.

The best scenario is that now the boss is happy and in a few days will try another three different queries, now broken and start the cycle again.

This ends up in a spiral of continuous patching of ad hoc solutions, creating a monster of Frankenstein [2] system that's not guaranteed to still work for some of the queries that were fixed in some previous iterations.

That's normally systemic: the search team may advise the boss they need to invest time to build an evaluation framework that will solidify progress and regression testing, but the immediate perceived benefit often outweighs mid/long-term solutions.

Underestimating this will cost: the more time passes, the harder it is to make sense of such systems; they become increasingly bad, unreliable and unreadable; maintenance collapses, and a reset is necessary.

And just adding large language models on top of this with no structured approach will just additionally deteriorate the situation: AI integrations must be the cherry on a delicious cake rather than a clumsy attempt to magically resurrect a rotten system.

What are the best practices, then?

First of all, it's important to come to terms with the fact that building a good information retrieval system is more difficult and costly than you expect.

If you are wise and already know this, recursively apply the statement four or five times, and you should be there.

So it's fundamental to protect the team and the development from entering these negative rabbit holes.

One of the very first questions should be: What does it matter for my search system?

An initial focus should be on online business expectations:

- I expect my users to find one relevant result, it should always be in the top position, and they should spend roughly 10 minutes on it.
- I expect my users to click on multiple results, they should be on the first page, and they should finalise an action (sale?) in the session.

6.1 Not Measuring Search Quality Metrics

- I expect my users to satisfy their information needs from a summary snippet, they should spend some time on it and finalise an action (a thumbs up for the summary) in the session.

These expectations must be translated into measurable signals that can be extracted and monitored from user interactions:

- Number of clicks on the position 1 result, time spent viewing the result
- Number of clicks on the first page, number of actioned sessions vs not actioned sessions (conversion rate)
- Time spent on the first page, number of thumbs-up sessions vs. non-thumbs-up

It's a vital exercise; I strongly recommend spending time with the stakeholders to understand their expectations and map them to measurable signals.

Once that is done, it's possible to build a monitoring system that collects these signals, aggregates them and shows a nice dashboard that can be used to have a view of how the online system is performing in production.

Achieving this is already a great success as it can give valuable insights on how your system is used by actual users (and trust me, this sometimes is way different from naive business expectations).

Having a visual on how the system is concretely performing in satisfying your business expectations is fundamental to monitoring and evaluating progress and regressions online after each important milestone, or in general to keep an eye on how the system is capable of scaling and adapting to the passing of time (with potential shifts in users' behaviour).

You shouldn't stop there.

Having your production system monitoring is fundamental, but it's not feasible to align development cycles to real-time online feedback: it takes too much time, and you risk exposing sub-optimal system candidates directly to your users.

Furthermore, you may be building a system from scratch, and you don't have real users yet.

Offline search quality evaluation comes to the rescue.

The fundamental entry point to a successful offline search quality evaluation system is a labelled dataset:

<query, document> pair with a relevance label associated.

This can be as simple as a binary relevance label (relevant/ irrelevant) or graded to the fine grain you like (from 0 to 10, from 1 to 5, etc.).

How should this dataset look?

Inferring relevance labels is complicated. What are the most common approaches for this task?

Explicit—Leveraging your team of experts to carefully assess the <query, document> pairs is expensive and takes time and effort, and humans are easy to get bored with such tasks, so you risk a not uniform quality of the rating set.

Implicit—Leveraging the online user interactions (if any), you can estimate relevance labels based on click-through rates, conversion rates, download rates, etc. This strictly depends on your online system and users' interaction, but it can be a viable option to accumulate a huge quantity of data with minimal human supervision. Noise is going to be bigger though, as users' interaction with the system is not an exact one-to-one match with the real quality of search results; there are biases, mistakes, perceived relevance that don't match the real one, etc.

Generated—Large language models can be used to assign ratings; this is similar to the explicit approach, it's certainly less expensive and less prone to the "getting bored" problem, but still, there's going to be noise and unpredictability. We explore this further in Sect. 4.10.

That's not the only problem, ideally, you want a query and document coverage as close to the production data as possible, but that's challenging both in terms of the time necessary to design, implement and set the processes needed to handle such data quantities and sourcing, as you don't always have the online data and you may need to resort to generate queries before you attempt to generate the relevance labels.

Once the dataset is ready, you need to choose the evaluation metrics that interest you.

Classic information retrieval metrics[1] have been studied deeply in the literature [1], and we won't go too much into the technical details here.

For the sake of this book, it's important to know that an evaluation metric takes in input the relevance-labelled query-document pairs and calculates a score that measures how well the information retrieval system performs from a specific angle.

What are the different perspectives we care about when evaluating an information retrieval system?

Precision—How many of the results returned are relevant to the query

Recall—How many of all the relevant results from the corpus of information are returned in the results

Different metrics offer detailed insights into different aspects of the system, including whether or not the ranking of search results matters for your business.

Once you have the dataset and the set of metrics to run, you are ready to integrate the offline evaluation with your development cycle.

The idea is that, iteration after iteration, along with the unit, integration and end-to-end tests, the system is also evaluated on the search quality metrics, allowing the developers to measure improvements and regressions quickly without affecting the end user.

More experiments can be done, and only the most promising versions of the system will reach production.

This is extremely valuable to shorten the feedback loop and have a global view of all the queries and use cases of interest, accumulated historically, avoiding the rabbit hole of random relevance tests and feedback with low reproducibility and tracking.

---

[1] https://www.pinecone.io/learn/offline-evaluation

Wrapping up, there's one additional consideration: in the era of artificial intelligence, having the ability to craft a labelled dataset is vital to building supervised machine learning models.

So dedicating the right effort to evaluation will also open the doors of many machine learning integrations, obtaining a duality of purpose for the evaluation dataset: measuring the quality and training models to improve it.

> **Key Takeaways**

- Without a systematic search quality evaluation in place, it's easy to end up in a spiral of regressions and never-ending bug-fixing iterations.
- Online search quality evaluation is fundamental to monitor how well the production system is satisfying the business expectations.
- Offline search quality evaluation allows for quicker development cycles and reduces the probability of sub-optimal system candidates being exposed to the final production users.
- The offline evaluation dataset can be used to train machine learning models that help improve the overall system.

6.2 Choosing the Wrong Tech Stack

When integrating large language models with a search project, nowadays, you have plenty of options to choose from. Should you use a search technology that includes interoperability out of the box, or should you connect with the LLM externally at the API level? Should you go with the latest and coolest vector database or opt for a solid traditional lexical solution that evolved over time? What are the consequences of bad decisions here? And how can you prevent them, avoiding the descent into the rabbit hole?

The first decision you need to make is architecturally where the LLM fits and how flexible you want your integration to look.

Do you want the large language model to be accessible by a SaaS endpoint (Software as a Service) or do you prefer to self-host it?

Various factors affect the decision here, as usual for this kind of question, you balance ease of access and ramp-up time with flexibility and performance tuning.

You should choose the SaaS approach if:

- You need a functioning LLM quickly
- You don't have the technical expertise, skills or energy to handle a self-hosting with all the scalability and deployment challenges that will come up (because even if the maturity of these technologies and open source frameworks improves by the day, challenges will come up)
- You don't care about fine-tuning performance, the throughput and service availability offered by the SaaS provider are enough
- You don't care to pay a likely higher monetary price in the long run
- You are ok to send your data to the SaaS provider (possibly they "guarantee" un-leakable silos... but you know...)

You should use self-hosting if:

- You can accept a longer ramp-up time, dedicate part of your team to the task or hire specialists to do it
- You enjoy the challenge of spinning up the service on your own, with deeper control over the technologies involved in the stack
- You care about top-notch performance, the throughput and service availability offered by the SaaS provider are not enough
- You are happy to pay more at the beginning but likely a lower monetary price in the long run
- You prefer to keep your data local

Going in the wrong direction will involve additional costs and confusion in the long term, not necessarily components developed to work in one scenario will fit the other, so extra care should be taken when going in one direction or the other.

On the other hand, based on my experience, it may happen that you start with a SaaS approach to quickly hit the market or the demo you need to secure further investment and then iterate, moving to self-hosting when you have the right capacity and energy to dedicate it.

The next step is the point of integration: Should you connect the LLM endpoint to your search engine through external APIs or just use out-of-the-box pluggable components?

Modern search engine technologies offer many features that integrate large language models out of the box: you select the feature, you choose the LLM and plug it in through endpoint configurations or model deployment, see Chap. 8 for plenty of details.

You won't have control over how the LLM is accessed by the application, but you can rely comfortably on what other search specialists have done for you.

You should go this route if:

- You are building a prototype, and having something quick to show to the team/stakeholders can be a good entry point for additional funding and work.
- You don't have much expertise in building such integrations, and the technical skills are necessary.
- You don't care about performance much.

6.2 Choosing the Wrong Tech Stack

An alternative is to integrate the LLM externally with the search engine, potentially both at query (runtime) and indexing (offline data structure preparation) time.

This means accessing the LLM directly with client libraries (open or proprietary) and fitting the integrations in the search API or in the indexing pipeline in the appropriate steps.

This guarantees much more control over the way your system interacts with LLM and opens the doors to much deeper flexibility, also in terms of performance, availability, failover management and retry policies.

You should go this route if:

- The search technology you are using doesn't meet your feature requirements, and you can afford (or don't want) a migration
- You need the fine-grained ability to scale up the LLM integrations differently from the rest of the search
- You care about performance, flexibility and the freedom to tune indexing/query performance deeply

Should you go with the latest and coolest vector database or opt for a solid traditional lexical solution that evolved over time?

The golden rule here is to never accept directions from non-technical stakeholders, and don't choose based on hype or marketing directions.

Blogs and press releases are cool, but they are meant to be shiny; it's their scope, they must be seducing, but we are here to build a pragmatic project and not to get seduced.

Choosing the search technology to use is a key milestone; getting it wrong will cause additional developments, back and forth, discussions, tension and in the long run, a necessary reset in the project.

Migrating the search technology will have a cost; you will have to:

- Ramp up the team on the new tech APIs and internals
- Adapt all the pipelines, frameworks and client applications interacting with it
- Re-index (including not only the inverted index but all the data structures necessary to power the full search experience)

Most of the time, you won't be able to tolerate downtime, so this means you'll also need to spin up entire environments in parallel, design a functional test strategy (to verify feature parity) and stress test the new technology to make sure to get comparable performance.

It's not a position you want to be in after the first few months of a project (and trust me, you need to be extra careful with the initial choice as I've seen this happening in the real world).

Nowadays, there are countless search engines that support flexible traditional and AI-based search, and if we also include the commercial ones (or the open source with some sort of paywall), the number increases.

Most of them offer the same core set of features, but the decision is not easy.

The focus here is on open source search technologies, as you have much more power in terms of exploring what's behind the curtain, to better understand the real status and value of the tech itself.

Some of them have been there for ages (Apache Lucene, Solr, Elasticsearch, Vespa), and others were born with the 2020 AI new spring.

The first due diligence you need to carry out is the analysis of your requirements.

Don't get fascinated by cool features you don't need and you don't even foresee needing them in the near future.

They will be nice to have, but shouldn't be your focus.

Once you have identified a set of candidate search technologies that match your requirements, you should assess the degree of familiarity your team has with each of them.

This is a key factor that should affect the decision; of course, it's not the only factor, but having a team that's already productive with technology and potentially knows the internals very well could be a game-changer for success.

The second aspect to evaluate is the community status for the project: how many committers/maintainers are active? In what capacity? How big is the contributor base? How alive is the community in terms of discussions, contributions and releases?

Make sure to dedicate a good amount of time to this exercise, don't rush to conclusions based on your feelings and perception, and allocate the right energy and time to carefully assess the situation as it is at the moment you need: the reputation of the project is important, but it's more valuable to have a recent snapshot of the situation.

What about the code quality? A key point of open source is that you have access to the code, sure you rarely need to modify that code if you are just an adopter of the solution, but still, it's very likely you will end up having to debug some weird edge cases and the ability to be able to pleasantly read and understand the code in there, it's not to underestimate.

Customisations may be needed, bug fixes, technical discussions with the community, etc., so make sure you are comfortable with the programming language used and the code quality of the technology when adopting it.

Only at this point, after all the previous considerations, you may look at the nice-to-have additional features available on the plate.

You may not need them now, but given that you have a limited possibility of extending an existing search technology, picking one that is more feature-rich can be a good idea, but you need a good balance with all the rest.

The focus of the section so far has been on the search technology itself, which is the core part of the decision, but there's more.

In case you plan to interact with the LLM externally (not relying on the out-of-the-box search technology integrations), what technology should you use?

We dedicate a chapter on the possible options in Chap. 7, but the main discriminant here is: single model client APIs vs flexibility.

6.2 Choosing the Wrong Tech Stack

If you plan to use just a single family of models, from a single supplier, it may be worth not investing in complicated orchestration frameworks: you should use the dedicated model client APIs and that's it.

Advanced orchestration libraries are a good idea when you need the additional abstraction layer, and you don't want to depend on a single LLM; that can be sensible, but always remember to focus the development on what you need rather than on possible future expectations.

When building client APIs, it's probably worth exploring more complicated and flexible solutions when the need arises and not from the beginning.

Another question I often receive is: "Should I have two separate search systems for traditional functionalities and AI-based ones?"

Vector databases marketing will try to push you in that direction, but don't get distracted; it's unlikely you need different technologies. Nowadays, the direction is towards complete offerings, so many open source solutions have solid traditional and AI features support.

It may be different in case you have a legacy system for your traditional keyword search, but in that scenario, I would carefully assess the situation and understand if a full migration to a single new technology may be more beneficial than just an added vector database.

Don't get me wrong, there may be edge cases where having a system dedicated to the AI-search part may be beneficial (e.g. in case you need to scale them differently and you don't find an all-in-one solution that aligns with your requirements), but don't do it lightly, always back your decision by a careful analysis, benchmark and rationale.

In conclusion, it's not easy to choose the right technology stack for a search project that involves the integration of search engines and LLM, but if you don't get seduced by fancy press releases and marketing advertisements and dedicate the right amount of time and effort to carry out the due diligence, you have many tools to face the decision process rationally.

> **Key Takeaways**

- Don't get seduced by marketing and press releases, focus on the features you need.
- The community health and activity are key points to choosing the right technology.
- Your team has a voice, make sure you listen to their needs and understand their skill level and knowledge.
- An open and high-quality code base can make the difference.
- Extra features are nice to have and can be tie-breakers.

6.3 Choosing the Wrong Large Language Model

> There are many types of large language models, depending on the task they are fine-tuned for. And to perform a single task, there are many to choose from, especially for general purposes such as instruction following or semantic vectorisation. Choosing the right one may be challenging, realising that you haven't chosen the right one may be difficult and recovering from the situation may be even more problematic.

Just on the public model repository Hugging Face[2] at the time of writing, there are almost 500,000 transformer-based models, 170,000 instruction following text generation models and 8000 text vectorisation models.

Given the current hot trend, these numbers are likely to increase, and that means that the task of choosing the right model for your use case is getting harder and harder with time.

We have dedicated an entire chapter to how to choose the right LLM for your use case in Chap. 5, so here we'll focus on what happens after that if you fail to do it and why it's so important to dedicate the right effort into choosing the right one.

The worst case scenario is that you choose the wrong LLM for the task you need and you don't even realise that, in production, you are not monitoring any signal that measures the users' happiness or profit of your business, offline you don't have functional tests that verify that your system is performing as expected, you lose users and in no time you are out.

That's an extreme, obviously, but it serves to highlight that you need to have a safety net in place: you need to be able to understand if the LLMs you employ in your system are bringing benefits, and you need to be able to discover problems as soon as possible.

The monitoring and evaluation metrics from Sect. 6.1 play a key role here.

You have red flags around that suggest that the large language model you chose doesn't perform as well as expected. What happens after that?

You have probably put some effort into plugging a certain LLM into your system, you may have various areas of your code base coupled with the decision, and even in situations where you went decently flexible, switching to a new model still costs some time and resources.

You are better off trying to make it work, and here you are, into the rabbit hole.

Especially if you opted for a general-purpose LLM, you can refine your prompt endlessly, solving a problem at each iteration and introducing tens of regressions.

---

[2] https://huggingface.co/

The fact that LLMs are probabilistic machines doesn't help; you will end up with prompts that grow in complexity patch after patch, ending again with something that's hardly readable and impossible to maintain.

Another rabbit hole you may end up in is adding post-processing components one after the other in order to manipulate and validate the output of the components interacting with the LLM.

Also in this case if the LLM chosen is not up to the task, you may end up with patches after patches of rule-based ad hoc modules that build on top of the LLM responses to solve an edge case after another, and this process the deeper you go will slowly defeat the entire idea of having the LLM in the first place.

Even if hard, you should accept the failure, raise your hand and go back to explore the LLM landscape to choose a better candidate model. Possibly, you don't need a generalist model at all, and you are better off with a small language model specifically fine-tuned for the task you need.

> **Key Takeaways**

- There is a multitude of LLMs to choose from; this activity must not be underestimated.
- You need a monitoring system in place to realise as soon as possible that the model chosen is not a good fit.
- You need to realise as soon as possible that you entered the rabbit hole and reconsider your choice.

References

1. Bama, S.S., Ahmed, M., Saravanan, A.: A survey on performance evaluation measures for information retrieval system. Int. Res. J. Eng. Technol. **2**(2), 1015–1020 (2015)
2. Shelley, M.: Frankenstein; or, The Modern Prometheus, 1st edn. Lackington, Hughes, Harding, Mavor & Jones, London (1818)

Part III

How to Use Open Source Software to Interact with Large Language Models

- How to interact programmatically with large language models?
- What LLM integrations are available in popular open source search engines, out of the box?

The third part of the book explores the most popular open source libraries you can use to interact with large language models and how this new technology is changing the landscape of open source search engines.

LLMs, fine-tuned for instruction following, are designed to follow natural language requests (prompts).

This design brought many interesting emergent capabilities in problem/task solving when scaled up to the sizes that brought the L (Large) to language models.

Researchers and practitioners started to see a huge benefit in accessing such technology in a programmatic way, to integrate it with many existing tools and software.

The huge momentum caused by the explosion of popularity of ChatGPT-like products raised an increased interest in the community to abstract and define common requirements for software integrations and implement them in the form of open source orchestration frameworks that encoded best practices and different layers of indirections to make simpler and more modular the construction of LLM-powered software.

We are going to explore the open landscape of these orchestration frameworks, analysing and comparing the most popular options out there, because with the flexibility of many alternatives also comes the difficulty of making the right decision for your project.

After that, the topic transitions to one that is greatly dear to the author: how are current open source search engines adapting to this innovation?

The LLM revolution stormed the (lexical) foundations of all the open source search engines dominating the market, and their developer communities had to adapt and start introducing features and integrations that leverage the additional capabilities of such powerful technology.

Part III is organised as follows:

- Chapter 7 presents the most popular orchestration libraries to use to interact programmatically with LLM: LangChain, Haystack and LangChain4j, among others.
- Chapter 8 is a survey of all the features introduced to support LLMs in popular search engines like Apache Lucene/Solr, Elasticsearch, OpenSearch and Vespa. The chapter wraps up by introducing promising vector search engines born in the last couple of years.

By the end of this part, the reader is expected to learn:

The *Open source LLM orchestration frameworks*—landscape, how they work, differences and when to use which.

The *Open source search engines and LLM*—landscape, the features they offer, the differences and when to use which.

7 Open Source Frameworks and Projects

Abstract

This chapter introduces the reader to the most popular open source orchestration frameworks around, including an analysis of their architecture, functionalities offered and differentiators. The chapter closes with a direct comparison that aims to help the reader identify which is the most appropriate library to use for their use case.

7.1 LangChain

LangChain is an open source, composable orchestration framework to build applications with LLMs.

It helps you chain together components and third-party integrations to simplify AI application development in Python and JavaScript/TypeScript.

Key components offered by the library help with interacting with LLMs through a chat API, handling the sequence of interactions in the context for short-term (in-process)/long-term (persisted) memory, defining tools for LLM function calling and working with the structured output functionalities.

LangChain also implements APIs to extract data from various data sources, enrich it through vectorisation and populate many databases and search engines.

The main benefit of LangChain is the great flexibility to switch LLMs and third-party integrations easily.

The overall LangChain ecosystem also includes paid services and platforms to evaluate, debug, deploy and observe stateful workflows.

The goal of LangChain, the Python/JavaScript package and LangChain the company, is to make it as easy as possible for developers to build applications that integrate with LLMs.

While LangChain originally started as a single open source package, it has evolved into a company and a whole ecosystem.[1]

The main targets of the open source library are:

Standardised component interfaces—Large language models, service providers (that offer multiple models as a choice) and vector storage solutions are growing in number by the day. Most of them use their own proprietary APIs (although some of them opted for the same structure to facilitate migrations and gain users).

LangChain unifies client APIs behind the same interfaces, making it easy for developers to build applications that need to interchange these components often, reducing the need to explore and learning each internal API.

Orchestration—There are a large number of modules in LangChain that implement specific LLM-based functionalities, which can be combined together to obtain an agentic workflow (where the LLM has access to information and tools).

Most of the times the low-level implementation goes back to some prompt template + boilerplate code: not to be seen as a negative point, it's just that in general most of the current strategies to get LLMs to solve complex tasks rely on describing the approach to follow via prompt rather than via specific programming instructions.

Abilities such as goal decomposition are implemented via detailed standard prompt templates aiming to activate chain of thought processes in the models, while better performance with tasks is achieved through few-shot prompting with positive and negative examples.

Not to be confused with internal chains of thought and self-reflecting models that encapsule these abilities via training and fine-tuning.

These approaches are interesting and currently addressed by the research community as they end up being more inherent abilities rather than something easily triggered by programming instructions.

Memory—Short-term memory is useful for LLM-based applications to keep track of the user agent's real-time conversation history.

It is supported by many LLMs, and generally speaking, it's implemented by a standard template for the input prompt (the context of the LLM text generation task).

Long-term memory is achieved by integrating persistence layers with the LLM interaction layer: LangChain offers many data storage/retrieval APIs to give users great flexibility in deciding where to store/retrieve such information.[2]

Tool use—Most modern LLMs give the possibility of defining tools via their APIs and then send prompt requests that can leverage the list of available tools.

LangChain offers a wrapper around these functionalities, unifying the interface across multiple vendors.

---

[1] https://www.langchain.com

[2] https://python.langchain.com/docs/integrations/vectorstores/

7.1.1 Should You Use LangChain?

From a very high level of abstraction, LangChain can be summarised as a sort of universal SDK for all the major LLMs.

A common API that also introduces additional layers of abstractions to cover the most popular use cases of interaction with such models.

It probably implements way more than you need and through way more stratified layers of indirection.

So, is it for you?

If you don't need the flexibility of supporting a plethora of LLMs, but you are focused on just one or a few, that's a first signal that you probably won't need it.

Additionally, if the module(s) of your application with the responsibility of interacting with LLMs do not perform any particularly complex tasks, the advantage of using LangChain would be minimal.

In general, at the beginning, it can be a nice time-saver, avoiding you from re-implementing many well-known patterns of interactions with LLMs, but when you end up having the need for more control or debugging a deep issue, the time-saving illusion may go away.

To be fair, this is valid for many libraries in general; they inevitably support many more functions than you need in your code, and if you end up using them for a while, the initial time-saving benefit normally goes away, and you realise you may need to go back to customisation or different solutions for certain problems.

Also, the benefit of having prompt catalogues and standard ways of achieving certain tasks on various LLMs is fading away at the same pace that more modern models learn how to deviate less from the user's intentions.

I don't like the fact that this framework (and many others) tries to solve via prompts, trial-and-error repetitions, tasks that should be solved by LLMs through an entirely different way of interacting with them, via programming them rather than "asking to solve a task via prompt".

Prompt engineering is not much engineering right now, and hard-coding sophisticated prompts that solve the problem **most** of the time with **most** of the LLMs is not good enough for workflows that need deterministic outcomes.

This is indeed another aspect to consider; this space is moving so fast that libraries such as LangChain end up changing their indirections and layers continuously, making it harder for developers to upgrade/migrate their applications and, in general, to use the library in the first place, without having to learn it again every two months.

My personal opinion is to use it for prototypes and quick models/storage comparisons, to then focus on your own code to build the production thing.

LangChain can definitely be good as a source of inspiration for the concepts it presents and the use cases it implements. It can introduce developers new to the field to the dos and don'ts and limitations of the underlying technology.

It may not be worth learning for building real-production grade applications: It provides good abstractions, code snippets and tool integrations for building demos;

however, you may be better off coding up your own implementations if you're developing a practical LLM-powered application and you don't need the level of flexibility.

> **Key Takeaways**

- LangChain is great if you need to be compatible with many LLMs and databases/search engines.
- LangChain is great for demos and prototypes, and to get inspiration to develop popular use cases.
- The steep learning curve, the amount of unnecessary flexibility, the frequency of major changes and refactors make LangChain not worth learning for everybody.

7.2 Haystack

> Haystack is an open source AI orchestration framework to build flexible and production-ready LLM applications.
>
> It consists of interoperable components (models, vector data stores, file processors) that can be connected into pipelines or agents.
>
> The main focus of the framework is building retrieval augmented generation, question answering, semantic search and conversational chatbot systems.

Haystack is an open source framework designed to facilitate the development of end-to-end AI-powered search systems that leverage natural language processing and machine learning techniques through large language models integrations.[3]

It is not a search engine library but an orchestration framework that introduces different layers of abstraction for its building blocks, giving the flexibility of switching models and search engines with ease.

Haystack is developed by Deepset, a company specialising in NLP and AI solutions starting from the end of 2019.

Over the years, the focus shifted towards mainstream LLMs providers to address the growing necessity for more sophisticated search systems that can handle unstructured data and provide more relevant and context-aware search results, often supporting natural language input/output (retrieval augmented generation).

---

[3] https://haystack.deepset.ai

With its modular building blocks, software developers can implement pipelines to address various search tasks over large document collections, such as document retrieval, semantic search, text generation, question answering or summarisation.

It integrates with many famous LLMs (Hugging Face Transformers, OpenAI, Cohere, Anthropic and others)[4] and search engines (Elasticsearch, OpenSearch and others).[5]

From a high-level summary, we can simplify the framework as three core components: embedding models, retrievers and LLMs.

Each of them is a unified interface with many different implementations, supporting the various LLM, vectorisation and search engine providers.

The project tends to be decently stable with a strong community both in terms of support and development: the code and interface stability is a key point to grant continuity to the community and avoid the need for practitioners and developers to constantly in the scenario of having to relearn things.

Starting from the open source library, Haystack now has a full ecosystem around it, that includes many third-party integrations:[6] mostly LLMs and document stores but also data ingestion, evaluation and monitoring solutions.

7.2.1 Should You Use Haystack?

As you can imagine, my feelings are pretty much the same as for LangChain.

The attempt here is pretty much the same, with a slightly better focus on the RAG scenario. But unifying so many different APIs and complex systems through the same wrapper inevitably will end up generalising too much, losing the ability of fine-grained interaction offered by each specific API.

I can see the same pattern here of a good time-saving benefit at the beginning, to then descend into a much higher complexity if you need to bring your project to production and have fine-grain control over the components' implementation you chose.

Even if all around the Haystack Web site, the core message is "Haystack is for production-ready systems", my feeling is that it fits better the quick prototype/demo/'I need to choose the technologies for my project' scenario.

Don't get me wrong, for sure it offers solid code foundations and a lot of good inspiration and code samples, especially though its cookbook,[7] but when approaching a serious integration project, I would prefer to fully explore the native libraries I choose, get control and familiarity with the official APIs and combine them at their best with custom ad hoc code.

---

[4] https://docs.haystack.deepset.ai/docs/generators

[5] https://docs.haystack.deepset.ai/docs/retrievers

[6] https://haystack.deepset.ai/integrations

[7] https://haystack.deepset.ai/cookbook

It's true that it opens the doors of information retrieval to casual practitioners, and there's merit there, but depending on the size, complexity and fine-grain control you need on each of the technologies involved, you may be better off with your own integration.

Haystack has been built by people fluent in search and can be extremely valuable to leverage the profuse expertise in their software **if** you are not that tech-savvy in the field.

Haystack can definitely help you move your minimum viable product to production quickly, with decent performance and features.

> **Key Takeaways**

- Haystack is an orchestration framework built with RAG in mind.
- It offers support for many vectorisation models, document retrievers (search engines) and LLM providers.
- Haystack is great for quick prototypes and demos.
- Although explicitly mentioned on their Web site multiple times, its usage for your production system should be carefully assessed.
- If you don't know much about information retrieval, Haystack can be a good entry point.

7.3 LangChain4j

LangChain4j developments started in 2023 with the objective of filling the Java gap for LLM orchestration libraries in the open source community.

Although present in the name, the project is not affiliated with LangChain but takes inspiration from it and other libraries from the LLM community.

The focus of LangChain4j is to provide unified Java APIs for both popular LLM providers and vector embedding data stores to ease the development of chatbots, function calling agents and retrieval augmented generation products.

The goal of LangChain4j is to simplify integrating LLMs into Java applications.[8]

LangChain4j history starts in early 2023 amid the ChatGPT popularity spike when the funding developers noticed a lack of Java counterparts to the numerous Python and JavaScript LLM libraries and frameworks blooming at the time.

---

[8] https://docs.langchain4j.dev/intro

7.3 LangChain4j

The project is a fusion of ideas and concepts from LangChain, Haystack, LlamaIndex and the broader community, enhanced by additional innovation introduced by its developers.

The first mission is to offer a unified API access to LLM providers and embedding vector storage solutions, effectively wrapping them through an indirection.

This allows you to experiment with different LLMs (both for text generation and text vectorisation) or embedding stores, easily switching between them without the need to rewrite your code.

This can be extremely beneficial if your code needs to be LLM/document storage agnostic (e.g. if you are writing a framework) or you need to quickly prototype to make a decision on the technologies to use.

The second focus of the project is to implement patterns and best practices for Java, regarding standard interaction with LLMs such as offering low-level prompt templates for various needs, implementing chat memory management, function calling and structured output.

Along with low-level components, LangChain4j also offers coordination capabilities to assemble RAG pipelines and agentic workflows where the LLM cooperates with third parties and tools.

To complete the ecosystem, LangChain4j presents a list of Java examples[9] that guides the user through tutorials and code to implement demo applications and use cases.

These examples need our attention as they can facilitate aspects of your project, without having to import the full library: sometimes a good inspiration is enough to start/unblock the progress without impacting the dependency complexity of your work.

7.3.1 Should You Use It?

LangChain4j is not much different from the other orchestration frameworks we have explored so far; hence, the same considerations apply here as well.

One main difference is that the Java programming language opened the doors to a series of interesting integrations in Apache Solr.

Aside from using it for quick prototypes and examples, LangChain4j unifies many proprietary LLM API, and this is extremely valuable if you need to build an integration that must be compatible with multiple LLM model choices, through the same code.

It's clear that generalising, you lose some of the flexibility of the original APIs for each implementation, but if that is acceptable and your solution is equally generic, you are good to go.

---

[9] https://github.com/langchain4j/langchain4j-examples

To give you a glimpse of a possible real-world use case, we used LangChain4j in the Apache Solr project to introduce support for text vectorisation.[10]

Apache Solr supports text vectorisation both at query time (through a query parser) and at indexing time (update request processor).

This means that Solr is capable of interacting with a text vectorisation endpoint offered by an LLM provider to encode text to vector and then run vector search on it.

Apache Solr is written in Java, and being a public open source project, the idea was to give the user the flexibility of using the LLM provider of their choice.

The indirection and Java programming language support of LangChain4j was the perfect match, and it was possible to implement a layer of abstraction where the user configures the LLM provider of their choice (from a list, subset of the supported providers of LangChain4j) to then be used to run the REST APIs interactions with no need of custom code personalised for each LLM solution.

This ended up being a clean solution for Apache Solr, generic and decently easy to maintain.

More will follow in regard to LangChain4j integrations in Apache Solr, so stay tuned!

> **Key Takeaways**

- LangChain4j is an independent project, not affiliated with LangChain.
- It offers a unified Java API to access popular LLM-based services and vector embeddings data stores.
- Through example and interface implementations, it facilitates the Java developer's work when building LLM-based applications.
- It's currently used in the Apache Solr project to support LLM integrations.

7.4 Comparisons

Most LLM orchestration frameworks share very similar traits, offering various indirection layers to plug alternatives for their components.

They are a reflection of this dynamic AI spring, where multiple equivalent solutions are approaching open source communities and the markets.

They have some minor differences, though, involving the programming language they support, the stability, the level of abstractions and the overall original focus.

---

[10] https://github.com/apache/solr/pull/2809

7.4 Comparisons

Let's start from the communities: LangChain, Haystack and LangChain4j have a descending size for their communities, showing the higher popularity of the first.

This doesn't mean the others have a small user base/developer base, but it's clear there are differences: to give some numbers at the time of writing, in the most recent one-month period, LangChain had 208 active pull requests and 74 contributors, Haystack had 72 active pull requests and 18 contributors and LangChain4j had 58 active pull requests and 22 contributors. This also acts as an indicator of the respective size and complexity of each project, but don't get fooled, bigger doesn't mean better, as we abundantly explained in each dedicated section.

My team at Sease preferred Haystack to develop a neural highlighter plugin for Apache Solr because it proved to be quite intuitive for supporting BERT-like models via Python, without the necessity of coupling the code to a single one (early 2023).

The observation comes from a quick investigation, but its documentation was immediately useful to build a prototype for our use case. The perception of LangChain was that it was more oriented to remote inference services (such as OpenAI ones), and it was bloated with too much indirection and complexity.

In general, LangChain appears as difficult to customise because of the many layers of abstraction, and releases happen frequently (with many breaking changes).

It's worth stressing again that Haystack was developed to support RAG and semantic search pipelines, while LangChain started as a much more general framework since its inception. This implies you don't need the additional layers and components if your use case is limited to search.

> **Key Takeaways**

- LangChain offers a huge variety of integrations at the cost of additional complexity and frequent breaking changes in their code releases.
- Haystack has a focus on RAG pipelines, with a more focused, smaller number of integrations.
- LangChain4j's main differentiator is the Java programming language.

Popular Open Source Search Engines

Abstract

This chapter aims to demystify the jungle of alternatives, giving a clear and pragmatic overview of the features supported by each solution, with a focus on the most comprehensive and established ones. Given the author's background in the Apache Lucene and Solr communities, there will be a bigger emphasis on Lucene-based search technologies. The chapter closes with an overview of the features supported by some of the new vector search engines, to check how far they are from the rest.

8.1 Apache Lucene

> The Lucene project is an information retrieval library from the Apache Software Foundation (written in Java but also includes Python bindings) that implements core indexing and search features along with auxiliary functionalities such as spellchecking, result snippets highlighting and advanced text analysis capabilities.
>
> With the recent new AI spring, many new LLM-related features have been added, including the support for vector search, vector quantisation and hybrid search.

Disclaimer The following section describes features up to Apache Lucene 10.2.1 (including some work in progress).

At the time of reading, make sure to check the latest available release version and the release notes: successive releases may bring new LLM-related features.

Apache Lucene support for LLM-based features focuses on pure vector-search capabilities (including quantisation) and hybrid search through reciprocal rank fusion.

Text-to-vector encoding needs to happen in your application outside Lucene's boundaries, and Lucene only stores and searches the resulting vectors.

Being Lucene a library, it won't be that easy to approach (in comparison to full Web server search engines, such as all the others).

There's still a benefit of guiding readers through the most important areas of code, so for a full understanding of this section, the reader is invited to exercise curiosity and check on the references and explore the Lucene code base for a better understanding.

The vector-search implementation in Lucene is based on hierarchical navigable small world graph [3, 4] (also known as the acronym HNSW).

The codec defines the format to use to build and read the data structures necessary for the vector graph and vector storage.

Codec

org.apache.lucene.codecs.lucene103.Lucene103Codec

```
public Lucene103Codec(Mode mode) {
    super("Lucene103");
    ...
    this.defaultKnnVectorsFormat = new Lucene99HnswVectorsFormat
        ();
}
```

HNSW vector formats define how to build and read the HNSW graph (where each vector ID is a node).

Flat vector formats define how to store the vectors themselves.

Lucene99HnswVectorsFormat uses Lucene99FlatVectorsFormat

- Store for each field the vector metadata (.vemf) and vector data (vec).
- It has a dedicated writer and reader, dependent on the vector encoding (BYTE or FLOAT32).
- It has its scorer (that just uses the supplied similarity).

Lucene99HnswScalarQuantizedVectorsFormat uses Lucene99ScalarQuantizedVectorsFormat (for scalar quantisation Sect. 4.1.2).

- Lossy compression from float32 to a number of bits (4 or 7).
- Raw disk increases (raw + quantized vectors).
- Off-heap memory decreases as quantised vectors are loaded.
- Search is faster.
- It has a dedicated writer and reader, dependent on the bits to use for quantisation.

8.1 Apache Lucene

org.apache.lucene.codecs.lucene99.Lucene99ScalarQuantizedVectorsFormat

```
/**
 * Constructs a format using the given graph construction
     parameters.
 *
 * @param confidenceInterval the confidenceInterval for scalar
     quantizing the vectors, when 'null'
 *     it is calculated based on the vector dimension. When
       '0', the quantiles are dynamically
 *     determined by sampling many confidence intervals and
       determining the most accurate pair.
 * @param bits the number of bits to use for scalar
     quantization (must be between 1 and 8,
 *     inclusive)
 * @param compress whether to compress the quantized vectors
     by another 50% when bits=4. If
 *     'true', pairs of (4 bit quantized) dimensions are
       packed into a single byte. This must be
 *     'false' when bits=7. This provides a trade-off of 50%
       reduction in hot vector memory usage
 *     during searching, at some decode speed penalty.
 */
public Lucene99ScalarQuantizedVectorsFormat(
    Float confidenceInterval, int bits, boolean compress) {
    ...
}
```

Lucene102HnswBinaryQuantizedVectorsFormat uses **Lucene102BinaryQuantizedVectorsFormat** (for binary scalar quantisation).

- Lossy compression from float32 to binary.
- Same observations from scalar quantisation apply.

Query
There are various queries supported by Lucene in the realm of vector search.

Knn Query
There are two variants, based on the data type of the element of the vector (supported 32 bits or 8 bits). They have identical parameters and behave the same.
org.apache.lucene.search.KnnByteVectorQuery
org.apache.lucene.search.KnnFloatVectorQuery

```
/**
 * Find the <code>k</code> nearest documents to the target
     vector according to the vectors in the
 * given field. <code>target</code> vector.
 *
 * @param field a field that has been indexed as a {@link
     KnnByteVectorField}.
 * @param target the target of the search
```

```
 * @param k the number of documents to find
 * @param filter a filter applied before the vector search
 * @param searchStrategy the search strategy to use. If null,
     the default strategy will be used.
 *     The underlying format may not support all strategies
     and is free to ignore the requested
 * strategy.
 * @lucene.experimental
 */
public KnnByteVectorQuery(
    String field, byte[] target, int k, Query filter,
    KnnSearchStrategy searchStrategy) {
    ...
}
```

Patience Knn Query

Wrapper of Knn query that implements an early termination approach [5].
org.apache.lucene.search.PatienceKnnVectorQuery

```
/**
 * Construct a new PatienceKnnVectorQuery instance for seeded
     vector field
 *
 * @param knnQuery the knn query to be seeded
 * @param saturationThreshold the early exit saturation
     threshold
 * @param patience the patience parameter that indicates how
     many saturations to accept before terminating
 * @return a new PatienceKnnVectorQuery instance
 * @lucene.experimental
 */
PatienceKnnVectorQuery(
    AbstractKnnVectorQuery knnQuery, double
        saturationThreshold, int patience) {
    ...
}
```

Seeded Knn Query

Wrapper of Knn query that implements an approach to start the graph exploration from entry points resulting from a seed query [2].
org.apache.lucene.search.SeededKnnVectorQuery

```
/**
 * Construct a new SeededKnnVectorQuery instance for a float
     vector field
 *
 * @param knnQuery the knn query to be seeded
 * @param seed a query seed to initiate the vector format
     search
 * @return a new SeededKnnVectorQuery instance
 * @lucene.experimental
```

8.1 Apache Lucene

```
 8    */
 9   public static SeededKnnVectorQuery fromFloatQuery(
         KnnFloatVectorQuery knnQuery, Query seed) {
10     return new SeededKnnVectorQuery(knnQuery, seed, null);
11   }
```

The idea is to initiate the graph vector search from entry points (vector nodes in the graph) that are not random but the results of a traditional Lucene query.

This is quite powerful, first of all to avoid starting the graph exploration randomly, but starting from a predictable seed and secondly to start from vectors that are expected to be relevant already.

This can both speed up vector search and also help with relevance, ideally expanding a set of documents that are coming from a solid lexical search query, with recall-optimised vector exploration.

With a certain degree of generalisation, we can consider it a form of hybrid search that happens on the fly directly on the HNSW graph.

Diversifying Children Knn Query

This query applies to the scenario where multiple vectors are children of the same document (e.g. when vectors are encoded from paragraphs, chunked from the original document).

The scope of this query is to be able to retrieve the best child for each parent document (avoiding the retrieval of multiple children of the same document).

There are two variants, based on the data type of the element of the vector (supported 32 bits or 8 bits).

They have identical parameters and behave the same.

org.apache.lucene.search.join.DiversifyingChildrenByteKnnVectorQuery
org.apache.lucene.search.join.DiversifyingChildrenFloatKnnVectorQuery

```
 1   /**
 2    * Create a DiversifyingChildrenByteKnnVectorQuery.
 3    *
 4    * @param field the query field
 5    * @param query the vector query
 6    * @param childFilter the filter to apply to children vectors
 7    * @param k how many parent documents to return given the
          matching children
 8    * @param parentsFilter Filter identifying all the parent
          documents.
 9    * @param searchStrategy the search strategy to use. If null,
          the default strategy will be used.
10    *     The underlying format may not support all strategies
          and is free to ignore the requested
11    *     strategy.
12    * @lucene.experimental
13    */
14   public DiversifyingChildrenByteKnnVectorQuery(
15       String field,
16       byte[] query,
17       Query childFilter,
```

```
18          int k,
19          BitSetProducer parentsFilter,
20          KnnSearchStrategy searchStrategy) {
21      ...
22      }
```

How to retrieve top-k documents, ranked by their best vector child?[1]

```
1   Query acceptedChildren =
2               getChildrenFilter(knnByteChildrenQuery.getFilter(),
                    parentsFilter, allParentsBitSet);
3   Query knnChildren =
4               new DiversifyingChildrenByteKnnVectorQuery(
5                   vectorField, queryVector, acceptedChildren, topK
                    , allParentsBitSet);
6   knnChildren = knnChildren.rewrite(req.getSearcher());
7   return new ToParentBlockJoinQuery(
8               knnChildren, allParentsBitSet, ScoreModeParser.parse
                    (scoreMode));
```

Vector Similarity Query

Search for all (approximate) vectors above a similarity threshold.

org.apache.lucene.search.ByteVectorSimilarityQuery
org.apache.lucene.search.FloatVectorSimilarityQuery

```
1   /**
2    * Search for all (approximate) vectors above a similarity
            threshold.
3    If a filter is applied, it traverses as many nodes as the
            cost of
4    * the filter, and then falls back to exact search if results
            are incomplete.
5    *
6    * @param field a field that has been indexed as a vector
            field.
7    * @param traversalSimilarity (lower) similarity score for
            graph traversal.
8    * @param resultSimilarity (higher) similarity score for
            result collection.
9    * @param filter a filter applied before the vector search.
10   */
11   AbstractVectorSimilarityQuery(
12       String field, float traversalSimilarity, float
                resultSimilarity, Query filter) {
13       ...
14   }
```

---

[1] https://github.com/apache/solr/pull/3316

8.1 Apache Lucene

Hybrid Search

Mixing lexical and vector results is supported through reciprocal rank fusion:[2] *org.apache.lucene.search.TopDocs#rrf*

```
/**
 * Reciprocal Rank Fusion method.
 *
 * <p>This method combines different search results into a
     single ranked list by combining their
 * ranks. This is especially well suited when combining hits
     computed via different methods, whose
 * score distributions are hardly comparable.
 *
 * @param topN the top N results to be returned
 * @param k a constant determines how much influence documents
     in individual rankings have on the
 *      final result. A higher value gives lower rank documents
     more influence. k should be greater
 *      than or equal to 1.
 * @param hits a list of TopDocs to apply RRF on
 * @return a TopDocs contains the top N ranked results.
 */
```

e.g. from *lucene/core/src/test/org/apache/lucene/search/TestTopDocsRRF.java*

```
TopDocs list1 =
        new TopDocs(
            new TotalHits(100, TotalHits.Relation.
                GREATER_THAN_OR_EQUAL_TO),
            new ScoreDoc[] {
                new ScoreDoc(42, 10f),
                new ScoreDoc(10, 5f),
                new ScoreDoc(20, 3f)
                });
TopDocs list2 =
        new TopDocs(
            new TotalHits(80, TotalHits.Relation.
                GREATER_THAN_OR_EQUAL_TO),
            new ScoreDoc[] {
                new ScoreDoc(10, 10f),
                new ScoreDoc(20, 5f)
                });

TopDocs rrf = TopDocs.rrf(3, 20, new TopDocs[] {list1, list2});
```

---

[2] https://github.com/apache/lucene/pull/13470

> **Key Takeaways**

- There's little implemented in Lucene to support LLMs in search: vector and hybrid search.
- On the other hand, vector search support is quite decent, including quantisation.

8.2 Apache Solr

> The Solr project is a search engine from the Apache Software Foundation (written in Java and exposing REST APIs) that provides traditional keyword-based search and vector search.
>
> It uses Apache Lucene as its core, so it inherits most of its vector search implementations. On top of it, it adds text vectorisation capabilities, interacting with hosted LLMs and more LLM-based features are coming.

Disclaimer The following section describes features up to Apache Solr 9.9 (including some work in progress).

At the time of reading, make sure to check the latest available release version and the release notes: successive releases may bring new LLM-related features.

Apache Solr support for LLM-based features focuses on text vectorisation (indexing and query time), pure vector-search capabilities and hybrid search through linear score combinations.

8.2.1 Text Vectorisation

Apache Solr can interact with LLMs fine-tuned for text vectorisation to encode text to vector at indexing and query time.[3]

Apache Solr itself doesn't operate the LLM in process but uses LangChain4j (see Sect. 7.3) to connect to inference APIs.

This functionality is provided through the "llm" module that needs to be enabled before use.[4]

---

[3] https://solr.apache.org/guide/solr/latest/query-guide/text-to-vector.html
[4] https://solr.apache.org/guide/solr/latest/configuration-guide/solr-modules.html#installing-a-module

8.2 Apache Solr

N.B. This module sends your documents and queries off to some hosted service on the Internet. There are cost, privacy, performance and service availability implications of such a strong dependency that should be diligently examined before employing this module in a serious way.

At the moment, these are the text vectorisation models supported by Solr:

- HuggingFaceEmbeddingModel
- MistralAiEmbeddingModel
- OpenAiEmbeddingModel
- CohereEmbeddingModel

To upload a model:
e.g.
curl -XPUT '.../solr/collection/schema/text-to-vector-model-store' –data-binary "@/path/myModel.json" -H 'Content-type:application/json'

```
{
  "class": "dev.langchain4j.model.huggingface.
      HuggingFaceEmbeddingModel",
  "name": "<an-identifier-for-your-model>",
  "params": {
    "accessToken": "<your-huggingface-api-key>",
    "modelId": "<a-huggingface-vectorisation-model>"
  }
}
```

To view all models:

```
../solr/collection/schema/text-to-vector-model-store
```

To delete the currentModel model:

```
curl -XDELETE '../solr/collection/schema/text-to-vector-model-
    store/currentModel'
```

To view the model you just uploaded:

```
../solr/collection/sschema/text-to-vector-model-store

{
  "class": "dev.langchain4j.model.openai.OpenAiEmbeddingModel",
  "name": "openai-1",
  "params": {
    "baseUrl": "https://api.openai.com/v1",
    "apiKey": "apiKey-openAI",
    "modelName": "text-embedding-3-small",
    "timeout": 60,
    "logRequests": true,
    "logResponses": true,
    "maxRetries": 5
  }
}
```

Indexing

To vectorise textual fields of your documents at indexing time, you need to configure an Update Request Processor Chain in the solrconfig.xml that includes at least one TextToVectorUpdateProcessor update request processor (you can include more than one, if you want to vectorise multiple fields):

```
<updateRequestProcessorChain name="textToVector">
  <processor class="solr.llm.textvectorisation.update.processor.
      TextToVectorUpdateProcessorFactory">
    <str name="inputField">_text_</str>
    <str name="outputField">vector</str>
    <str name="model">dummy-1</str>
  </processor>
  <processor class="solr.RunUpdateProcessorFactory"/>
</updateRequestProcessorChain>
```

The TextToVectorUpdateProcessor update request processor vectorises the content of the "inputField" for each document processed at indexing time.

The resulting vector is added as a value for the "outputField".

To perform the vectorisation, it leverages a "model" you have previously uploaded to the text-to-vector-model-store.

Querying

To run a query that vectorises your query text, using a model you previously uploaded, is simple:

```
?q={!knn_text_to_vector model=a-model f=vector topK=10}hello
    world query
```

The search results retrieved are the k=10 nearest documents to the vector encoded from the query "hello world query", using the model "a-model".

8.2.2 Vector Search

Apache Solr leverages the internals of Lucene to provide vector search.[5]

Generally speaking, a feature is first released in Lucene and then exposed in Solr, but it takes a bit of time, though, as Apache Lucene and Solr are not the same project anymore (they've been for many years).

As a rule of thumb, expect any Lucene breakthrough to reach Solr sooner or later.

Indexing

The DenseVectorField gives the possibility of indexing and searching dense vectors of float elements. For example: [1.0, 2.5, 3.7, 4.1]

Here's how DenseVectorField should be configured in the Solr schema:

---

[5] https://solr.apache.org/guide/solr/latest/query-guide/dense-vector-search.html

8.2 Apache Solr

```
<fieldType name="knn_vector" class="solr.DenseVectorField"
    vectorDimension="4" similarityFunction="cosine"/>
<field name="vector" type="knn_vector" indexed="true" stored="
    true"/>
```

And this is an example of how a Solr document with a vector field looks:

```
[{ "id": "1",
"vector": [1.0, 2.5, 3.7, 4.1]
},
{ "id": "2",
"vector": [1.5, 5.5, 6.7, 65.1]
}
]
```

Solr also offers additional parameters to potentially customise the HNSW graph building. Take a look at the official documentation if you want to know more.

Querying

Apache Solr provides two query parsers to implement vector search: the KNN query parser and the vectorSimilarity query parser. All parsers return scores for retrieved documents that are the approximate distance to the query vector (the similarity metric is defined by the similarityFunction configured at indexing time), and both support pre-filtering the document graph to reduce the number of candidate vectors evaluated (without needing to compute their vector similarity distances).

```
?q={!knn f=vector topK=10}[1.0, 2.0, 3.0, 4.0]
```

Here's an example of a simple vector similarity search:

```
?q={!vectorSimilarity f=vector minReturn=0.7}[1.0, 2.0, 3.0,
    4.0]
```

The search results retrieved are all documents whose similarity with the input vector [1.0, 2.0, 3.0, 4.0] is at least 0.7 based on the similarity function configured at indexing time.

It's also possible to combine lexical and vector search queries via filtering and hybrid search queries. It's not that related to LLMs per se, but if you are curious, this blog gives more details.[6]

8.2.3 Future Work

Being myself the current VP of Apache Solr and chair of the Solr Project Management Committee (PMC), I can give some glimpses into what's coming next for Apache Solr in the space of LLMs.

---

[6] https://sease.io/2023/12/hybrid-search-with-apache-solr.html

The first priority is to expose all Lucene goodies in a usable and flexible way, which includes nested vector support, scalar quantisation and KNN optimisations. Keep an eye on the Solr pull requests to see the progress.[7]

Secondly, there is a bunch of LLM-related functionalities that would be a nice complementary fit in Apache Solr:

- Retrieval augmented generation (see Sect. 4.2)
- Semantic highlighting (see Sect. 4.4)
- LLM query parser (see Sect. 4.8)

Some of these are already work in progress at the time of writing, and with the right sponsorship, may come soon to Apache Solr.

Bear in mind that Apache Solr is fully open source and exists thanks to volunteers and donations; this means that it's not easy to estimate when new features and releases will come.

> **Key Takeaways**

- Apache Solr only support LLMs fine-tuned for text vectorisation and vector search.
- It relies on Lucene as its internal library (inheriting its vector search goodies).
- Reach out if you want to sponsor any of the new contributions!

8.3 OpenSearch

The OpenSearch project is a search engine originally forked from Elasticsearch (written in Java and exposing REST APIs) that provides traditional keyword-based search and vector search.

It uses Apache Lucene as its core (plus another couple of vector engines), so it inherits most of its vector search implementations and more.

On top of it, it adds text/multi-modal vectorisation capabilities, interacting with hosted LLMs and retrieval augmented generation.

Disclaimer The following section describes features up to OpenSearch 3.0 (including some work in progress).

---

[7] https://github.com/apache/solr/pulls

8.3 OpenSearch

At the time of reading, make sure to check the latest available release version and the release notes: successive releases may bring new LLM-related features.

OpenSearch support for LLM-based features focuses on:

- Text/multi-modal vectorisation (indexing and query time)
- Pure vector-search capabilities (including quantisation)
- Learned sparse retrieval
- Cross-encoders reranking
- Semantic highlighting
- Hybrid search through linear score combinations and fusion techniques
- Retrieval augmented generation with message history

8.3.1 Text/Multi-modal Vectorisation

OpenSearch can interact with locally or remotely hosted LLMs fine-tuned for vector embedding generation to provide users with a transparent semantic search experience.[8]

This applies to both text and multi-modal, giving the possibility of also encoding images/audios/videos to vector.

The first step involves defining the model(s) to use.[9]

OpenSearch gives the possibility of hosting certain families of models directly in process (be aware that this is computationally expensive and cool for prototyping, but not recommended in production) or interacting with remotely hosted models.

We'll go through the main concepts, but won't go through low-level details, as there are plenty of official tutorials on the OpenSearch documentation, and they are a better resource if you plan to code and spin up a search solution following a guide.

This chapter is more to give you an understanding of the current state of the art of open source search engines in terms of capabilities and discussions, rather than being an exhaustive snapshot of the official documentation and tutorials.

Let's see how to implement text vectorisation and semantic search in OpenSearch: we'll take a text vectorisation use case as an example, but the process to do multi-modal is quite similar:

Create a Model Group This is a container for models that may be used to solve similar problems.

---

[8] https://docs.opensearch.org/docs/latest/tutorials/vector-search/semantic-search/index/
[9] https://docs.opensearch.org/docs/latest/ml-commons-plugin/integrating-ml-models/#choosing-a-model

Create a Model Connector This details how to connect to a model (remote or self-hosted, if running the model in process, be aware that there are other steps necessary to deploy and run it).

Register the Connector to the Model Group This adds a specific model connector to a group.

At this point, the model is usable through the predict API, and its ID can be used to integrate it in search functionalities:

Indexing

To vectorise textual fields of your documents at indexing time, you need to configure an ingest pipeline:

```
PUT /_ingest/pipeline/nlp-ingest-pipeline
{
  "processors": [
    {
      "text_embedding": {
        "model_id": "modelID",
        "field_map": {"passage_text": "passage_embedding"}
      }
    }
  ]
}
```

Querying

To vectorise your textual query:[10]

```
"query": {
    "neural": {
        "<vector_field>": {
            "query_text": "<query_text>",
            "model_id": "<model_id>",
            "k": 100
        }
    }
}
```

8.3.2 Vector Search

OpenSearch implements vector search leveraging three internal libraries as options:

---

[10] https://docs.opensearch.org/docs/latest/query-dsl/specialized/neural/

8.3 OpenSearch

- Apache Lucene (see Sect. 8.1)
- Faiss[11]
- NMSLIB[12]

In terms of vector data types support OpenSearch supports 32-bit float, 8-bit byte and binary elements.

At indexing time, the first step is to configure the mapping for the field you intend to use to store (and search) vectors:

```
PUT my-knn-index-1
{
  "settings": {
    "index": {
      "knn": true,
      "knn.algo_param.ef_search": 100
    }
  },
  "mappings": {
    "properties": {
      "my_field_vector": {
        "type": "knn_vector",
        "dimension": 100,
        "space_type": "innerproduct",
        "method": {
          "name": "hnsw",
          "engine": "faiss",
          "parameters": {
            "ef_construction": 128,
            "m": 24
          }
        }
      }
    }
  }
}
```

As in many other open source engines you'll see in this chapter, the field definition is quite standard: It requires the user to specify:

- dimension → the vector dimensionality
- space_type → the vector similarity metric
- method.name → the approximate nearest neighbour algorithm to use
- method.engine → the internal library implementation
- method.parameters → and potentially some advanced parameters depending on the algorithm

---

[11] https://github.com/facebookresearch/faiss
[12] https://github.com/nmslib/nmslib

OpenSearch offers three alternative implementations: This is extremely good for flexibility, but it introduces a plethora of parameters for each of them and going beyond the default would be quite intense for a non-expert user.

With flexibility, you sacrifice usability; this is generally true in information technology, and OpenSearch vector search is a clear example: powerful and flexible but much more error-prone for users and vulnerable to bugs (as maintaining three different internal implementations may end up with more frailty).

Indexing documents with vectors is nothing fancy:

```
POST _bulk
{ "index": { "_index": "my-knn-index-1", "_id": "1" } }
{ "my_vector1": [1.5, 2.5], "price": 12.2 }
{ "index": { "_index": "my-knn-index-1", "_id": "2" } }
{ "my_vector1": [2.5, 3.5], "price": 7.1 }
{ "index": { "_index": "my-knn-index-1", "_id": "3" } }
{ "my_vector1": [3.5, 4.5], "price": 12.9 }
...
```

By default, OpenSearch supports the indexing and querying of vectors of 32-bit float elements.

OpenSearch supports many varieties of quantisation. In general, the level of quantisation will provide a trade-off between the accuracy of the nearest neighbour search and the size of the memory footprint consumed by the vector search (see Sect. 4.1.2).

Leveraging its internal libraries, OpenSearch provides:

- Apache Lucene scalar quantisation[13]
- Faiss scalar quantisation[14]
- Faiss product quantisation[15]
- Faiss binary quantisation[16]

There's no quick recommendation on which quantisation to use, in general or applied to OpenSearch.

The rule of thumb is to start looking at quantisation if you are unhappy with the query time latency and memory footprint of your vector search.

Quantisation is lossy, so it's a matter of compromise.

You can experiment iteratively and measure how much quantising is impacting your recall at the benefit of reduced resource cost.

---

[13] https://docs.opensearch.org/docs/latest/vector-search/optimizing-storage/lucene-scalar-quantization/

[14] https://docs.opensearch.org/docs/latest/vector-search/optimizing-storage/faiss-16-bit-quantization/

[15] https://docs.opensearch.org/docs/latest/vector-search/optimizing-storage/faiss-product-quantization/

[16] https://docs.opensearch.org/docs/latest/vector-search/optimizing-storage/binary-quantization/

You may stop with scalar quantisation or go deep up to binary depending on your use case and the compromises you are willing to accept to get acceptable resource consumption.

Querying

To query your vector field, you can run k-nearest neighbour retrieval or similarity-based search.[17] OpenSearch also supports filtering and post-filtering to combine vectors with lexical search and hybrid search.[18]

```
GET /my-nlp-index/_search
{
  "query": {
    "knn": {
      "<vector_field>": {
        "vector": [<vector_values>],
        "k": <k_value>,
        "max_distance": <threshold>,
        "min_score": <threshold>,
      }
    }
  }
}
```

8.3.3 Nested Vectors Search

Vector embedding models are LLMs fine-tuned for sentence similarity, and most of the time, they work better on shorter texts.

The recommendation is always to carefully look at the model you choose, verifying its fine-tuning dataset (where available) to have a clear understanding of the sentence length the model is best suited for.

Taking a look at the sample datasets that were used for training can give you a better insight into the kind of data the model is fine-tuned to work on: the closer your data is, the better.

Generally, if the query and the documents present similar textual length, it's more likely you'll get a successful semantic search implementation.

For this reason is very common to split long documents into chunks, vectorise chunks and then perform vector search.

The idea is to retrieve the best chunks and then return the original parent document.

For this reason, it's a common need to offer the possibility of nesting vectors (with potential additional metadata) in documents, where each vector represents a chunk of the document itself.

---

[17] https://docs.opensearch.org/docs/latest/query-dsl/specialized/k-nn/index/
[18] https://docs.opensearch.org/docs/latest/vector-search/ai-search/hybrid-search/index/

Indexing

To index nested vectors, first you need to define a nested mapping where the nested document has at least one vector field:

Mapping

```
PUT my-knn-index-1
{
  "settings": {
    "index": {
      "knn": true
    }
  },
  "mappings": {
    "properties": {
      "chunk": {
        "type": "nested",
        "properties": {
          "my_vector": {
            "type": "knn_vector",
            "dimension": 3,
            ...
          },
          "color": {
            "type": "text",
            "index": false
          }
        }
      }
    }
  }
}
```

And index documents following the nested field standard:

```
PUT _bulk?refresh=true
{ "index": { "_index": "my-knn-index-1", "_id": "1" } }
{"chunk":[
    {"my_vector":[1,1,1], "color": "blue"},
    {"my_vector":[2,2,2], "color": "yellow"},
    {"my_vector":[3,3,3], "color": "white"}
    ]}
{ "index": { "_index": "my-knn-index-1", "_id": "2" } }
{"chunk":[
    {"my_vector":[10,10,10], "color": "red"},
    {"my_vector":[20,20,20], "color": "green"},
    {"my_vector":[30,30,30], "color": "black"}
    ]}
```

Querying

To query your vector field, you can run k-nearest neighbour retrieval or similarity-based search on the nested field (using a nested query).

Syntactically, there's not much difference with any other nested query, but behind the scenes, OpenSearch uses the Lucene DiversifyingChildrenFloatKnnVectorQuery (or the byte implementation, depending on your vector element data type) and an equivalent implementation in Faiss.

This means that the user doesn't see this complexity and, out of the box, gets the most efficient implementation that guarantees the top-k parents retrieval.

That's the key aspect, as while retrieving chunks from the nearest neighbour candidates, the algorithm needs to pay attention to their relation with the parents, making sure that only the best chunk is kept for a single parent (replacing it with a new, better one if found).

```
GET my-knn-index-1/_search
{
  "query": {
    "nested": {
      "path": "nested_field",
      "query": {
        "knn": {
          "nested_field.my_vector": {
            "vector": [1,1,1],
            "k": 2
          }
        }
      }
    }
  }
}
```

Out of the box, this query will just return the parent documents (the document the nested field/chunk belongs to).

OpenSearch also supports the possibility of returning the best/all chunks for a given returned document, which can be quite handy if you also need to return the chunks to the user to explain why the top document was chosen.

Especially in the domain of vector search, explainability is extremely important: potentially, there is no keyword match at all, and, being the document potentially long, showing the paragraph with the highest semantic similarity to the user can give a glimpse of why the document was returned in the first place.

Another important aspect is the filtering support; it's very common to have the necessity to mix vector search with lexical filters, and OpenSearch supports that in nested vector search for both parents and children:

This means you can retrieve children filtering by lexical conditions while performing vector search and then further refine the parents based on filtering conditions that apply to the parent metadata.

8.3.4 Learned Sparse Retrieval

OpenSearch supports some learned sparse retrieval models (to refresh on the concept, see the dedicated Sect. 4.1.3).

They have been specifically trained by the OpenSearch team on public datasets.[19]

Their approach is built upon SPLADE with several contributions [1].

Indexing

To build a sparse vector representation of a field, this is the ingest pipeline configuration:

```
PUT /_ingest/pipeline/nlp-ingest-pipeline
{
  "processors": [
    {
      "sparse_encoding": {
        "model_id": "<bi-encoder or doc-only model ID>",
        "field_map": {
          "passage_text": "passage_embedding"
        }
      }
    }
  ]
}
```

The learned token weights (that form the sparse vectors) are stored in Lucene org.apache.lucene.document.FeatureField.

Querying

At query time, the query text is encoded to a sparse vector and then the inverted index is accessed for the retrieval phase.

OpenSearch supports two search modes:

Bi-encoder mode (requires a sparse encoding model): A sparse encoding model generates sparse vector embeddings of both documents (fields) and query text.

After encoding the query to a sparse vector, it's parsed into Lucene disjunctive feature queries (FeatureQuery(termA) OR FeatureQuery(termB) OR FeatureQuery(termC) ...).

Each FeatureQuery looks through the corresponding token's posting list.

Similarly to traditional lexical inverted index approaches (such as BM25), the search time complexity depends on the number of query terms (accesses to the inverted index) and each term's posting list length.

Learned sparse encoding is generally less sparse than traditional lexical approaches (effectively, both query and document expansion happen).

The result is that the latency is increased in comparison to the traditional inverted index approach.

---

[19] https://huggingface.co/opensearch-project/opensearch-neural-sparse-encoding-v2-distill

Doc-only mode (requires a sparse encoding model and a tokeniser): The query is just tokenised, and for each token the associated weight is extracted from a lookup table.

It's cheaper as no query expansion happens, but this also impacts relevance.

An example of a query follows:

```
GET my-nlp-index/_search
{
  "query": {
    "neural_sparse": {
      "passage_embedding": {
        "query_text": "Hello world",
        "model_id": "<ID of the model>"
      }
    }
  }
}
```

In terms of performance, OpenSearch also supports GPU acceleration, so keep an eye on it if you have the possibility for your project.

If you are curious about some benchmarks and additional details, this blog proved quite useful.[20]

8.3.5 Cross-encoders for Reranking

We talked about cross-encoders when exploring various alternatives in terms of how to fine-tune and use LLMs for first-stage retrieval or reranking (see Sect. 4.1.5).

To refresh a bit on them, they are LLMs fine-tuned to be able to return a similarity score for a query concatenated to a document in input; the higher the score, the more semantically similar the query is to the document.

Being more expensive than bi-encoders (that encode the query and document separately to vectors), cross-encoders are normally used for reranking a subset of the first-stage retrieval candidate results.

Cross-encoders tend to be better at capturing semantic similarity between pieces of text.

They can be configured in OpenSearch as a specific rerank processor, with the "ml_opensearch" type.[21]

Specify the document field that will be used to calculate the reranking score. The query context will be passed dynamically at query time.

---

[20] https://opensearch.org/blog/A-deep-dive-into-faster-semantic-sparse-retrieval-in-OS-2.12/
[21] https://docs.opensearch.org/docs/latest/search-plugins/search-relevance/rerank-cross-encoder/

Rerank Definition

```
PUT /_search/pipeline/my_pipeline
{
  "response_processors": [
    {
      "rerank": {
        "ml_opensearch": {
          "model_id": "cross-encoder-Id"
        },
        "context": {
          "document_fields": [
            "passage_text"
          ]
        }
      }
    }
  ]
}
```

At query time, the documents resulting from the query are rescored with the similarity score processed by the cross-encoder.

Rerank Query

```
POST /my-index/_search
{
  "query": {
    "match": {
      "passage_text": "how to welcome in family"
    }
  },
  "ext": {
    "rerank": {
      "query_context": {
        "query_text": "how to welcome in family"
      }
    }
  }
}
```

Aside from a couple of small cross-encoders trained on MS-Marco,[22] openSearch supports the TorchScript and ONNX formats to deploy your own cross-encoder.

---

[22] https://github.com/microsoft/MSMARCO-Passage-Ranking

8.3.6 Semantic Highlighting

We talked about the application of LLMs for semantic highlighting already (see Sect. 4.4).

The idea of it in OpenSearch is to process the search results, document by document, segmenting each sentence and applying a classifier that assesses if the sentence is relevant or not for the query.[23]

The concept is similar to cross-encoding, but the underlying models supported are different.

First of all, OpenSearch leverages an internal text segmentation algorithm to build a candidate list of sentences for each document.

It's a pretty old-style approach based on regular expressions and heuristics to handle abbreviations and quotes; it's unclear why a dedicated library was not used.

In terms of model support, a pre-trained one is available directly in OpenSearch, but very little information is shared on its internals.[24]

Given that we talked about this in the dedicated chapter, it was worth mentioning the feature, but it's uncertain whether it uses some sort of fine-tuned LLM for the task.

For sure, it doesn't use general-purpose remotely hosted LLMs.

8.3.7 Retrieval Augmented Generation with Conversation History

The idea is to support conversational search, allowing the user to send queries in natural language and refine the results and generated snippets by asking follow-up questions.

It uses explicitly general-purpose LLMs, enriching each request with a context coming from your OpenSearch corpus of information (retrieved results) and your current session interactions (conversation history).

The conversation history is just a storage for messages (including the user query and the response), grouped by conversation session.

The Retrieval Augmented Generation pipeline is implemented through a search pipeline containing a retrieval-augmented generation processor.

The processor intercepts the OpenSearch query results, retrieves previous messages from the conversation history and sends both of them as additional context in the prompt to the LLM.

After the processor receives a response, it saves the response in the conversation history and returns both the query results (used as context) and the generated snippet.

---

[23] https://docs.opensearch.org/docs/latest/tutorials/vector-search/semantic-highlighting-tutorial/
[24] https://huggingface.co/opensearch-project/opensearch-semantic-highlighter-v1

To enable such functionality, the first step is to activate both components:

```
PUT /_cluster/settings
{
  "persistent": {
    "plugins.ml_commons.memory_feature_enabled": true,
    "plugins.ml_commons.rag_pipeline_feature_enabled": true
  }
}
```

The part related to the model definition is pretty much the same we've seen with the vector embedding models; the difference here is that the model connector points to a remotely hosted general-purpose LLM.

The next step is to configure a search pipeline:

```
PUT /_search/pipeline/rag_pipeline
{
  "response_processors": [
    {
      "retrieval_augmented_generation": {
        "model_id": "modelId",
        "context_field_list": ["text"],
        "system_prompt": "You are a helpful assistant",
        "user_instructions": "Generate a concise and informative
            answer in less than 100 words for the given
            question"
      }
    }
  ]
}
```

Aside from boilerplate and obvious parameters, we should focus on the:

- "context_field_list"—That defines the fields from the search result documents, used as context for the RAG prompt.
- "system_prompt"—That defines the tone for the response; this is customisable, but there's not really a list of supported personas to choose from right now when we interact with general-purpose LLMs, so its utility and accuracy are debatable.
- "user_instructions"—That's the prompt, customisable as well.

Once the response processor is set up, we can configure the conversation history session:

```
POST /_plugins/_ml/memory/
{
  "name": "Conversation session 1"
}
```

Be aware that it's your responsibility to group the interactions within the same "memory".

This means that your application layer should manage sessions and recognise when it's needed to create a new one.

Be careful with that or you risk creating increasingly long and mixed-up contexts that get sent to the LLM (with performance and costs impact).

The more cohesive the context, the better the response from the LLM, so pay attention to keep each memory focused.

The last step is to make a query that uses the memory created and the RAG pipeline:

```
GET /my_rag_test_data/_search
{
  "query": {
    "match": {
      "text": "What's the population of London in 2025"
    }
  },
  "ext": {
    "generative_qa_parameters": {
      "llm_question": "What's the population of London in 2025",
      "memory_id": "memoryId",
      "context_size": 5,
      "message_size": 5,
      "timeout": 15
    }
  }
}
```

- llm_question → the main natural language query to send to the LLM.
- memory_id → the pipeline retrieves the "message_size" most recent messages in the specified memory and adds them to the LLM prompt.
- context_size → the number of search results sent to the LLM.
- message_size → the number of messages from the memory sent to the LLM. The default is set to 10.

Particular attention should be paid to the context and message size as they mitigate the problem of excessively long memory sessions, and keep the context length (and related costs/latency) under control.

> **Key Takeaways**

- OpenSearch offers deep support for dense vector search through Lucene, Faiss and NMSLIB libraries.
- Text and multi-modal vectorisation are supported both through in-process and remotely hosted models.
- Cross-encoders are supported for reranking.
- OpenSearch supports the interaction with general-purpose, remotely hosted LLMs to provide retrieval augmented generation with chat memory.

8.4 Elasticsearch

> The Elasticsearch project is a search engine server (written in Java and exposing REST APIs) that provides traditional keyword-based search and vector search.
>
> It uses Apache Lucene as its core, so it inherits most of its vector search implementations. Focusing on the open source version, Elasticsearch offers vector search only.

Disclaimer The following section describes features up to Elasticsearch 9.0 (including some work in progress). At the time of writing, the only LLM-related feature offered by the open source version of Elasticsearch is vector search.

Everything else is under Platinum/Enterprise licenses, so it won't be covered here. It was not that easy to navigate this information, as the blog and the documentation are quite fuzzy about it. After several investigations, the results were that:

When downloading Elasticsearch, it comes with a one-month trial license that includes all Elastic features. After the trial period, the license reverts to Free and open—Basic.[25] Refer to Elastic subscriptions for more information.[26] At the time of reading, make sure to check the latest available release version and the release notes: successive releases may bring new LLM-related features.

8.4.1 Vector Search

Elasticsearch implements vector search leveraging the internal Apache Lucene implementation.

In terms of vector data types support Elasticsearch supports 32-bit float, 8-bit byte and binary elements.[27]

At indexing time, the first step is to configure the mapping for the field you intend to use to store (and search) vectors:

```
PUT my-index-2
{
  "mappings": {
    "properties": {
      "my_vector": {
```

---

[25] https://github.com/elastic/elasticsearch

[26] https://www.elastic.co/subscriptions

[27] https://www.elastic.co/docs/reference/elasticsearch/mapping-reference/dense-vector#dense-vector-params

8.4 Elasticsearch

```
      "type": "dense_vector",
      "dims": 3,
      "similarity": "dot_product"
}}}}
```

As in many other open source engines you'll see in this chapter, the field definition is quite standard: It requires the user to specify:

- dims → the vector dimensionality
- similarity → the vector similarity metric

Indexing documents with vectors is nothing fancy:

```
POST /my-vectors/_bulk?refresh
{"index": {"_id" : "1"}}
{"my_vector": [127, -127, 0, 1, 42]}
{"index": {"_id" : "2"}}
{"my_vector": [127, 55, 0, 1, 42]}
...
```

By default, Elasticsearch supports the indexing and querying of vectors of 32-bit float elements, using 8-bit scalar quantisation: "int8_hnsw".

Elasticsearch supports three varieties of quantisation. In general, the level of quantisation provides a trade-off between the accuracy of the nearest neighbour search and the size of the memory footprint consumed by the vector search (see Sect. 4.1.2).

- **int8**—Quantises each dimension of the vector to 1-byte integers. This reduces the memory footprint by 75% (or 4×) at the cost of accuracy.
- **int4**—Quantises each dimension of the vector to half-byte integers. This reduces the memory footprint by 87% (or 8×) at the cost of accuracy.
- **bbq**—Better binary quantisation which reduces each dimension to a single bit precision. This reduces the memory footprint by 96% (or 32×) at a larger cost of accuracy. Generally, oversampling during query time and reranking can help mitigate the accuracy loss.

There's no quick recommendation on which quantisation to use, as already stated for OpenSearch.

You can experiment iteratively and measure how much quantising is impacting your recall at the benefit of reduced resource cost.

When using a quantised format, at query time you could retrieve more results (higher top-k) and rescore the results using the original raw vector.[28]

N.B. When using quantisation, the original float vector values are kept on disk for reranking, reindexing and quantisation improvements over the lifetime of the data.

---

[28] https://www.elastic.co/docs/solutions/search/vector/knn#dense-vector-knn-search-rescoring

This means disk usage in comparison to not using quantisation will increase by ~25% for int8, ~12.5% for int4 and ~3.1% for bbq due to the overhead of storing the quantised vectors on top of the original ones.

Querying

To query your vector field, you can run k-nearest neighbour retrieval or similarity-based search. Elasticsearch also supports filtering and post-filtering to combine vectors with lexical search.

```
POST image-index/_search
{
  "knn": {
    "field": "image-vector",
    "query_vector": [-5, 9, -12],
    "k": 10,
    "num_candidates": 100,
    'similarity': 0.7
  }
}
```

From the above, at this point of the book, you should be familiar with all the parameters except "num_candidates" and possibly "similarity".

This is the number of nearest neighbour candidates to consider per shard while doing knn search, while "k" is the number of results that will be returned.

Also, "similarity" may be a bit misleading; that's the minimum acceptable similarity score, in case we want to exclude results that don't meet the bar.

8.4.2 Nested Vectors Search

Offering the possibility of indexing and querying nested vectors is practical for scenarios where long documents get chunked into paragraphs and users need to retrieve the top-k parent documents based on the top matching children.

We've talked about this extensively, so let's jump to the details:

Indexing

To index nested vectors, first you need to define a nested mapping where the nested document has at least one vector field:

Mapping

```
PUT my-knn-index-1
{
    "mappings": {
        "properties": {
            "chunk": {
                "type": "nested",
                "properties": {
                    "my_vector": {
                        "type": "dense_vector",
```

8.4 Elasticsearch

```
            "dims": 3,
        },...
}}}}}
```

And index documents following the nested field standard:

Indexing

```
PUT _bulk?refresh=true
{ "index": { "_index": "my-knn-index-1", "_id": "1" } }
{"chunk":[
    {"my_vector":[1,1,1]},
    {"my_vector":[2,2,2]},
    {"my_vector":[3,3,3]}
]}
{ "index": { "_index": "my-knn-index-1", "_id": "2" } }
{"chunk":[
    {"my_vector":[10,10,10]},
    {"my_vector":[20,20,20]},
    {"my_vector":[30,30,30]}
]}
```

Querying

To query your vector field, you can run k-nearest neighbour retrieval or similarity-based search on the nested field (using a nested query).

Syntactically, there's not much difference with any other nested query, but behind the scenes, Elasticsearch uses the Lucene DiversifyingChildrenFloatKnnVectorQuery (or the byte implementation, depending on your vector element data type).

This means that the user doesn't see this complexity and, out of the box, gets the most efficient implementation that guarantees the top-k parents retrieval.

That's the key aspect, as while retrieving chunks from the nearest neighbour candidates, the algorithm needs to pay attention to their relation with the parents, making sure that only the best chunk is kept for a single parent (replacing it with a new, better one if found).

```
POST my-knn-index-1/_search
{
    ...
    "knn": {
        "query_vector": [
            0.45,
            45
        ],
        "field": "chunk.my_vector",
        "k": 2,
        "num_candidates": 2
    }
}
```

Out of the box, this query will just return the parent documents (the document the nested field/chunk belongs to).

Elasticsearch also supports the possibility of returning the best/all chunks for a given returned document, which can be quite handy if you also need to return the chunks to the user to explain why the top document was chosen.

Especially in the domain of vector search, explainability is extremely important: potentially, there is no keyword match at all, and being the document potentially long, showing the paragraph with the highest semantic similarity to the user can give a glimpse of why the document was returned in the first place.

Another important aspect is the filtering support; it's very common to have the necessity to mix vector search with lexical filters, and Elasticsearch supports that in nested vector search for both parents and children:

This means you can retrieve children filtering by lexical conditions while performing vector search and then further refine the parents based on filtering conditions that apply to the parent metadata.

> **Key Takeaways**

- There's little implemented in open source Elasticsearch to support LLMs in search: just vector search.
- Vector search support is quite decent, including all the Lucene variations of quantisation.
- Platinum and Enterprise versions of Elasticsearch offer more features, but are not open source.

8.5 Vespa

The Vespa project is a search engine (written in Java and C++ and exposing REST APIs) that enables organisations to efficiently manage and analyse large, evolving datasets using a combination of vector/traditional search, structured data handling and machine-learned model inference. It has dedicated modules to use local and remote general-purpose LLMs for retrieval augmented generation and document enrichment.

Disclaimer The following section describes features up to Vespa 8.530.11 (including some work in progress).

Vespa development is based on a solid continuous integration/continuous deployment philosophy, which means that "new versions" are much more frequent than other open source search engines (with fewer press releases and release notes). Their

8.5 Vespa

GitHub[29] and their building framework[30] should guide you into finding new features released after the time of writing.

Vespa support for LLM-based features focuses on:

- Text/multi-modal vectorisation (indexing and query time)
- Pure vector-search capabilities (including quantisation and GPU acceleration)
- Learned sparse retrieval
- Cross-encoders and late interaction models reranking
- Hybrid search through linear score combinations and fusion techniques
- Retrieval augmented generation
- Document enrichment through LLMs

8.5.1 Text/Multi-modal Vectorisation

Vespa can interact with locally or remotely hosted LLMs fine-tuned for vector embedding generation to provide users with a transparent semantic search experience.[31]

This applies to both text and multi-modal, giving the possibility of also encoding images/audios/videos to vector.

Vespa can host certain families of models directly in process through ONNX files (be aware that this is computationally expensive) or interact with external models.

This means you can rely on a set of embedders explicitly supported that can run in the Vespa process or create a customised embedder implementation that calls models external to Vespa (potentially self-hosted locally or hosted remotely as a service).

When encoding text to vector internally in Vespa, if possible, you should use GPU acceleration to improve performance and reduce costs.

As for the other open source search engines, we'll go through the main concepts, but won't go through low-level details as there are plenty of official tutorials on the Vespa documentation and blog, and they are a better resource if you plan to code and spin up a search solution following a guide.

Let's see how to implement text vectorisation and semantic search in Vespa: we'll take a text vectorisation use case as an example, but the process to do multi-modal is quite similar. The first step involves defining the embedder to use in the "services.xml".

```
<container id="default" version="1.0">
    <component id="hf-embedder" type="hugging-face-embedder">
        <transformer-model path="my-models/model.onnx"/>
```

---

[29] https://github.com/vespa-engine/vespa
[30] https://factory.vespa.ai/
[31] https://docs.vespa.ai/en/embedding.html

```
            <tokenizer-model path="my-models/tokenizer.json"/>
            <prepend>
                <query>query:</query>
                <document>passage:</document>
            </prepend>
        </component>
        ...
</container>
```

N.B. The main configuration involves loading the model files (transformer and tokeniser); some additional parameters may be necessary depending on the model.

In the above example, a prefix is concatenated to the text to encode to differentiate the query from the document encoding. Some models may give this possibility, always check the model you aim to use and read its documentation.

At this point, the embedder is usable and can be used to integrate it in search functionalities:

Indexing

To vectorise textual fields of your documents at indexing time, you need to configure the schema:

```
schema doc {

    document doc {

        field title type string {
            indexing: summary | index
        }

    }

    field embeddings type tensor<bfloat16>(x[384]) {
        indexing {
            input title | embed embedderId | attribute | index
        }
    }

}
```

We'll see more about pure vector search in a later section, but to give more context, this configuration defines the vector element data type (bfloat16) and dimensionality (384).

Querying

To vectorise your textual query:

```
{
    "yql": "select * from doc where {targetHits:10}
        nearestNeighbor(embedding_field, query_embedding)",
    "text": "my text to embed",
```

```
4        "input.query(query_embedding)": "embed(@text)",
5    }
```

8.5.2 Vector Search

Vespa implements vector search through both exact (very expensive) and approximate nearest neighbour (using Hierarchical Navigable Small World graph under the hood).

In terms of vector data types support Vespa supports 64-bit double, 32-bit float, 16-bit float and 8-bit signed integer.

For binary vectors, the 8-bit signed integer type is used.[32]

At indexing time, the first step is to configure the schema for the field you intend to use to store (and search) vectors:

```
1  schema product {
2
3      document product {
4          ...
5          field text_embedding type tensor<float>(x[384]) {
6              ...
7              attribute {
8                  distance-metric: prenormalized-angular
9      }}}}
```

As in many other open source engines you'll see in this chapter, the field definition is quite standard: It requires the user to specify:

- float → 32-bit vector element type
- x[384] → the vector dimensionality
- distance-metric → the vector similarity metric to use at indexing time to build the HNSW graph

Indexing documents with vectors is nothing fancy:

```
1   [
2       {
3           "put": "id:shopping:product::998211",
4           "fields": {
5               ...
6               "text_embedding": [0.07, 0.32, 0.65, ..]
7           }
8       },
9       {
10          "put": "id:shopping:product::97711",
11          "fields": {
```

---

[32] https://docs.vespa.ai/en/binarizing-vectors.html

```
12              ...
13              "text_embedding": [0.03, 0.24, 0.61, ..]
14          }
15      }
16  ]
```

By default, Vespa supports the indexing and querying of vectors of 64-bit double elements. For production use cases, it's recommended to start your benchmarks with a 32-bit float data type.

Vespa supports many varieties of quantisation. In general, the level of quantisation will provide a trade-off between the accuracy of the nearest neighbour search and the size of the memory footprint consumed by the vector search (see Sect. 4.1.2).

Vespa out of the box supports only naive binary quantisation through "converters".[33]

This is extremely lossy when applied to standard embedding models (not specifically trained to work on binary elements) but brings huge benefits in memory: it just encodes the vector element to 0/1 depending on whether the element is higher or lower than a threshold. Then multiple elements of the original vector are packed into 8-bit integers for storage (they will be unpacked at query time). This means there is a compression of the vector element type (up to 8-bit integers) and vector dimensionality.

For the rest, you should quantise outside Vespa or use embedding models that are already returning certain element types in output.

Querying

To query your vector field, you first need to define a rank profile for nearest neighbour search:

```
1  rank-profile semantic_similarity {
2      inputs {
3          query(query_embedding) tensor<float>(x[384])
4      }
5      first-phase {
6          expression: closeness(field, text_embedding)
7      }
8  }
```

To run the query:

```
1  {
2      "yql": "select * from product where
3      {targetHits: 100}nearestNeighbor(text_embedding,
          query_embedding)",
4      "input.query(query_embedding)": [ 0.22, 0.11, 0.94, ...],
5      "ranking.profile": "semantic_similarity",
6      "hits": 10
7  }
```

---

[33] https://docs.vespa.ai/en/reference/indexing-language-reference.html#converters

Vespa also supports filtering and post-filtering to combine vectors with lexical search and hybrid search.[34]

8.5.3 Multi-vectors Search

As seen in other open source search engines, it is very common to split long documents into chunks, vectorise chunks and then perform vector search.

The idea is to retrieve the best chunks and then return the original parent document.

Vespa supports this via multi-valued vectors per field in the document.

Schema
To index multi-value vectors, first you need to define the schema:

```
schema wiki {
  document wiki {
    field title type string {}
    field paragraphs type array<string> {}
    field paragraph_embeddings type tensor<float>(p{},x[384]) {}
  }
}
```

This definition states that the field "paragraph_embeddings" stores an undefined number of vectors of 384 dimensions.

The documents are indexed following the multi-valued field standard:

Indexing

```
{
  "put": "id:wikipedia:wiki::Metric_space",
  "fields": {
    "title": "Metric space",
    "paragraphs": [
      "In mathematics, a metric space...",
      "strings can be equipped with the Hamming distance, which
          measures the number.. "
    ],
    "paragraph_embeddings": {
      "0": [0.12,0.03,....,0.04],
      "1": [0.03, 0.02,...,0.02]
    }
  }
}
```

The label for the vector is useful when returning the result snippets.

---

[34] https://docs.vespa.ai/en/tutorials/hybrid-search.html

Querying

The query won't change, except for the ranking profile that can add the "match-features" parameter, responsible for returning the label of the closest vector, which can be later used to return the best matching paragraph in the response.

```
rank-profile semantic inherits default {
  inputs {
    query(q) tensor<float>(x[384])
  }
  first-phase {
    expression: cos(closeness(field, paragraph_embeddings))
  }
  match-features: closest(paragraph_embeddings)
}
```

8.5.4 Learned Sparse Retrieval

Vespa supports SPLADE models for learned sparse retrieval (to refresh on the concept, see the dedicated Sect. 4.1.3).

They can be used both for retrieval and reranking.

Indexing

To build a sparse vector representation of a field, the configuration involves defining an embedder:

```
<container version="1.0">
    <component id="splade" type="splade-embedder">
        <transformer-model path="models/splade_model.onnx"/>
        <tokenizer-model path="models/tokenizer.json"/>
    </component>
</container>
```

And then using the embedder to encode text to a sparse vector (this is pretty much the same we've seen for vector search.

Out of the box, the embedder output is a tensor that can be used for reranking.[35]

To use a learned sparse representation for top-k retrieval, Vespa supports the weighted set feature and the wand query:[36]

```
schema doc {

  field sparse_rep type weightedset<int> {
      indexing: summary | attribute
      attribute: fast-search
  }
}
```

---

[35] https://github.com/vespa-engine/sample-apps/tree/master/splade
[36] https://blog.vespa.ai/redefining-hybrid-search-possibilities-with-vespa/

8.5.5 Cross-encoders and Late Interaction Models for Reranking

We talked about cross-encoders when exploring various alternatives in terms of how to fine-tune and use LLMs for first-stage retrieval or reranking (see Sect. 4.1.5).

To refresh a bit on them, they are LLMs fine-tuned to be able to return a similarity score for a query concatenated to a document in input; the higher the score, the more semantically similar the query is to the document.

Being more expensive than bi-encoders (that encode the query and document separately to vectors), cross-encoders are normally used for reranking a subset of the first-stage retrieval candidate results.

Cross-encoders tend to be better at capturing semantic similarity between pieces of text.

Vespa supports cross-encoders through the Open Neural Network Exchange (ONNX[37]) format.

Each model depends on a tokeniser approach, so it's also needed to pass it to Vespa to make sure they are aligned.

For the full details, the recommendation is to follow the documentation guide.[38]

An interesting optimisation offered by Vespa is the possibility of pre-tokenising the documents and query, so that when the similarity score happens, that passage can be skipped and performance optimised. Normally, tokenisation is repeated for each pair of query and document in cross-encoding.

On the other hand, late interaction models encode both the query and the documents into a multi-vector representation (see Sect. 4.1.4).

They tend to be less expensive than cross-encoders but still more costly than running approximate nearest neighbour on bi-encoders' vectorised text.

For this reason, they are generally employed as rerankers as well.

As a first step, it's necessary to define the ColBERT embedder. The component has the responsibility of encoding a text into an array of vectors.

```
<container version="1.0">
    <component id="colbert" type="colbert-embedder">
        <transformer-model url="https://huggingface.co/colbert-
            ir/colbertv2.0/resolve/main/model.onnx"/>
        <tokenizer-model url="https://huggingface.co/colbert-ir/
            colbertv2.0/raw/main/tokenizer.json"/>
        <max-query-tokens>32</max-query-tokens>
        <max-document-tokens>128</max-document-tokens>
    </component>
</container>
```

The parameters are self-explicit but pay particular attention to the max tokens (both at query and document time) as this regulates how much of the text is vectorised (impacting both performance and quality of your results).

---

[37] https://onnx.ai/
[38] https://docs.vespa.ai/en/cross-encoders.html

Then, the embedder is added to the schema:

```
schema doc {
    document doc {
        field text type string {..}
    }
    field colbert_tokens type tensor<float>(token{}, x[128]) {
        indexing: input text | embed colbert | attribute
    }
}
```

Encoding a vector per token, the cardinality of the tensor is the number of tokens (token) while each vector has a dimensionality that depends on the model (128 in this example).

The query time implementation for the max similarity is defined in a rank profile:

```
# See https://docs.vespa.ai/en/ranking.html
    rank-profile default inherits default {
        inputs {
            query(queryTokens) tensor<float>(queryTokens{}, x
                [128])
            query(q) tensor<bfloat16>(x[384])
        }
        function unpack() {
            expression: unpack_bits(attribute(colbert))
        }

        function max_sim() {
            expression {
                sum(
                    reduce(
                        sum(
                            query(queryTokens) * unpack() , x
                        ),
                        max, documentTokens
                    ),
                    queryTokens
                )
            }
        }
```

For a better understanding of the formula, I encourage you to look back at the max similarity definition in Sect. 4.1.4 and the Vespa tutorial.[39]

8.5.6 Local or Remote LLMs

Vespa supports the integration with general-purpose LLMs directly in process or through external services (self-hosted or remote APIs).

---

[39] https://github.com/vespa-engine/sample-apps/tree/master/colbert

8.5 Vespa

Running LLMs locally offers various advantages, particularly in terms of data security and privacy; sensitive information remains within the confines of the application or network, eliminating the risks associated with sharing delicate data with external services.

To set up an inference engine in Vespa,[40] the first step is the "services.xml":

```xml
<services version="1.0">
    <container id="default" version="1.0">

        ...

        <component id="local" class="ai.vespa.llm.clients.
            LocalLLM">
            <config name="ai.vespa.llm.clients.llm-local-client"
                >
                <model url="..." />
            </config>
        </component>

        ...

    </container>
</services>
```

Internally, Vespa uses llama.cpp,[41] so all their supported models are compatible.

Running the model within Vespa is extremely useful to have a self-contained app, especially for quick prototyping.

Should you use this paradigm in production?

Probably not: you may want more flexibility in the design of your inference code, potentially using other libraries rather than llama.cpp, and potentially fine-tuning the resource management and scalability ad hoc for the inference part only, keeping it separate from the search engine.

Vespa also gets you covered in this scenario as it allows the configuration for remote LLMs (running outside Vespa).

Vespa provides a client compatible with OpenAI-style APIs.

This includes, but is not limited to, OpenAI, Google Gemini, Anthropic, Cohere and Together.ai, or you can also host your own OpenAI-compatible server using VLLM or llama-cpp-server.[42]

The first step, as usual, is in the "services.xml":

```xml
<services version="1.0">
    <container id="default" version="1.0">

        ...

```

---

[40] https://docs.vespa.ai/en/llms-local.html
[41] https://github.com/ggml-org/llama.cpp
[42] https://docs.vespa.ai/en/llms-external.html

```
 6        <component id="openai" class="ai.vespa.llm.clients.
             OpenAI">
 7
 8           <!-- Optional configuration: -->
 9           <config name="ai.vespa.llm.clients.llm-client">
10              <apiKeySecretName> ... </apiKeySecretName>
11              <!-- endpoint example: https://openai-compatible
                   -api.com/v1/ -->
12              <endpoint> ... </endpoint>
13           </config>
14
15        </component>
16
17        ...
18
19     </container>
20  </services>
```

For the full list of parameters, please refer to the documentation.

The important bit here is to know that the compatibility is with the API rather than the LLM service itself: if it's compatible with the input/output, it's usable.

8.5.7 Retrieval Augmented Generation

We've talked extensively about retrieval augmented generation in Sect. 4.2.

In Vespa, the RAGSearcher first performs the query as specified by the user, creates a prompt based on the results and queries the language model to generate a response.[43]

To enable such functionality, the first step is to specify the LLM connection and the searcher:

```
1  <services version="1.0">
2     <container id="default" version="1.0">
3        <component id="LLM" class="ai.vespa.llm.clients.OpenAI">
4           <!-- Configure as required -->
5        </component>
6     </container>
7  </services>
```

Searcher

```
1  <services version="1.0">
2     <container id="default" version="1.0">
3        ...
4        <search>
5           <chain id="rag" inherits="vespa">
```

---
[43] https://docs.vespa.ai/en/llms-rag.html

```
            <searcher id="ai.vespa.search.llm.RAGSearcher">
                <config name="ai.vespa.search.llm.llm-
                    searcher">
                    <providerId>LLM</providerId>
                </config>
            </searcher>
        </chain>
    </search>
  </container>
</services>
```

You can use any type of search in Vespa with the RAGSearcher, including text search based on BM25, advanced approximate vector search or anything in between.

Behind the scenes, Vespa uses the retrieved documents to build a simple prompt by default.

This can be customised explicitly at runtime:

```
$ vespa query \
    --header="X-LLM-API-KEY:..." \
    yql="select title,body from msmarco where userQuery()" \
    query="what was the manhattan project?" \
    prompt="{context} @query Be as concise as possible." \
    searchChain=rag \
    format=sse
```

where the "context" is the list of results (restricted to the fields defined in the YQL).

8.5.8 Document Enrichment

Document enrichment enables automatic generation of document field values using LLMs or custom code during feeding.[44]

Examples of enrichment tasks include:

- Named entity recognition (e.g. extracting people, organisations, locations, etc.).
- Categorisation and tagging (e.g. sentiment and topic analysis) to be later used for filtering and faceting
- Generation of relevant keywords, queries and questions to do document expansion
- Translation of content for multi-lingual search

---

[44] https://docs.vespa.ai/en/llms-document-enrichment.html

It's the user's responsibility to craft the prompt they need, directly passing it in the services file or through dedicated template files:

```
<services version="1.0">
    ...
    <container id="container" version="1.0">
        ...
        <component id="questions_generator" class="ai.vespa.llm.
            generation.LanguageModelFieldGenerator">
            <config name="ai.vespa.llm.generation.language-model
                -field-generator">
                <providerId>LLM</providerId>
                <promptTemplate>Generate 3 questions relevant
                    for this text: {input}</promptTemplate>
            </config>
        </component>
        ...
    </container>
    ...
</services>
```

In the schema:

```
schema passage {
    ...
    # Generate relevant questions to increase recall and search
        suggestions
    field questions type array<string> {
        indexing: input text | generate questions_generator |
            summary | index
        index: enable-bm25
    }
    ...
}
```

> **Key Takeaways**

- Vespa offers strong support for vector search, including text and multi-modal vectorisation through embedders.
- Learned sparse retrieval models, such as SPLADE, are supported both for retrieval and reranking.
- Cross-encoders and late interaction models (like ColBERT) are supported for reranking.
- Both in-process and external general-purpose LLMs are supported to build retrieval augmented generation and document enrichment pipelines.

8.6 Qdrant

> The Qdrant project is a vector search engine (written in Rust and exposing REST APIs) that provides a production-ready service to store, search and manage vectors and metadata.

Disclaimer The following section describes features up to Qdrant 1.14.1.

At the time of reading, make sure to check the latest available release version and the release notes: successive releases may bring new LLM-related features.

The main focus of Qdrant is purely on vector search with a secondary support for text/multi-modal vectorisation.

It's intended to be a component to store vectors in your LLM-powered search architecture rather than the entire solution.

For the vectorisation part, Qdrant released FastEmbed,[45] a lightweight text vectorisation library to be used in conjunction with the main search engine.

In regard to vector search, Qdrant supports:

- Exact and HNSW-based vector search for 32-bit, 16-bit float and 8-bit integers vector elements.
- Scalar quantisation to compress vector to 8-bit integers, naive binary quantisation and product quantisation.[46] Qdrant also supports oversampling to then rescore using the original vector.
- Hybrid search (also including SPLADE sparse vectors).[47]
- GPU acceleration.[48]
- Late interaction models for first-stage retrieval and reranking.[49]
- Cross-encoders[50] for reranking.

---

[45] https://github.com/qdrant/fastembed
[46] https://qdrant.tech/documentation/guides/quantization/
[47] https://qdrant.tech/documentation/concepts/hybrid-queries/
[48] https://qdrant.tech/documentation/guides/running-with-gpu/
[49] https://qdrant.tech/documentation/fastembed/fastembed-colbert/
[50] https://qdrant.tech/documentation/fastembed/fastembed-rerankers/

> **Key Takeaways**

- There's little implemented in Qdrant to support LLMs in search: vector and hybrid search.
- Vector search is the focus of the technological solution and includes decent support for popular features (first-stage retrieval and reranking).

8.7 Milvus

The Milvus project is a vector search engine (written mostly in Go and exposing REST APIs) that provides a production-ready service to store, search and manage vectors and metadata with a focus on scalability.

Disclaimer The following section describes features up to Milvus 2.5.13.

At the time of reading, make sure to check the latest available release version and the release notes: successive releases may bring new LLM-related features.[51]

The main focus of Milvus is purely on vector search with a secondary support for text/multi-modal vectorisation.

It's intended to be a component to store vectors in your LLM-powered search architecture rather than the entire solution.

For the vectorisation part, Milvus released pymilvus,[52] a lightweight Python SDK for text vectorisation to be used in conjunction with the main search engine.

In regard to vector search, Milvus supports:

- Exact and approximate vector search (vector element bits supported varies from 32-bit up to binary depending on the quantisation)
- Scalar quantisation, product quantisation[53] and binary quantisation coming in 2.6
- Hybrid search (also including SPLADE sparse vectors)[54]

---

[51] https://milvus.io/docs/roadmap.md
[52] https://github.com/milvus-io/pymilvus
[53] https://milvus.io/docs/index.md?tab=floating
[54] https://milvus.io/docs/multi-vector-search.md

- GPU acceleration[55]
- Cross-encoders[56] for reranking

> **Key Takeaways**

- There's little implemented to support LLMs in search: vector and hybrid search.
- Vector search is the focus of the technological solution and includes decent support for popular features (first-stage retrieval and reranking).

8.8 Weaviate

The Weaviate project is a vector search engine (written in Go and exposing REST APIs) that provides a production-ready service to store, search and manage vectors and metadata. It integrates with LLMs to offer text/multi-modal vectorisation and retrieval augmented generation pipelines.

Disclaimer The following section describes features up to Weaviate 1.30.7.

At the time of reading, make sure to check the latest available release version and the release notes: successive releases may bring new LLM-related features.

The main focus of Weaviate is on vector search, but it also supports semantic search (via text/multi-modal vectorisation behind the scenes) and retrieval augmented generation integrations out of the box.

Specifically it supports:

- Text/multi-modal vectorisation integrating with self-hosted or remote embedding models.[57]
- Retrieval augmented generation integrating with self-hosted or remote LLMs.[58]
- Exact and HNSW-based vector search for 32-bit elements.

---

[55] https://milvus.io/docs/gpu_index.md
[56] https://milvus.io/docs/rerankers-cross-encoder.md
[57] https://weaviate.io/developers/weaviate/model-providers
[58] https://weaviate.io/developers/weaviate/search/generative

- Scalar quantisation to compress vector to 8-bit integers, naive binary quantisation and product quantisation.[59] Weaviate also supports over-fetching to then rescore using the original vector.
- Hybrid search.[60]
- Late interaction models for first-stage retrieval.[61]
- Cross-encoders[62] for reranking.

> **Key Takeaways**

- Weaviate offers semantic search (through text and multi-modal vectorisation) and retrieval augmented generation out of the box through self-hosted or remote LLMs.
- Vector search is the focus of the technological solution and includes decent support for popular features (first-stage retrieval and reranking).

References

1. Geng, Z., Ru, D., Yang, Y.: Towards competitive search relevance for inference-free learned sparse retrievers (2024). https://arxiv.org/abs/2411.04403
2. Kulkarni, H., MacAvaney, S., Goharian, N., Frieder, O.: Lexically-accelerated dense retrieval. In: Proceedings of the 46th International ACM SIGIR Conference on Research and Development in Information Retrieval, SIGIR '23, pp. 152–162. ACM, New York (2023). https://doi.org/10.1145/3539618.3591715
3. Malkov, Y.A., Yashunin, D.A.: Efficient and robust approximate nearest neighbor search using hierarchical navigable small world graphs (2018). https://arxiv.org/abs/1603.09320
4. Malkov, Y., Ponomarenko, A., Logvinov, A., Krylov, V.: Approximate nearest neighbor algorithm based on navigable small world graphs. Inform. Syst. **45**, 61–68 (2014) . https://doi.org/10.1016/j.is.2013.10.006
5. Teofili, T., Lin, J.: Patience in proximity: a simple early termination strategy for HNSW graph traversal in approximate k-nearest neighbor search. In: Hauff, C., Macdonald, C., Jannach, D., Kazai, G., Nardini, F.M., Pinelli, F., Silvestri, F., Tonellotto, N. (eds.) Advances in Information Retrieval. pp. 401–407. Springer, Cham (2025)

---

[59] https://weaviate.io/developers/weaviate/configuration/compression
[60] https://weaviate.io/developers/weaviate/concepts/search/hybrid-search
[61] https://weaviate.io/developers/weaviate/tutorials/multi-vector-embeddings
[62] https://weaviate.io/developers/weaviate/model-providers/cohere/reranker

Glossary

Algorithm Sequence of mathematically rigorous instructions to solve a problem.

Artificial intelligence It is a branch of computer science that aims to reproduce human-like intellectual capabilities through computers.

Artificial general intelligence It's one of the goals of artificial intelligence, meaning to reproduce artificially the ability to perform **any** task effectively and efficiently.

Machine learning It is a sub-discipline of artificial intelligence that studies the design, development and application of statistical algorithms that learn from (past) data to predict unseen data without explicit new instructions.

Large language model It is a type of artificial intelligence software designed to model the human language. The "large" attribute comes from its size (both at the training level and computational complexity level).

Pre-training Unsupervised training phase of a large language model, on a Web-scale quantity of data. It aims to capture the structure of language patterns.

Fine-tuning Supervised or semi-supervised training phase of a large language model, on a reduced quantity of data. It aims to specialise the model to solve a specific task.

General purpose/instruction following LLM A large language model fine-tuned to follow instructions and respond with text or multi-modal generation to natural language requests.

Generative pre-trained transformer Large language models based on the autoregressive foundation, which means that they are trained to predict the next word based on all the preceding words.

Model distillation Technique to build a smaller model from a bigger one, extracting a subset of its original capabilities.

Prompt A request to a large language model, expressed in natural language and aiming to obtain specific information from the model.

Zero-shot prompting A prompt that just asks the large language model to perform some task, with no examples or step-by-step definition.

Few-shot prompting A prompt that asks the large language model to perform some task, giving a few specific examples of input/expected output.

Chain-of-thoughts prompting A prompt that asks the large language model to perform some task, giving a few specific examples of input/expected output with a step-by-step explanation of how to reach the output for each of the sample inputs.

Open source Open source in computer software means that access to code (read) and contribution (write) is permitted to anyone for free by the copyright owner under a permissive license that offers the possibility of using, studying, modifying and re-distributing the code for any purpose.

Open weight A large language model is considered open weight if only the learned weights of the neural network model are released with an open source license.

Lexical search Synonym of traditional keyword search, the information is retrieved from a corpus of information matching query keywords with document terms.

Vector search Vector search (also known as neural search or dense retrieval) aims to represent the semantics of text (both the query and the documents) as a numerical vector and perform a nearest neighbour search using a similarity metric based on vector distance.

Sparse vector A vector with pretty much all zeroes, only a few (sparse) elements are different from zero. The number of dimensions is generally quite high (corresponding to the term dictionary cardinality), and the vector for any given document contains mostly zeros (hence it is sparse, as only a handful of terms that exist in the overall index will be present in any given document).

Dense vector The number of dimensions in this approach is generally much lower than the sparse case, and the vector for any given document is dense, as most of its dimensions are populated by non-zero values.

GPSR Compliance

The European Union's (EU) General Product Safety Regulation (GPSR) is a set of rules that requires consumer products to be safe and our obligations to ensure this.

If you have any concerns about our products, you can contact us on ProductSafety@springernature.com

In case Publisher is established outside the EU, the EU authorized representative is:

Springer Nature Customer Service Center GmbH
Europaplatz 3
69115 Heidelberg, Germany

Batch number: 09544540

Printed by Printforce, the Netherlands